This work makes important contributions to th
Book of Leviticus, the place of chapter 17 withi
of Leviticus 17, and its application to the practice of eating blood in Chinese culture. Dr. Chang has argued her case well. Her work will repay serious consideration in the academy as well as the church in China and around the world.

Richard E. Averbeck, PhD
Professor Emeritus of Old Testament and Semitic Languages,
Trinity Evangelical Divinity School, Illinois, USA

This thought-provoking study on Leviticus 17 not only resides within biblical-theological academia but transcends cultural boundaries. It offers a robust theological response to the consumption of blood in Chinese culture, whether for nutritional purposes, healing, or even as a ritual practice in folk religions. Dr. Chang challenges Chinese Christians to re-evaluate their attitudes towards this cultural norm, providing a solid foundation for a more comprehensive and nuanced theological understanding of the atonement of sin, which was ultimately realized in Christ's death on the cross. This book is a must-read for theologians, pastors, and anyone interested in a deeper understanding of the theological implications of Leviticus in our multicultural society and globalized world.

Clement Mook-Soo Chia, PhD
Principal,
Singapore Bible College

Written by one who is at home in both the world of Leviticus and the contemporary struggles of Chinese culture, this book offers a solid and insightful theological resolution to the practice of "eating blood." Dr. Chang skillfully helps us to bridge the gaps among Ugaritic insight, the worldview of Leviticus, and the Asian context in a thoughtful and cogent way.

Lawrence M. H. Ko, PhD
Chair, Division of Biblical Studies,
Alliance Bible Seminary, Hong Kong

Dr. Chang is to be commended for this excellent literary and theological analysis of Leviticus 17 and its contribution to a biblically incisive, culturally astute understanding of the complex cultural phenomenon of eating blood. Her work throughout is a judicious blend of extensive, all-encompassing scholarly research, keen literary sensibility, exegetical acumen, and probing cultural and personal insight. Her scholarship is especially evident in her thorough analysis of the Hebrew text and relevant Ancient Near Eastern parallels. This volume is an exceptional and welcome resource for reexamining and rethinking a long-standing controversial topic, and its practical and theological implications.

Dennis R. Magary, PhD

Chair, Department of Old Testament and Semitic Languages,
Trinity Evangelical Divinity School, Illinois, USA

The Power and Purpose of Blood in God's Design

Leviticus 17 and Its Implications for Christian Engagement with Chinese Culture

Cynthia Hsing-Wei Chang

Langham
ACADEMIC

Published 2024 by Langham Academic
An imprint of Langham Publishing
www.langhampublishing.org

Langham Publishing and its imprints are a ministry of Langham Partnership

Langham Partnership
PO Box 296, Carlisle, Cumbria, CA3 9WZ, UK
www.langham.org

ISBNs:
978-1-83973-256-0 Print
978-1-78641-012-2 ePub
978-1-78641-013-9 PDF

British Library Cataloguing-in-Publication Data
A catalogue record for this book is available from the British Library

ISBN: 978-1-83973-256-0

Cover & Book Design: projectluz.com

To my beloved husband Amos, who has more than anyone provided
the sacrifices and support that have made this effort possible.
To my two beautiful children, Clement and Priscilla, who
have supported me with their patience and prayers
in this *long* journey of completion.
You are the best! And,
you deserve this.

Contents

Abstract

The need for this study arose from personal experience regarding the unfamiliar and impractical nature of the ritual teachings in the book of Leviticus for Christians, the list type of Leviticus, and the common practice of eating cooked blood pudding in Chinese culture. It aims to explore the issues involved in the literary structure of Leviticus, emphasizing the role of Leviticus 17, thus paving the way to reinvestigate two exegetical issues more comprehensively and thoroughly. The study concludes with a solid suggestion for Chinese Christians regarding the attitude they should have toward the practice of eating blood in Chinese culture.

Three basic principles for distinguishing the structure of Leviticus in view of the role of Leviticus 17 form the framework of the first part of this book: (1) the relationship between laws and narratives in the Pentateuch, (2) the literary flow and characteristics of Leviticus 17 and its literary contexts, and (3) the critical function of introductory speech formulas in compiling the regulations in Leviticus.

The second part of this book discusses two issues in the interpretation of Leviticus 17. First, a comparison is made between well-being offerings in the Old Testament and two representative Ugaritic sacrificial documents in light of the altar centralization emphasized by the regulation of well-being offerings in Leviticus 17. The debate on altar centralization is then reexamined with regard to the literary contexts of Leviticus 17 and Deuteronomy 12. Second, the prohibition of eating blood is treated grammatically, syntactically, contextually, and in relation to the meaning of rituals.

This book's primary contributions include reexaming the literary function of Leviticus 17 in the book of Leviticus, reconsidering the interpretation of the regulations of altar centralization in the Pentateuch with comparison to some representative Ugaritic ritual documents, and probing the meaning of blood atonement in rituals in relation to rhetorical techniques and the relationship between narrative and law in the Sinai covenant.

This interpretation is applied to Chinese Christians, revealing the need for – and attempting to provide – a more comprehensive theological response to the practice of eating blood in Chinese culture.

Acknowledgments

This research has been made possible by the support and assistance of many people. I am deeply indebted to my supervisor, Dr. Richard E. Averbeck. His patience, kindness, and encouragement have warmed my heart and enabled me to finish this difficult task. His insightful, critical comments, and careful scrutiny of my thesis have been invaluable. I have benefited greatly from his guidance and direction throughout my studies.

I would like to acknowledge the support and encouragement of the former and the present interim principals (Dr. Albert Ting and Dr. Michael Shen) of Singapore Bible College. I also want to acknowledge Dr. Clement Chia, the Dean of School of Theology Chinese, who has been considerate of my teaching load and has supported me in numerous ways as I worked on my thesis alongside carrying out my teaching responsibilities over these past five years. I am grateful to my colleagues at Singapore Bible College who have supported me, especially through prayers and sharing the workload, and to Mrs. Jan Shen, the Library Coordinator, who has always supported me by getting the resources I needed for my research on time.

Thanks are due to the Langham Partnership for the provision of scholarship funds during my PhD studies from 2006 to 2010. In addition to financial support, John Stott Ministry has provided a supportive community of scholars with consultation, prayers, and friendship. Thank you, Ginny and Earle Combs, Dr. Elaine Vaden, Dr. Ian Shaw, and Dr. Paul Barker.

I would also like to express my appreciation to my beloved brothers and sisters in Christ in our spiritual home in Illinois, Chinese Christian Fellowship Church South Lake Branch. In this family of Christ, we grew spiritually together with joy and tears during my five and a half years of residential study.

These treasured memories of fellowship will remain deep in our hearts. Thank you for your prayers and countless kinds of support.

I want especially to thank my husband, Amos, and our two wonderful children, Clement and Priscilla, for their understanding and unfailing support. To my dear husband, thank you so much for your willingness to sacrifice more than seven years to accompany me for ThM and PhD studies just because of the conviction you have shared with me: "Let the one who is able to study to finish the equipment as her response to God's calling." To my lovely kids, thank you for bearing with me to fulfill God's calling in my life. For this goal in my life, you two have been willing to move around the world to live in four different countries at your young age, and still try your best to adjust in a different educational system in Singapore. No matter where we stay, we are family as long as we bond together in love. Yes, by God's grace I completed my study. Finally! It is a long-awaited ending.

Finally, I am grateful to God. It was by his providence that I was able to complete this challenging task. בָּרוּךְ יְהוָה אֵלִי

Abbreviations

ANE	Ancient Near East(ern)
b. Šabb.	Babylonian Talmud *Šabbat*
HALOT	*The Hebrew and Aramaic Lexicon of the Old Testament*
KTU	*Die keilalphabetischen Texte aus Ugarit*. Edited by Manfried Dietrich, Oswald Loretz, and Joaquín Sanmartín.
Mo'ed Qaṭ.	*Mo'ed Qaṭan*
NIDOTTE	*New International Dictionary of Old Testament Theology and Exegesis*. Edited by W. A. VanGemeren.
NT	New Testament
OT	Old Testament

Signs on Ugaritic transliteration

italics	word or phrase where the spelling is not the issue
ALL CAPS	root
[x]	sign entirely destroyed
⸢x⸣	sign partially preserved, reading not epigraphically certain but restorable from context.
⸢_⸣	lacuna, estimated numbers of signs missing indicated by dash(es)
[ ]	lacuna of known length but the number of signs missing may not be estimated with any precision
[. . .]	lacuna of unknown length
. . . .	unknown number of lines missing

CHAPTER 1

Introduction and Methodological Considerations

In Christian churches, Israel's ritual regulations in Leviticus are often ignored and considered unimportant.[1] Undoubtedly, the concepts of the atonement,[2] expiation, holiness, and the presence of God are critically important in both the Hebrew Scriptures and the New Testament (NT), as well as later Jewish and Christian literature, and these themes are largely based on the book of Leviticus. The strong emphasis in Leviticus on these themes supports Jacob Milgrom's high view of the theological nature of Leviticus,[3] and Paul

1. Averbeck pertinently states, "As important as they are in the Old Testament law, rituals often seem to be magical or superstitious. . . . Most Christians find such regulations uninteresting if not confusing, if they pay attention to them at all. No wonder most readers never make it through the Book of Leviticus!" Averbeck, "Law," 50. House observes that Leviticus is a literary world foreign to even many trained biblical scholars. House, *Old Testament Theology*, 126. Mann points out that "many a pious vow to read straight through the Bible from cover to cover has foundered in the shoals of Leviticus. It is difficult to think of a book in the Bible that is less inviting to twentieth-century readers. . . . Few people would want to revive such rituals, but even fewer have dispensed with the theological concerns those rituals express." Mann, *Book of the Torah*, 113. J. C. Powys's remark amplifies this dismissive attitude toward the laws in the Pentateuch: "Exodus, Leviticus, Numbers, and Deuteronomy . . . are by far the least inspiring and the least interesting books in the whole Bible." Powys, *Enjoyment of Literature*, 16.

2. "As for the NT, a foundational truth of Christianity is that final atonement *has been made*." Brown, "*Kippēr* and Atonement," 202.

3. "Theology is what Leviticus is all about. It pervades every chapter and every verse. . . . Indeed, every act, whether movement, manipulation, or gesticulation, is pregnant with meaning." Milgrom, *Leviticus 1–16*, 42. "The book of Leviticus is a rich treasure house of truth about the Israelite sanctuary and the system of salvation it portrayed in type during the era it functioned. An examination of this spiritual heritage should, therefore, offer assistance in studying the working out of salvation themes in the later literature of the OT and in the grand fulfillments of the NT." Shea, "Literary Form," 135.

R. House's conviction that Leviticus is one of the most theologically-oriented books in Scripture.[4] Scholarly interest in the study of Israel's cult and rituals has recently increased to become more proportionate to the emphasis placed on such matters by the biblical authors or editors themselves. As Christian scholars, we should prepare ourselves "to debate not only with Christian theologians, but also with Jewish scholars and philosophers who have now joined the conversation."[5]

Problem Statement

Scholars have endeavored to establish the literary macrostructure of Leviticus, but have not arrived at a consensus on the role of Leviticus 17 in this macrostructure. Moreover, scholars have not treated the exegetical debates regarding altar centralization and the prohibition against the consumption of blood in relation to each other or in relation to the role of Leviticus 17 within Leviticus. The holistic framework of the Mosaic covenant at Sinai in Exodus 19–Numbers 10 has not been considered in the treatment of these two major exegetical issues.

Research Methodology

This research will pursue a synchronic and text-oriented reading,[6] focusing on rhetorical analysis, comparative study, and exegetical work on the final form of the Old Testament (OT) rather than following the historical-critical agenda.[7] However, engagement in conversation with those who adopt the

4. "Though it is hard to envision at first because of its unfamiliar subject matter, even simple reflection on Leviticus quickly demonstrates that this is one of the most theologically oriented books in Scripture." House, *Old Testament Theology*, 126.

5. The OT interpretation and theology done in Christian circles could be different from that done by Jewish scholars, although both sides base their findings on the same texts. Brett, "Future of Old Testament," 484.

6. "Synchronic analysis concentrates on the question, how a text can be read on the basis of linguistic knowledge and knowledge of rhetorical patterns, admitting that in the case of ancient texts this is historical knowledge." Talstra, "Deuteronomy 9 and 10," 207.

7. This study will consider House's conviction that Leviticus should be examined in its canonical context – particularly in the Pentateuch and other related OT passages – first so that the uniformity and uniqueness of Leviticus may be better appreciated. House, *Old Testament Theology*, 126.

historical-critical method will be important to this research, which attempts to consider and respond to such scholars' viewpoints from an evangelical perspective.[8] The rhetorical approach, which focuses on the dynamics between narrative and ritual woven together in Leviticus,[9] will be one of the prominent methodological concerns. To search out the literary function of Leviticus 17, other texts such as Leviticus 8–10 and 16 will be discussed within the rhetorical analysis.

In its exegetical discussion of altar centralization and the prohibition of consuming blood, the scope of this study will extend to related texts in the Pentateuch, such as Genesis 9,[10] Exodus 19–20, and Deuteronomy 12. On the other hand, when it comes to the meaning of a specific ritual (for e.g. the rite of dealing with blood in the animal sacrifice, especially in the discussion of the well-being offerings in Leviticus 17), I believe that the main purpose of rituals in Leviticus is to communicate the symbolic meanings inherent in the rituals and revealed in their social contexts. In the case of Levitical studies, this could be understood in the textual contexts in Leviticus.[11] Although I accept that it is possible to interpret a ritual action as having different

8. We should seriously reexamine the historical-critical method while we are engaged with the findings from this method. Barr highlights this need in his article: "Actual historical criticism worked in a rather empirical, trial-and-error, manner. . . . People came to accept critical approaches as effective practice, whether they troubled with the method or not. To this day there does not exist any really clear and philosophically valid account of what traditional biblical criticism was doing." Barr, "Synchronic, Diachronic and Historical," 9.

9. Despite holding a critical view of how the narratives and ritual material came to appear together in the book of Leviticus, Smith admits that "through these narratives, matters of ritual prescription were grounded in a literary context." Smith, *Priestly Vision of Genesis 1*, 124. Moreover, Bibb argues that "narrative texts from Ugarit provide a better historical parallel to Leviticus than do ritual texts. If this is true, however, we must discern to what extent one can consider Leviticus to be a ritual text." Bibb, *Ritual Words*, 35. Bibb seems to regard Leviticus as a narrative with ritual words. In other words, Bibb uses the narrative scope to interpret the ritual described within. However, since only Leviticus 8–10 and 24:10–12 are conspicuous narrative passages, while the rest of Leviticus tends toward more prescribed ritual or moral regulations introduced by the short speech formula, I would propose that the text of Leviticus consists of narrative and ritual or moral regulations woven together, rather than simply a narrative. Chapter 3 will be devoted to comparing the well-being offerings in Leviticus and the Ugaritic sacrificial documents.

10. Carmichael expands his discussion of the blood taboo in Leviticus 17:10–16 to consider Genesis 9. Carmichael, *Illuminating Leviticus*, 71–74.

11. G. A. Klingbeil asserts that "ritual does not happen in a vacuum or a black hole. Generally it occurs in a specific context and often represents the collective (or individual) response to a particular situation. Some rituals represent the response to a specific event in the life of an individual or community. Others appear as highly conventionalized markers in life." Klingbeil, *Bridging the Gap*, 134.

meanings in different textual contexts, I will argue that the symbolic meaning of any specific rite in Leviticus must have been assigned by God when he appointed it[12] and that this should be the very same meaning comprehended by the priest (the performer), the congregation of Israel (the observers), and readers of Scripture as well.

Furthermore, this study will seek a balanced comparative methodology concerning the Ancient Near Eastern (ANE) context. As William W. Hallo proposes, this will be a "contextual method" observing both comparisons and contrasts in the ANE context to obtain a better understanding of biblical rituals.[13] The similarities show us that there is a close connection between biblical and ANE texts,[14] whereas the differences between them show us the uniqueness of God's special revelation in the Bible.[15] In this regard, as we investigate the well-being offerings in Leviticus 17, Ugaritic documents such as *KTU* 1.40 (RS1.002),[16] *KTU* 1.109 (RS 24.253),[17] and *KTU* 1.115 (RS 24.260: 9–10), will be highlighted, and other ANE sources investigated.[18]

---

12. As Douglas says, "rituals of purity and impurity create unity in experience. So far from being aberrations from the central project of religion, they are positive contributions to atonement. By their means, symbolic patterns are worked out and publicly displayed." Douglas, *Purity and Danger*, 2–3.

13. Hallo, "Compare and Contrast," 1–26. "In the last century, we have learned about legal cultic instructions in the Ancient Near East that have affinities to Israelite priestly prescriptions (cf. Weinfeld 1983a). Furthermore, we now have an Ancient Near Eastern literary type of cultic prescriptive and descriptive documents that are identical to those found in Israelite priestly literature (Levine 1963, 1965; Rainey 1970)." Weinfeld, *Place of the Law*, 74.

14. Under the inspiration of the Lord, the human authors of the Bible – who were indeed living in an ANE context – used these common ideas or traditions to tell the Israelites that they worshiped not pagan deities but the true and only God who rules over the world. For an example comparing ideas in biblical and other ANE documents, see Averbeck, "Ancient Near Eastern Mythography," 328–56.

15. Talmon, "'Comparative Method,'" 345. Since the Bible is simultaneously in its world and against its world, we should pay equal attention to differences and similarities when we apply the comparative method to biblical studies. Averbeck, "Sumer, the Bible," 91. Averbeck observes that "there is a tendency, sometimes blatant, to allow the data from the Ancient Near East to overwhelm the biblical basis of the discussion or push it aside in favor of the worldviews reflected in texts outside the Bible. It is important to resist this temptation and, instead, allow the Hebrew Bible to carry its own weight within the conceptual world of its ancient west Asian environment." Averbeck, "Ancient Near Eastern Mythography," 344–45.

16. Merlo and Xella, "Ugaritic Cultic Texts," 293; De Moor and Sanders, "Ugaritic Expiation Ritual," 283–300; Pardee, *Ritual and Cult*, 77–83.

17. Clemens, *Sources for Ugaritic Ritual*, 1200.

18. Merlo and Xella, "Ugaritic Cultic Texts," 293. The Ugaritic texts found at Ras Shamra regarding ¬*lmm* have also been discussed in De Vaux, *Les sacrifices*, 44–48. Cf. De Vaux,

As the discussion touches upon well-being offerings and blood atonement, ritual theories – including the anthropological approaches and related issues pertaining to the history of religions – will also be explored.

Literature Review

Among the various issues that draw scholarly attention to Leviticus 17, the following assume the greatest prominence.

The Division of the Priestly Document and the Holiness Code

The debate over the structure of the book of Leviticus – especially the division of the so-called "two major parts": the Priestly Document and the Holiness Code – has continued throughout the recent decades.[19] According to the traditional historical-critical view,[20] Leviticus 1–16 belongs to the Priestly Document (P), which originates with a priestly writer or priestly tradition and was probably written or compiled during or after the exile, whereas Leviticus 17/18–26 belongs to the Holiness Code (H), an exilic source.[21] P is not restricted to the book of Leviticus, but is a longer narrative work that traces a continuous chronology beginning with creation. Although legal material predominates in P, it is interwoven with a narrative that provides the framework for the laws.

According to the historical-critical theory, P was written to stir up zeal for the postexilic temple and its ritualistic worship so that Judah, a Persian province, might be reorganized as a theocracy. The argument for a late dating of P is based on at least two main factors: linguistic criteria, and the history

Studies in Old Testament, 46–51. Wright contends that his main goal in Ugaritic ritual study is to examine how ritual functions within the context of stories. Wright, *Ritual in Narrative*, 6.

19. For a brief introduction to the debate, see Hildenbrand, *Structure and Theology*, 75–81.

20. Bruce C. Birch, Walter Brueggemann, Terence E. Fretheim, and David L. Petersen hold this traditional historical-critical view on Leviticus. See Birch et al., *Theological Introduction*, 135–39. For a summary of and response to the critical view, see Ross, *Holiness to the LORD*, 35–41.

21. Graf attempted to demonstrate that Ezekiel is the author of Leviticus 18–26, and thus dated H to the early exilic period. Graf, *Geschichtlichen bücher*, 81–82. Milgrom argues in a recent essay that P and H date to the preexilic and exilic period, respectively. Milgrom, "Case for Pre-exilic," 48–56. See also Milgrom, *Leviticus 1–16*, 27.

of the Israelite religion.[22] Some historical-critical scholars argue that "P, although a product of the exilic community, projected its material back into the past to present it as having been given by God in remote antiquity at Sinai."[23]

On the other hand, Leviticus 17/18–26 is generally referred to as the Holiness Code in the historical-critical theory. In its general form, it corresponds to P, but it is distinguished from the rest of the priestly document in the Pentateuch by its vocabulary, style, and theology.[24] Israel Knohl holds that Leviticus 17/18–26 was the work of a "holiness school" that came after the Priestly and Deuteronomistic schools.[25] Recent research on the structural reconstruction of Leviticus tends to divide the "Holiness Code" into several redaction layers acquired from different sources.[26] The modern trend is to accept the diversity of the "Holiness Code" rather than maintaining the hypothesis of an originally independent legal corpus lying behind Leviticus 17/18–26.[27]

---

22. "For the documents which according to the canonical theory all came down directly from the time of Moses, were now considered to be much later, and were assigned to what could in no way be called creative periods in the history of the law: Deuteronomy to the seventh century B.C., the legal documents in the 'Priestly writing,' whether the Holiness Code was included or not, as late as the sixth or fifth century B.C." Alt, "Origins of Israelite Law," 83. Scholars who hold to the late dating of P include: Patrick, *Old Testament Law*, 146–47; Blum, *Studien zur komposition*, 221–28; Levinson, "Right Chorale," 148–49; Blenkinsopp, *Pentateuch: Introduction*, 217, 238; Doorly, *Laws of Yahweh*, 49, 63–73.

23. Brueggemann agrees with this view. Brueggemann, *Introduction to Old Testament*, 67; Cf. Nicholson, *Pentateuch in Twentieth Century*, 220. Daly also comments on the first seven chapters in Leviticus by saying that "most scholars agree that these chapters were written down in the form in which we now have them some thousand years after the time of Moses by the so-called 'Priestly Writers' who projected their own concerns and issues back into the time and mouth of Moses." Daly, *Sacrifice Unveiled*, 30. See the explanation of the critical view in Ross, *Holiness to the LORD*, 36. Cf. Eissfeldt, *Old Testament: Introduction*, 207.

24. Ross, 36. H is considered to be an independent collection of laws edited with hortatory additions by a compiler and then gathered into P with some adjustments made to reflect the spirit and system of P. Since its inception in the later nineteenth century, research on H as a distinct entity has been characterized by growing complexity in the reconstruction of its redaction history. Joosten, *People and Land*, 7. Also see Milgrom, *Leviticus 1–16*, 35–38; Milgrom, *Leviticus 17–22*, 1319–32.

25. Knohl, *Sanctuary of Silence*, 70–71. See also the summary of Knohl and Milgrom's view in Smith, *Priestly Vision of Genesis 1*, 172.

26. For example, Cholewinski holds this view in Cholewinski, *Heiligkeitsgesetz*, 11–141. Sailhamer and Sun mention this phenomenon as well. Sailhamer, *Pentateuch as Narrative*, 343; Sun, "Investigation," 32–34.

27. See Sun, 40; Davies and Rogerson, *Old Testament World*, 143; Rendtorff, *Old Testament: Introduction*, 145.

The Structure of the Book of Leviticus

Several scholars have recently put forward another theory that differs from the documentary hypothesis, suggesting that there may have been a literary structure in Leviticus besides the major distinguishing features of P and H.[28] These scholars have begun to explore the possibility of reading Leviticus as a separate book.[29] It is also noteworthy that some scholars regard Leviticus as the center of the compositional structure of the Pentateuch. Erich Zenger posits that the editor of the Pentateuch built a twofold frame around the book of Leviticus by drawing significant parallels between Genesis and Deuteronomy and between Exodus and Numbers, thereby making Leviticus the editorial and theological center of the Pentateuch.[30]

In terms of the structure of Leviticus, Richard E. Averbeck proposes that we should understand all of the OT laws under the framework of the Mosaic covenant at Sinai, which defines the limits of the content and primary application of the law. Averbeck argues that the material in Exodus 25–Leviticus 25 initiates the tabernacle and priestly ritual system (Exod 25–Lev 9), defines the priestly conception of things (Lev 10–16), and works out the implications

---

28. Christophe Nihan believes that "the distinction between 'cultic laws' in ch. 1–16 and 'holiness laws' in 17–27, for instance, is much too general and imprecise to be regarded as the major organizing principle of the book." Nihan, *Priestly Torah to Pentateuch*, 77.

29. Bibb, for example, claims that "Leviticus can, in fact, stand as a separate book in the intellectual sense because it bears a narrowly defined objective that is fulfilled within its own, closed literary universe." Bibb, *Ritual Words*, 20, 22. Campbell and O'Brien also suggest that "the Sanctuary Narrative ends here, at Exod 40:38. The book of Leviticus has its own integrity." Campbell and O'Brien, *Rethinking Pentateuch*, 87. Rendtorff, M. Douglas, Milgrom, B. A. Levine, J. E. Hartley, K. Gutzwiller, and G. Auld also deal with Leviticus as a separate book. See Rendtorff, "Is It Possible?", 22, 27; Douglas, "Forbidden Animals in Leviticus," 3–23; Milgrom, *Leviticus 17–22*, 1364; Levine, *Leviticus*, xvi–xvii, xxv, 48; Hartley, *Leviticus*, xxx; Gutzwiller, "Comments on Rolf Rendtorff," 37; Auld, "Leviticus at the Heart," 49; Auld, "Leviticus: After Exodus," 43. Consistent with the characterization of the Pentateuch as a unified whole, however, Sailhamer contends that "Leviticus is a continuation of Exodus. We should not, in fact, think of it as a new book." Sailhamer, *Pentateuch as Narrative*, 323. In my opinion, we cannot claim that Leviticus is not a separate book solely because of its close relationship with Exodus. As for the argument about not regarding Leviticus as a book, see Erhard S. Gerstenberger's comment: "Leviticus is not a 'book' at all but rather a fairly artificial excerpt from a larger narrative and legislative work, sewn together like a patchwork quilt from many different, individual pieces." Gerstenberger, *Leviticus*, 2.

30. He claims, "Die fünf Bücher sind chiastisch/spiegelbildlich um das Buch *Levitikus als theologisches Zentrum* angeordnet." Zenger, *Einleitung*, 69. Birch, Brueggemann, Fretheim, and Petersen also claim in their book that "the book of Leviticus is the center of the Pentateuch. This placement conveys the importance of worship for the life and well-being of the community." Birch et al., *Theological Introduction*, 135.

for Israelites in each aspect of their daily life (Lev 17–25).[31] James W. Watts also contends that, based on the style and content, Exodus 25–Numbers 9 is a normal delineation of the Levitical law.[32] David A. Dorsey treats Exodus 19:3–Numbers 10:10 as the treaty at Sinai and contends that the narratives woven in with this section of laws serve not only as the mark of the beginning and end of the laws but also as a breaking sign to prevent the laws from being a long, boring compilation.[33] He divides Leviticus into three major sections – Leviticus 1–10, 11–18, and 19–26 – and believes that Leviticus 17–18 both serve as the conclusion of Leviticus 11–18 and constitute a significant bridge between ritual and moral purity.[34]

Some scholars emphasize the literary artistry of Leviticus as they investigate its structure. Mary Douglas, who takes an "anthropological" and rhetorical approach,[35] claims that Leviticus contains several interlocked "ring structures."[36] John E. Hartley divides Leviticus into six sections: chapters 1–7, 8–10, 11–15, 16, 17–26, and 27.[37] Using a linguistic approach, Wilfried

31. The beginning of the framework of the Mosaic covenant is recorded in Exodus 19–24, in which the Lord proposed a relationship between himself and the Israelites in Exodus 19 and they solemnized the covenant commitment through the stipulations, oath, and covenant meal in Exodus 24. Furthermore, Averbeck contends that the theology in Leviticus 10–16 "is pivotal to understanding priestly theology at its most basic level." Averbeck, "Law," 116–23.

32. Watts suggests that in one respect it is more difficult to define the boundary of the rhetorical context of the priestly legislation, since it is less obvious. He also observes that one can find descriptions of threats to the divine-human communion in the two main sections of narrative that are inserted in the ritual lists: Exodus 32–34 and Leviticus 8–10. Watts argues that the material "uses the rhetoric of story and list to develop a dialectical tension between the idealistic version of a divine-human communion and realistic warnings of its dissolution." Watts, *Reading Law*, 52, 55.

33. Dorsey treats the Pentateuch as a united book called "The Book of the Law of Moses." Dorsey, *Literary Structure*, 72, 76–83.

34. Dorsey, 76–83. Dorsey regards Leviticus 19–Numbers 10:10 as a unit called "holiness laws." He sees Leviticus 19–26 as the first section and Leviticus 27–Numbers 10:10 as the second section within this unit.

35. Douglas, *Leviticus as Literature*, 7.

36. Douglas, 50–53. Douglas believes that the writer has embedded the theological lessons of the book within its literary structure. Douglas, *Leviticus as Literature*, 12. Milgrom also relies on Douglas's ring structure. Milgrom, *Leviticus 17–22*, 1364, 1366. Watts comments that Douglas "outlined the literary structure of Leviticus in a form that mirrors the architectural structure of the Tabernacle, so that reading the book becomes analogous to touring that sanctuary. The initial problem with this proposal has already been mentioned: nowhere does Leviticus make any of these analogies explicit, as Douglas admitted." Watts, *Ritual and Rhetoric*, 20.

37. Hartley, *Leviticus*, xxx–xxxv. House holds to a structure of Leviticus similar to Hartley's: Leviticus 1–7, 8–10, 11–15, 16, and 17–26. House, *Old Testament Theology*, 126–27.

Warning concludes that the thirty-seven occurrences of divine speech in Leviticus serve to structure the entire book.[38] Didier Luciani suggests that Leviticus consists of three units: 1–15, 16, and 17–27, with an axle center in Leviticus 16.[39] Christophe Nihan also proposes a threefold structure of Leviticus: Leviticus 1–10, 11–16, and 17–26, with Leviticus 16 constituting the center of the book.[40]

The Ambiguous Location of Leviticus 17 in the Book of Leviticus

The location of chapter 17 in the book of Leviticus is ambiguous, and scholars have proposed at least four different explanations. First, some include it in the Holiness Code. August Kayser was the first to include Leviticus 17 in the Holiness Code by extending the observation of the linguistic descriptions in Leviticus.[41] John H. Sailhamer also groups Leviticus 17 with Leviticus 18–26 in his most recent book.[42] Second, some scholars exclude chapter 17 from

---

It seems that Hartley still holds that the block of text known as the "Holiness Code" is a distinct portion in the structure. Hartley, *Leviticus*, 249.

38. Warning, *Literary Artistry*, 37–63.

39. See Luciani, *Sainteté et pardon*, 1: 243–334. Luciani discusses the microstructure of Leviticus according to the speech discourses. He further suggests that there are nine sections in the book of Leviticus, namely, Leviticus 1–7(A), 8–10(B), 11–12(C), 13–15(D), 16(X), 17–22:16(D'), 22:17–22:33(C'), 23–24(B'), and 25–27(A'). Luciani, *Sainteté et pardon*, 1:326–28. For the structure of Leviticus 17, see Luciani, *Sainteté et pardon*, 2:388–89.

40. Nihan, *Priestly Torah to Pentateuch*, 95–110.

41. Kayser concluded that "Der Versuch das Räthsel der sich aughebenden sprachlichen Erscheinungen, in Leviticus 17–26, durch Scheidung zweier Urkunden zu lösen, hat sich als ausführbar und damit als berechtigt erwiesen." [The attempt to solve the riddle of the linguistic phenomena that arise in Leviticus 17-26 by separating two documents has proved to be feasible and thus justified.] Kayser, *Vorexilische buch*, 78. Other scholars representing this view include Wellhausen, Kilian, Knohl, Joosten, and Levine. See Wellhausen, *Prolegomena*, 376–85; Wellhausen, *Composition des Hexateuchs*, 149–72. However, Kilian thought that Leviticus 17 was redacted into the Holiness Code later. Kilian, *Literarkritische*, 164–79; Cf. Whybray, *Making of Pentateuch*, 31; Knohl, *Sanctuary of Silence*, 70–71; Joosten, *People and Land*, 6; Levine, "Leviticus: Its Literary History," 13–23.

42. The strategy of placing Leviticus 17 as an introduction to the following laws in Leviticus 18–26 is presented in Sailhamer's new book about the composition of the Pentateuch, in which he recognizes Exodus 25–Leviticus 16 as the Priestly Code and Leviticus 17–26 as the Holiness Code. Sailhamer, *Meaning of Pentateuch*, 42–47, 360–65. In his earlier (1992) book, however, Sailhamer, divides the book into two sections: chapters 1–17 and 18–27. This shows that at that time he viewed Leviticus 17 as the conclusion of the first section of the book of Leviticus. Sailhamer, *Pentateuch as Narrative*, 323, 345. He further argues that there are six subsections in each of the two parts. Sailhamer, 323–67. Nevertheless, it is not clear why he would regard Leviticus 17 as a conclusion, given that his discussion of this chapter focuses

the Holiness Code. Karl Heinrich Graf was the first to argue that Leviticus 18–23 and 25–26 constitute an independent corpus of law in Leviticus.[43] August Klostemann took this a step further when he labeled this material *das Heiligkeitsgesetz*, "the Holiness Code."[44] Third, some see Leviticus 17 as a transition between Leviticus 1–16 and 18–26. Michael Dean Hildenbrand, for example, concludes that Leviticus 17 "is a transition chapter between chapters 1–16 and the rest of the book and should not be included as part of the unit of chapters 18–26."[45]

---

for the most part on how it serves as an introduction to subsequent chapters rather than a conclusion to previous ones. After a detailed discussion, Sailhamer concludes that "Leviticus 17 plays a strategic role as a prologue to the laws that follow (Leviticus 18–26)." Sailhamer, *Pentateuch as Narrative*, 343–45.

43. "Zunächst lassen sich im Leviticus zwei durch klar hervortretende Unterschiede als verschiedener Hand angehörende Haupttheile unterscheiden, einerseits die Opfer - und Priestergesetze nebst den Reinigkeitsgesetzen C. 1–16, andrerseits eine durch Eigenthümlichkeiten im Ausdrucke und in gewissen Formeln ausgezeichnete Gesetzsammlung C. 18–26, welche schon vorher ein Ganzes gebildet zu haben und als solches, wenn auch vorher ein Ganzes gebildet zu haben und als solches, wenn auch mit einzelnen Zusätzen erweitert, aufgenommen worden zu sein scheint." Graf, *Geschichtlichen bücher*, 75. Graf has pointed to the use of the participle forms of קדשׁ – an attribute of Yahweh, the קרת penalty, and the use of numerous expressions from Leviticus 18–25 in Leviticus 26. Graf, 75–83. Feucht also dates some parts of the Holiness Code, including Leviticus 18–23A (H1) and 25, to the early seventh century. Feucht, *Untersuchungen*, 176–77.

Graf excludes Leviticus 24 from the corpus of Leviticus 18–26 because, on the one hand, he believes that Leviticus 23 and 25 have a better and closer relationship with each other because of their similar concerns (namely, the Sabbatical year and the Jubilee year) and, on the other hand, he regards Leviticus 24:1–9 as describing the arrangement of equipment in the holy place and Leviticus 24:10–23 as listing the latest legal additions because of the linguistic characteristic of the name of God. "Das Gesetz vom Sabbathjahr und Jubeljahr C. 25 schliesst sich seinem Inhalte nach an C. 23 an; C. 24, 1–9 und 24, 10–23 sind dagegen Zusätze von anderer Hand, die in keinem Zusammenhange damit stehen: 24, 1–9 gehört zu den Anordnungen über die Einrichtungen des Heiligthums überhaupt Ex. 25 ff. vgl. Ex. 25, 30. 40, 4, und 24, 10–23 scheint zu den spätesten gesetzlichen Zusätzen zu gehören, denn nur hier V. 11 und 16, sonst nirgends im A. T., wird nach späterm jüdischen Sprachgebrauche הַשֵּׁם zur Bezeichnung des Namens Gottes gebraucht." Graf, *Geschichtlichen bücher*, 79.

44. This was an aside to Klostermann's main point refuting the thesis that Ezekiel wrote these chapters of Leviticus. Klostermann, *Pentateuch*, 385; See also Sun, "Investigation," 4–5.

45. Hildenbrand, *Structure and Theology*, 83; See also Averbeck, "Leviticus," in VanGemeren, *NIDOTTE* 4:914. Milgrom also regards Leviticus as a transitional chapter between Leviticus 1–16 and 18–26. Milgrom, *Leviticus 17–22*, 1364–66. Wolf agrees with Gordon Wenham's view that chapter 17 belongs to the section of chapters 17–27; however, in this section, chapter 17 "is something of a hinge linking the chapters on ritual regulations (chs. 1–16) with those dealing with more personal matter." Wolf, *Introduction to Old Testament*, 163–64; See also Wenham, *Book of Leviticus*, 241.

Finally, some scholars hold that Leviticus 16–17 plays a special role in the whole of Leviticus 1–27.[46] John H. Walton and Andrew E. Hill regard Leviticus 1–17 as the first sequence in the divine equilibrium section. They observe that "as chapter 16 moves from the center zone to outside the camp, chapter 17 moves from outside the camp to the center zone."[47] The movement from the center to the outside in Leviticus 16 matches the movement in Leviticus 1–16, whereas the movement from outside to the center in Leviticus 17 matches the movement in Leviticus 18–22. Moreover, Walton and Hill claim that the purpose of Leviticus 26 is similar to Leviticus 16, while Leviticus 27 parallels chapter 17, since both are concerned with the movement of objects across zones – from outside the camp to the inside zone. In terms of the concern of space in the tabernacle, then, Leviticus 16–17 illustrates movements in opposite directions and seems to serve as an important transitional pivot between Leviticus 1–15 and 18–22.[48] Zenger also proposes that Leviticus 16–17 is the center of the sevenfold structure of Leviticus.[49]

Ritual Theories

Rituals in general possess some common prominent characteristics.[50] These elements and their symbolic meanings are critical for conveying the significance of rituals to those who observe them.[51] Although the rituals in Leviticus

46. Gerstenberger asserts that there is a very close relationship between Leviticus 16 and 17. Gerstenberger, *Leviticus*, 17–19, 211, 234.

47. Walton and Hill, *Old Testament Today*, 101.

48. Walton and Hill, 102–4.

49. Zenger's sevenfold structure is arranged as follows: 1–7, 8–10, 11–15, 16–17, 18–20, 21–22, and 23–26/27. Zenger, "Buch Levitikus," 65–70; See also Zenger, *Einleitung*, 65.

50. Kertzer, *Ritual, Politics, and Power*, 9.

51. Malul discusses the symbolic acts in Mesopotamian law. Malul, *Studies in Mesopotamian Legal*. I would agree with Turner and Turner, who regard the ritual actions as symbols rather than signs. According to Turner and Turner, "in symbols there is some kind of likeness (either metaphoric or metonymic) between the thing signified and its meaning; signs need bear no such likeness. . . . Signs are almost always organized in 'closed' systems. . . . The symbol's meaning is not absolutely fixed. New meanings may be added by collective fiat to old symbol vehicles. Moreover, individuals may add personal meaning to a symbol's public meaning, either by utilizing one or another of its standardized modes of association." Turner and Turner, *Image and Pilgrimage*, 245. Malina also notes that "symbols are notorious for being polyvalent, fused, and multi-meaninged." Malina, "Mediterranean Sacrifice," 37. Roland Grimes lists the following extended qualities of rituals: performed, embodied, enacted, gestural, repetitive, redundant, rhythmic, collective, institutionalized, consensual, patterned, standardized, ordered, rehearsed, meaningful, serious, condensed, multilayered, symbolic, referential, dramatic, paradigmatic, and so on. Grimes, *Ritual Criticism*, 14.

are set out in great detail, the interpretation of many aspects of the Levitical sacrificial system remains uncertain.[52] In part, this is because the rituals stem from a priestly circle that was very familiar with sacrifice and did not feel the need to question or explain it.[53] Gordon J. Wenham comments that "it was understood by everyone what a burnt offering symbolized, why the priest could eat of the flesh of the sin offering and guilt offering but not of the burnt offering. It was plain to the worshipers of ancient Israel why sometimes the sacrificial blood was poured out at the foot of the altar, why at others it was smeared on the horns of the altar. . . . But these points mystify us."[54] Therefore, several interpretive approaches have emerged from scholarly circles. I would now like to briefly introduce three major perspectives by which Levitical rituals are interpreted in academic circles.

The Religious Perspective

When W. Robertson Smith proposed his communion theory of the sacrifices in 1894, he claimed from the perspective of Semitic religious studies that the main purpose of animal sacrifices in ANE culture was not to give gifts to the god but to achieve communion between the god and the worshipers by partaking in flesh and blood.[55] Smith argued that the understanding of sacrifice

---

52. Gluckman suggests that "complex problems are involved in the question of when actions referring to beliefs in occult power occur, and how they operate. It therefore seems advisable to use a more complicated vocabulary in discussing these problems. The term *ceremonial* may be used to describe all actions which involve symbolic statements of social status. . . . As a further distinction, *ceremoniousness* could be used to describe ceremonial where the practitioners have no idea of occult powers being involved. . . . Ritual describes ceremonial where ideas of occult power are present." Gluckman, "Ritual," 44.

53. Jenson, "Levitical Sacrificial System," 25.

54. Wenham, "Theology of Old Testament," 77. Kiuchi agrees with Wenham's view on this issue. Kiuchi, "Spirituality in Offering," 23.

55. Smith, *Religion of Semites*, 226–27. Smith further explains that "the sacrificial meal was an appropriate expression of the antique ideal of religious life . . . the very act of eating and drinking with a man was a symbol and a confirmation of fellowship and mutual social obligations. The one thing directly expressed in the sacrificial meal is that the god and his worshippers are *commensals.*" Smith, 269.

Regarding animal sacrifices, Smith notes that it was not enough for the food to be shared; it had to be slaughtered: "There is no sacrificial feast according to Semitic usage except where a victim is slaughtered." Smith, *Lectures on Religion*, 280.

as a gift, which was proposed by Edward Burnett Tylor in 1871,[56] must have come later, for a gift is intended to alleviate guilt and to secure forgiveness.[57]

As we investigate the meaning of rituals from the perspective of religious studies, we should recognize that some scholars assert that strong connections exist in ancient religions between mythology and the meaning of ritual practices.[58] Because of this connection, myth, and ritual practice became the two most important elements in ancient religions.[59] Smith, however, claims that even though myth took the place of dogma in ancient religions, myth should not itself be the focus of the study of such religions, for myth merely explains ritual.[60] According to Smith, one could not interpret the meaning of ritual through myth as if the ritual was based on the myth; rather, the myth was derived from the ritual.[61] As for the meaning of any specific rite, Smith maintains that one should not attempt to assign a definite meaning to any of the developments of ancient rituals. All one can do is trace the meaning of the ritual and its influence on successive phases of thought in order to obtain a more holistic understanding of the ritual's meaning.[62]

---

56. Tylor, *Primitive Culture*, 461–96.

57. Smith, *Religion of Semites*, 226–27.

58. For a brief review of the close relationship between myth and ritual in the primitive culture, see Doty, *Mythography*, chapter 5: "Comparativism and the Functional Contexts of Myths and Rituals," 125–56.

59. Smith, *Religion of Semites*, 17. Durkheim defines religion as "a unified system of beliefs and practices (rites) relative to sacred things, that is to say, things set apart and forbidden – beliefs and practices which unite into a single moral community called a Church, all those who adhere to them." Durkheim, *Elementary Forms*, 47. For Durkheim, rites are "the rules of conduct which prescribe how a man should comport himself in the presence of these sacred objects." Durkheim, *Elementary Forms*, 41.

60. Smith, *Religion of Semites*, 17–20. In his introduction to Smith's *Religion of Semites*, Robert A. Segal comments that "Smith's focus on practice rather than belief as the core of primitive and ancient religion is revolutionary." Smith, x. Tylor, on the other hand, devotes only a small section of *Primitive Culture* to ritual, and sees ritual as the mere application of belief. Tylor, *Primitive Culture*, 2:362-442.

61. Smith contends that "it may be affirmed with confidence that in almost every case the myth was derived from the ritual, and not the ritual from the myth; for the ritual was fixed and the myth was variable . . . the myth itself requires to be explained . . . not in arbitrary allegorical theories, but in the actual facts of ritual or religious custom to which the myth attaches. The conclusion is, that in the study of ancient religions we must begin, not with myth, but with ritual and traditional usage." Smith, *Religion of Semites*, 18. "The rite, in short, was connected not with a dogma but with a myth. In all antique religions, mythology takes the place of dogma. . . . But, strictly speaking, this mythology was no essential part of ancient religion, for it had no sacred sanction and no binding force on the worshippers." Smith, 16–17.

62. Smith, 399.

Milgrom, on the other hand, identifies the purpose behind the institution of sacrifice in Israel as a means of giving gifts to God to induce his aid both externally, through blessings, and internally, through expiation.[63] Hartley mentions that the rituals practiced in the tabernacle from the time of Moses were designed to promote the relationship between God and his people, the Israelites, through a formal and standardized worship sequence.[64] In other words, Hartley recognizes that communion between God and his people became the primary purpose of the ritual practices of the Israelites. Based on this understanding, Hartley suggests that at least three dimensions exist within this foremost purpose of the sacrificial system: "sacrifice as a gift to God," "sacrifice as a means of expiation," and "sacrifice as a means of communication between God and members of the community."[65]

In terms of ritual texts, Wesley J. Bergen asserts that a text about ritual is not a ritual itself, but rather a sign of the absence of ritual. Bergen further claims that the *reading* of the text *becomes* a ritual as "readers are given the opportunity to stand in the place of Moses while speaking these words [the ritual regulations in Leviticus] to the people. Thus, the textualization of the ritual is balanced by the ritualization of the text."[66] Therefore, Bergen insists that modern readers of Leviticus participate in the ritual performance by imagining themselves as the ritual performers or participants in the audience.[67]

The Social-Psychological Perspective

When Clyde Kluckhohn proposed his social-psychological perspective on the meaning of ritual in 1942, he demonstrated an understanding that, from the point of view of society, myth and ritual are adaptive in that they contribute to social solidarity, enhance the integration of the society by promoting its values, and so on, thereby protecting cultural continuity and stabilizing the society.[68] Raymond Firth discussed the role of rituals as symbolic acts,

---

63. Milgrom, *Leviticus 1–16*, 440–41.

64. Hartley, *Leviticus*, lxvii.

65. Hartley, lxvii–lxxii.

66. Bergen, *Reading Ritual*, 7–8.

67. Bergen, 8–9. Bergen gives Leviticus 7 as an example and shows how different readers – a scholar, a pastor, and a poet – could contribute their understanding of this chapter from their own perspective. Bergen, *Reading Ritual*, 107–23.

68. Kluckhohn, "Myths and Rituals," 64–65.

stressing that the major function of symbols is to communicate meaning. According to Firth, "a major function of symbols is in facilitating communication. Utterance of words – a basic form of symbolic action – allows us to dispense with many kinds of manual and bodily actions in providing stimulus or conveying meanings. . . . In a ritual field, performance of a symbolic act allows ideas to be shared and reformulated without use of words, or with minimal verbalization."[69] Catherine Bell also argues that the primary function of ritual is to communicate, noting that it affects social realities, as well as the perceptions of those realities.[70]

Bruce J. Malina seems to relate the meaning of sacrifices to social systems. "Sacrifice is a pattern of human behavior. . . . This pattern labeled sacrifice, like every other pattern of human behavior, encodes meaning from the social system and concretely realizes that meaning in the persons, places, and things of sacrificial interaction."[71] Malina points out that the Levitical practice of offering sacrifices at a central place represents a form of political sacrifice similar to practices in Greek temple worship and Roman public sacrifice.[72] This practice of connecting Levitical sacrifices to the political sense understands God in political terms: "He is no longer 'patron' (a kinified relationship), but 'king' or 'lord' (a politified relationship)."[73] Malina concludes that because "sacrifice is about the interaction of persons in society, it points to the value of taking a social-psychological perspective to explain the behavior called sacrifice."[74] Finally, Janzen claims that, due to this close bond between rituals and their social realities, no ritual has a fixed meaning. He considers

69. Firth, *Symbols*, 79.

70. Bell, *Ritual Theory, Ritual Practice*, 43. Bell claims that "the value of the offerings to any one group is a function of that group's place in the whole system of offerings. Likewise, the system of offerings communicates about the relative status of the invisible recipient." Bell, *Ritual: Perspectives and Dimensions*, 67–68. Rappaport also points out that "to understand ritual to be a mode of communication does not restrict its scope . . . communication includes not only simple 'saying,' but also the sorts of 'doing,' in which the efficacious principle is informative rather than powerful." Rappaport, *Ritual and Religion*, 51. Leach observes that "most modern anthropologists would agree that culturally defined sets of behaviors can function as a language, but not all will accept my view that the term *ritual* is best used to denote this communicative aspect of behavior." Leach, "Ritual," 524.

71. Malina, "Mediterranean Sacrifice," 27.

72. Malina, 33.

73. Malina, 35.

74. Malina, 37. Malina also cites Gamson's view that "social psychology in fact 'is about the mesh between the self and society.'"

the meaning of sacrifice to be like the meaning of a word that changes with time and context.[75]

The Anthropological Perspective

Many modern anthropologists borrow the systems theory from the humanities and use it to interpret rituals in different religions.[76] This theory originates with sciences such as mathematics and physics. In the 1970s, anthropologist Monica Wilson used the system theory to investigate the religious system of the Nyakyusa, a tribe in Africa.[77] In 1987, Joannes Snoek, another anthropologist, tried to use a scientific approach to classify and define religious rituals. He described his methodology in the study of rituals as a systematic science of religion in general.[78]

A similar case can be found in the work of Frits Staal, who proposed the concept of the meaninglessness of ritual.[79] Staal believed that if a particular ritual itself bears no meaning and it is possible to make generalizations about rituals in human societies,[80] it must be possible to know what the rules of that ritual are.[81] Staal held that scholars who saw ritual as meaningless neglected

---

75. Janzen, *Social Meanings of Sacrifice*, 1–5.

76. Lemche, "On Use of 'System Theory,'" 77–79.

77. Wright, "Nyakyusa Cults and Politics," 156–59.

78. Snoek, *Initiation*, 2–3.

79. Staal, "Meaninglessness of Ritual," 2–22. Staal is an anthropologist who studies Indian religion. He inquires into the structural aspects of Indian ritual based on contemporary modes of linguistic analysis. Miller, "Review," 392–93. Scharfe, an anthropologist who has done research in Indian religion, criticizes Staal's hypothesis that rites are meaningless. He concludes that "one should wonder, if nature would have permitted such exuberant growth of something completely devoid of meaning, as according to Staal, rituals are amongst men and animals alike." Scharfe, "Great Rituals?" 96.

80. "Among students of ritual – whether religiously, anthropologically or psychologically inspired – we mostly meet with generalities." Staal, "Meaninglessness of Ritual," 15.

81. Staal, 15. Staal realizes that there are two different perspectives on the rules of ritual. One considers rituals as lacking clear structures. For example, Lévi-Strauss argues that fragmentation and repetition are two basic operations in rituals in general. The other perspective regards rituals as having inherited clear procedural structures. That means there is a beginning, middle, and an end in every ritual process. This view is held by Hubert and Mauss. Bell mentions that "after Lévi-Strauss . . . religious ideas and symbols (high gods, ancestors, food offerings, etc.) were regarded as systems in themselves; the meaning of any one symbol depended on the logic of its relationships to other symbols. . . . The real meaning of the system was thought to lie in the message communicated by the invisible structural patterns." Bell, *Ritual: Perspectives and Dimensions*, 63.

to develop a science of ritual. He believed that ritual itself is certainly amenable to precise investigation – just like physics, mathematics, or grammar.[82]

Based on these presuppositions, Staal adopted the General System Theory in his study of Indian religious rituals.[83] He also developed an analysis system called "Ritual Syntax," which understands rituals in terms of a complex tree-view structure and sees the related action as meaningless.[84] In other words, ritual activities are meaningless in themselves; they are composed of their activities and attached meanings. Roy Gane embraced this idea in 2005 to develop his exegesis on purification offerings in Leviticus.[85]

Likewise, in 1977, Victor Turner noted that different levels of senses are attached to the meaning of ritual.[86] Turner believes that "ritual is not just a concentration of referents, of messages about values and norms; nor is it simply a set of practical guidelines and a set of symbolic paradigms for everyday action. . . . It is also a fusion of the powers believed to be inherent in the persons, objects, relationships, events, and histories represented by ritual symbols. It is a mobilization of energies as well as messages."[87]

---

82. Staal, "Meaninglessness of Ritual," 15.

83. Staal, 15–19.

84. Staal, 15–21.

85. Gane, *Cult and Character*, 6–9.

86. Turner believes that "a single symbol, in fact, represents many things at the same time: it is multivocal, not univocal. Its referents are not all of the same logical order but are drawn from many domains of social experience and ethical evaluation." Turner, *Ritual Process*, 52. Based on his observation of African religious rituals, Turner claims that "the same symbol vehicles can represent different, even disparate, processes." Turner, "Symbols in African Ritual," 61. According to Turner and Turner, a symbol can be interpreted at three levels. First, there is the exegetic meaning given by those inside the ritual system. The exegetic level consists of four categories of meaning: (a) nominal – the name of the symbol, which may be heavily charged with meaning; (b) substantial – the physical and biological characteristics of the symbol; (c) artifactual – the symbol as a product of human fashioning or an object of culture; (d) historical – the origins and subsequent history, often dramatic or moving, of the symbol. Second, there is the operational meaning, which is derived from use of the symbol and the social composition of the groups performing the ritual. Third, the positional meaning is revealed in the relationship of the symbol to other symbols in the total ritual system. Turner and Turner, *Image and Pilgrimage*, 247–48; Cf. Shorter, "Symbolism, Ritual and History," 140; Staal, *Rules Without Meaning*, 152–55.

87. Turner, "Symbols in African Ritual," 59. Turner also suggests that "ritual symbolism is the means by which a man shares his inmost experiences with other men." Furthermore, Turner proposes that "the meaning of a ritual, therefore, cannot be limited to any one of its structures, but is the product of all of them." Shorter, "Symbolism, Ritual and History," 140. Since Turner has suggested that ritual serves as a vehicle for unfolding social dramas, Bell regards him as one of those scholars who use the performance theory to approach rituals. Bell, *Ritual Theory, Ritual Practice*, 41–43. Regarding the "inner power," characteristic of the religious symbol, Paul Tillich also notes that "the third characteristic of the symbol is its innate power. This implies

In conclusion, the search for the meaning of rituals has revealed the following: first, since the rituals were prescribed to the Israelites in the OT within the context of their relationship-building with God, the communion or communication function of the rituals is properly emphasized by scholars. Second, regarding the biblical ritual texts, although the biblical texts convey only a limited sense of the lively reality of ritual performance in ancient Israelite history, they describe the rituals well enough that modern readers can understand the contextualized information and obtain a holistic conception of the meaning of the ritual. I would, however, caution modern readers not to impose other imaginative interpretations on these rituals, but rather to discover the meaning conveyed by the author through the texts. Third, because rituals are only prescribed from within specific historical contexts, I concur with scholars working from a social-psychological perspective that a close relationship exists between rituals and their societies. Moreover, when considering ritual texts, we should also pay attention to their textual context.[88] Fourth, even if rituals are symbols attached to meanings that might differ due to their diverse backgrounds, I will argue that the meaning of a specific ritual in the text can usually be discerned through its immediate textual context. However, because I believe the meaning of rituals in the biblical text have been assigned by the text's author from within its own context, I will be cautious about making direct and strong connections to similar ritual actions in other cultures when considering the meaning of biblical rituals.[89]

Origin of the Argument of Altar Centralization

In the nineteenth century, the study of Israelite religion emerged as the result of the rise and flourishing of sociology and anthropology.[90] The origin of the argument for altar centralization in Israelite history has been traced back primarily to de Wette's argument regarding the place of worship. In 1805, De Wette argued in his doctoral thesis that the book of Deuteronomy was not

---

that the symbol has a power inherent within it that distinguishes it from the mere sign, which is impotent in itself." Tillich, "Religious Symbol," 76.

88. "Ritual pragmatics tries to describe the illocutionary force of a given ritual or subrite and seeks to locate it in the larger societal context." Klingbeil, *Bridging the Gap*, 205.

89. Regarding my approach to the meaning of ritual, please refer to the discussion in the section on "Research Methodology" on pp. 2–4 of this book.

90. See Hess, *Israelite Religions*, 25–41.

composed in the Mosaic time but much later, during the period of Josiah's reform in the divided kingdom of Israel. De Wette claimed that Deuteronomy was most likely related to the book of the Law found at that time (2 Kgs 22:8), since the books of Samuel and Kings portray kings offering sacrifices in a variety of locations, and the concept of the centralization of the sanctuary in Deuteronomy seemed to fit the emphasis of Josiah's reform.[91] De Wette's work was later taken up by scholars such as J. F. L. George,[92] Wilhelm Vatke, and refined by Graf and Julius Wellhausen in the late 1860s.[93]

Wellhausen considered the cult of Israel to be a natural religion; however, it was a religion of worshiping the true God, not animism. He, therefore, believed that the earliest Israelites worshiped their God everywhere: at field altars, high places, local sanctuaries, and so on. Josiah's reform put an end to these inclusive settings and based worship exclusively in the Jerusalem temple.[94] His understanding of Israelite religious development led Wellhausen to the conclusion that the doctrine of worship centralization embodied in the Deuteronomic Code and pervasive in P actually produced P's image of the tabernacle.[95] Thus, by projecting the tabernacle back into the period of the desert wanderings, P aimed to show that the centralization of the cult was prevalent in Israel from the beginning of its history. From this perspective, historical critics argue that the tabernacle is a fictitious creation of a postexilic scribe.

Weinfeld responds by saying, "The Tabernacle as presented in P is anachronistic and has utopian features. However, this does not permit us to consider the Tabernacle as pure fiction, being – as it were – a retrojection of Solomon's Temple, as Wellhausen contends."[96] When Weinfeld argues against the pos-

91. Gignilliat, *Brief History*, 44.

92. Rogerson, "Bible and Theology," 456.

93. Gignilliat, *Brief History*, 57.

94. Wellhausen, *Prolegomena*, 19–28. Wellhausen bases his reasoning regarding the multiple places of worship in the earlier years of Israelite history partly on Exodus 20:24–26. He concludes that "it is obvious that a multiplicity of altars is not merely regarded as permissible, but assumed as a matter of course."Wellhausen, 29. This concept might be influenced by evolutionary theory, which is seen as the foundation of the development of religion – religion developed later in history is more complex, whereas religion developed earlier in history is simpler. Monotheism is viewed as a later development in the history of religion because it is more complex.

95. Wellhausen, *Prolegomena*, 33–38.

96. Weinfeld, *Place of the Law*, 19.

sibility of regarding the tabernacle as an invention of the Second Temple period, he contends that "the Tabernacle as presented in P, absorbed some characteristic features of the Hurrian-Hittite cult prevailing in pre-Davidic Jerusalem. Nevertheless, the basic concept of the Tabernacle as a shelter for the Ark of YHWH of the ancient tribal confederacy has not been changed."[97] Therefore, as James K. Hoffmeier determined after his discussion on the wilderness tradition and the origin of Israel, "it seems to me easier to believe that the Bible accurately preserves an authentic picture of the travels and life in the Sinai wilderness than to suppose that authors six to seven hundred years later, writing in ignorance of the past and using creative imagination, got so much certifiably correct as the investigation has demonstrated."[98]

In terms of the apparent discrepancy between Exodus 20:24–26 and Deuteronomy 12:5–28 regarding the place of the altar,[99] the critical scholarly consensus has been that "the place" and "the altar of the LORD your God" (Deut 12:5, 27) referred to the temple and altar in Jerusalem, respectively, and that Deuteronomy was written in the seventh century BC to support Josiah's centralization of worship (2 Kgs 22–23).[100] Wellhausen claimed that "in that book [Deuteronomy] the unity of the cultus is *commanded*; in the Priestly Code it is *presupposed*. Everywhere it is tacitly assumed as a fundamental postulate, but nowhere does it find actual expression."[101] Wellhausen, therefore, argued the chronological relationship between D and P and arrived at the result in the well-known sequence: J, E, D, and P.[102]

97. Weinfeld, 25.

98. Hoffmeier, *Ancient Israel in Sinai*, 249. As William Dever asserts, "They knew a lot; and they knew it early, based on older and genuinely historical accounts, both oral and written. One simply cannot force all the biblical texts down into Persian, much less the Hellenistic, period." Dever, *What Did Biblical Writers?* 273.

99. Exodus 20:24 permits a multiplicity of simple altars in various locations, but Deuteronomy 12:5–28 seems to allow for only one altar and sanctuary. See discussion in Averbeck, "מִזְבֵּחַ," in VanGemeren, *NIDOTTE* 2:893.

100. Wellhausen, *Prolegomena*, 35.

101. Wellhausen, 35. Wellhausen notes, "the small body of legislation contained in Lev. xvii.–xxvi. is the transition from Deuteronomy to the Priestly Code." Wellhausen, 35, n.1.

102. Wellhausen, 35–51. Averbeck concludes that "this is one of the first and most important lines of evidence and argumentation that results in the well-known sequence: J, E, D, P." Averbeck, "מִזְבֵּחַ," 893.

The Prohibition of the Consumption of Blood in Leviticus 17

Turning to the prohibition of eating blood in Leviticus 17:10–12, the preposition ב in the clause נֶפֶשׁ הַבָּשָׂר בַּדָּם הִוא literally means "in or contained."[103] Allen P. Ross regards the blood as not only the symbol of life but as life itself.[104] In other words, when the blood is gone, there is no life.[105] Joe M. Sprinkle has argued that "the blood, symbolic of the life, had to be poured back to God even for non-atoning slaughter to symbolize that only by divine permission could even animal life be taken."[106] Sprinkle contends that the blood is prohibited because God gave it to humans by ordering it to be placed on the altar to make atonement.[107] Schwartz disagrees and contends that the prohibition of eating blood in Leviticus 17 is restricted and applies only to sacrificial animals rather than to all animals.[108]

Projection of Research Significance

The role of Leviticus 17 in the macrostructure of Leviticus is still ambiguous. In my view, discussion of the literary function of Leviticus 17 and these two major interpretive issues (altar centralization and the prohibition of consuming blood) in this chapter will help us rethink and sharpen the interpretive methodology with which we approach OT ritual regulations through the analysis of narrative and ritual woven together in Leviticus.[109] In other words, identifying the macrostructure of Leviticus will help us approach the message

---

103. Daly, *Sacrifice Unveiled*, 38–39.

104. Ross, *Holiness to the LORD*, 335. Carmichael also holds this view, contending that "the blood constitutes the soul or life of the animal." Carmichael, *Spirit of Laws*, 128–29.

105. Schwartz, "Prohibition Concerning 'Eating,'" 49.

106. Sprinkle, *Biblical Law*, 114. Goldingay believes that in all the Israelite rituals in the OT, the blood is regarded as a symbol of life. See Goldingay, *Israel's Faith*, 639. Merrill also contends that the principle of the sanctity of life is symbolized by the disposition of blood. Merrill, *Everlasting Dominion*, 295.

107. Sprinkle, *Biblical Law*, 114. Ross contends that "it is this higher use for shed blood that greatly enhanced the prohibition against eating blood. Since God had designed blood for atonement, it had to be brought to God. Eating it made common or profane something that God had intended for the sanctuary." Ross, *Holiness to the LORD*, 336.

108. Schwartz, "Prohibition Concerning 'Eating,'" 60–61.

109. The importance of engaging in the study of biblical laws and the narrative surrounding them has been stressed in Stahl, *Law and Liminality*, 11–26.

of Leviticus as a whole, and will also help us clarify to which literary subunit Leviticus 17 belongs. Through this contextual identification, we may secure a better comprehension of these exegetical issues.[110]

This improved understanding may in turn provide a solid answer for Chinese Christians regarding the decision they must make about the OT prohibition of consuming blood. These believers live every day in a social context where eating cooked solid blood is widespread due to the common conception that the consumption of blood has health benefits. Tracing this practice back to ancient Chinese literature in order to gain a better understanding of the common cultural heritage will also be of interest.

110. "Recent literary studies have shown that literary and syntactic design did not 'just occur' but that the author or editor employed well-considered patterns that provide clues for the interpretation of the relevant section. Thus literary and syntactic patterns help us to understand the performance of ritual texts." Klingbeil, *Bridging the Gap*, 148.

CHAPTER 2

The Role of Leviticus 17 in Leviticus

After embarking upon the journey of reading the Pentateuch, sooner or later one will notice that lists of laws are interwoven with the historical context provided in the narratives. These lists seem to interrupt the narrative storyline.[1] Some scholars, such as Harold Bloom, dismiss the priestly regulations in Leviticus in their discussions of the Pentateuch.[2] Others observe that the exodus theme provides one of the most prominent patterns reflected in the legal documents that follow, namely, the Covenant Code, the Priestly Documents, the Holiness Code, and Deuteronomy.[3] As a reader considers the literary structure of Leviticus, he or she will also notice that the book's rhetorical context is made more difficult to discern by the book's indistinct literary boundaries. In this study, however, the context of the Sinai covenant from Exodus 19 to Numbers 10:10 will be regarded as the outer framework of the book of Leviticus in regard to its literary grounds of style and content.[4]

1. As Hillers notes, "to study law and covenant we must look at the lists of laws that stud the book of Moses. The reader who tries to read the Bible like other books is apt to be confused or annoyed at the interruption of the story by bodies of laws – indeed it would be abnormal not to feel something approaching a personal dislike for the author of Leviticus." Hillers, *Covenant*, 87.

2. Harold Bloom dismisses the priestly regulations in Leviticus and elsewhere as pitifully belated attempts to domesticate the numinous, uncanny, and poetic essence of the Pentateuch, the Yahwistic narratives. Bloom, "'Before Moses Was,'" 8–9.

3. Preuss comments that, in Deuteronomy, "election and the gifts of both the commandments and the land are related to the exodus out of Egypt." Preuss, *Old Testament Theology*, 45; Also see Preuss, "Deuteronomium," 187. However, Watts argues that P's Sinai material in its present form seems to have a broader context in mind, namely, the content of the entire Pentateuch. Watts, *Reading Law*, 52–53.

4. In taking this approach, Watts consciously assumes that in regard to the rhetorical context of the priestly legislation, "its usual delineation as Exodus 25 to Numbers 9 makes

The Relationship of Law and Narrative in the Pentateuch

A vast amount of the Pentateuch is woven together by the laws and the narratives. How does the arrangement of the laws and narratives in the present shape of the Scriptures affect the interpretation of the laws? Did a compositional purpose guide the author or editor in choosing this specific arrangement? Scholars generally admit that, because the texts are positioned as they are, one should approach the two genres of law and narrative with the relationship between them in mind, though some scholars have analyzed the laws in the Pentateuch without considering their connections to the narratives woven within them.[5] Bratcher reveals his understanding of the laws given by Moses in the Pentateuch by showing that the history of the exodus – Yahweh's historical deliverance of the Israelites and their encounter with Yahweh – is the foundation of the Sinaitic covenantal laws as God built the relationship between the Israelites and himself.[6] Bratcher further explains that the laws are a response to, as well as a means to further nurture, the relationship between God and the Israelites as the result of his initiating love and grace through the historical deliverance in exodus. Because of the laws given to them, the Israelites could live out the implications of the covenantal relationship in history.[7] As Sprinkle astutely observes, "For Israel, a personal relationship

---

sense on grounds of style and content, but ignores the fact that this material shares the same temporal and physical setting as the preceding chapters. The priestly legislation continues the description of the Sinai event which begins in Exodus 19–24." Watts, *Reading Law*, 52. Ruwe also points out that Leviticus is not an independent narrative but a part of Sinai pericope – Exodus 19–Numbers 10:10. He claims that "an analysis of Leviticus that is satisfying with regard to the narrative respect, should therefore in any case start from the consideration of the immediate narrative context of Exod 19:1–Num 10:10." Ruwe, "Structure of Book of Leviticus," 58.

5. See, for example, Falk, *Hebrew Law in Biblical Times*; Doorly, *Laws of Yahweh*, 47–79. Moreover, some scholars ignore the narratives interwoven with the ritual regulations in the book of Leviticus and assume that in Leviticus there is almost no narrative. For instance, Radday claims that "while Deuteronomy contains a few passages which are narrative in parts, Leviticus has almost none, so that we would be justified in the present study in passing it over." Radday, "Chiasmus in Hebrew Biblical," 87.

6. "First, the simple observation that exodus precedes the giving of *torah* at Sinai should be allowed to have its full import. God initiated a relationship with this people by entering history and hearing the cries of oppressed slaves. He revealed himself in history, not only through the words to Moses but by the exodus itself. . . . The Sinai narratives are rooted in that historical deliverance and encounter. The introductory speech to these narratives is important (Exod 19:4–6)." Bratcher, "Torah as Holiness," n.p.

7. Bratcher points out that "Israel took the historical nature of its relationship with God seriously. That is, she understood that relationship with God as His people meant translating

with God places every facet of life under faithful response to God. This is the reason why the laws cover various aspects of life: moral, social, and religious."[8]

The Relationship between Law and Narrative in the Sinai Pericope (Exodus 19–Numbers 10:10)

Pertaining to the intertwined structure of the laws and narratives of the Sinai pericope, scholars debate the framework of Exodus 19–24.[9] Some stretch the narratival context of the laws to span from Genesis to 2 Kings. For example, Carmichael accepts that the collection of biblical laws is embedded in the narratives stretching from Genesis to 2 Kings, but further claims that the rules are not necessarily connected with their immediate narratival contexts. He asserts, rather, that they can be freely related to the initial stories recorded in this long pericope of narrative collections.[10] Carmichael not only proposes to freely connect the rules to the narratives in Genesis–2 Kings, but also denies the historicity of the pericope of Genesis–2 Kings,[11] regarding these books as a legendary history made up by later national or ethnic groups in Israelite history in order to locate the foundation of the laws.[12] In other

---

it into the very arena in which He had revealed Himself to initiate the relationship: the real life arena of human history. Relationship with God was never left in abstracted categories, nor could it be mythicized into a cosmic realm, nor could it be encompassed by legal requirements. It must be lived in real time, in real place, in changing human existence. That meant that relationship with God was dynamic as the community moved through history. Walking in God's ways became a suitable metaphor to capture this dynamic dimension of God's interaction with the people, and their response." Bratcher, "Torah as Holiness," n.p.

8. Sprinkle, *Biblical Law*, 50.

9. Blenkinsopp observes that "bracketing of laws with the early narrative sources, especially the so-called covenant law book (Exod 20–23) with E and the so-called ritual Decalogue (Exod 34:11–26) with J, has never been successfully demonstrated. The entire issue of the relation between law and narrative still remains to be clarified." Blenkinsopp, *Pentateuch: Introduction*, 26–27.

10. Carmichael, *Illuminating Leviticus*, vii, 1.

11. Carmichael, 1. "The scribes responsible for this merging of law and narrative, adopting a convention common in the ancient world, attributed their own creation to a great figure of the past. Thus they made of Moses a legendary figure who, in the rules he enunciated, judged past and contemporary developments in his nation's history as recorded in Genesis–Deuteronomy (the Pentateuch) and also anticipated future ones as recorded in Joshua–2 Kings (the Historical Literature). This legendary Moses took up problems that existed among his ancestors (the kidnapping of Joseph, for instance), that occurred in his own time (his sister's leprosy), and that would occur long after he lived (the appointment of a king in Israel)."

12. Carmichael, vii–viii. Carmichael insists that "I do not agree with the common view that the rules found in the Bible are responses to issues that came up at different times during the actual history of ancient Israel. Rather, the rules exhibit a feature that so often underlies

words, Carmichael believes that the scribes created a fiction and carefully wove the narratives and rules together to present the purpose of the rules from their point of view.[13] Thus, Carmichael claims that "the literary traditions in Genesis–2 Kings contain all of the issues taken up in the laws, legendary history and law being intimately linked."[14]

Therefore, even though Carmichael advocates examining "every law in the Pentateuch with a view to demonstrating that each is linked to a narrative,"[15] the validity of "jumping" among texts from Genesis to 2 Kings instead of focusing on the immediate narratival contexts of the laws should be seriously reconsidered.[16] In regard to the ritual regulations in Leviticus, Carmichael freely links the ritual laws in Leviticus 10–27 with other narratives in Genesis–2 Kings. For example, when he deals with the rules in Leviticus

---

legal systems. National and ethnic groups attempt to link their laws to legendary history and to locate the foundations of their laws as far back in time as possible. In the case of ancient Israel, scribes created, I submit, a fiction about the origin of their nation's laws. . . . When combining the stories from Genesis to 2 Kings, the scribes carefully wove together laws and narratives by placing collections of rules at points of crucial beginning in the flow of the overall narrative. . . . They formulated, for example, the deity's rules about killing animals and humans at the fresh beginning of the world after the Flood (Genesis 9). The Decalogue, the Book of Covenant (rules in Exodus 21–23), and the succeeding rules about the institution of the cult they placed at the start of the nation after the exodus from Egypt. The laws of Leviticus they put immediately after the setting up of the Tabernacle." This kind of idea is also evident in Carmichael's earlier writings. See Carmichael, *Law and Narrative*, 18–19. "My view of how biblical laws came to be set down in writing differs radically from the long-standing view of other scholars who assume that the laws are responses to issues and problems that arose in the lives of lawgivers. For these scholars, the laws reflect live history, whereas for me they reflect a long lost past." Carmichael, *Illuminating Leviticus*, 9.

13. His view of the fictional Mosaic character preserved in the Pentateuch is also present in his early writings. See Carmichael, *Law and Narrative*, 19–23. Regarding narratives in the Pentateuch as mythic or fictive compositions, Bibb reveals a similar perspective by arguing that "Leviticus narrates a mythic tale of ritual founding, itself the heart of the nation's founding." Bibb, *Ritual Words*, 35. Bibb further supports his view by asserting that "the process of ritualization explains not only the development of Israel's ritual system but also the presentation of that system in narrative form. The ritual prescriptions are placed in the mouth of Yahweh and of Moses, and are delivered at a specific moment in the mythic past. This transformation of ritual description into prescriptive formulation, and finally into a transformed fictive description, has a dramatic impact on the nature of these ritual elements." Bibb, *Ritual Words*, 73.

14. Carmichael, *Illuminating Leviticus*, 1. Carmichael argues that "the key to comprehending biblical legal material is the recognition that what inspires the formulation of biblical rules are incidents in biblical narratives, not the actual history of ancient Israel that scholars infer from these rules and narratives." Carmichael, *Illuminating Leviticus*, viii.

15. Carmichael, viii.

16. Averbeck astutely notes that "the relationship between the narrative framework and the laws is a subject that needs serious reconsideration." Averbeck, "Form Critical, Literary," 1, n.3.

10–14 regarding clean and unclean food, childbirth, and skin diseases, he turns to the stories of the flood, the wickedness of the priestly house of Eli, and the plagues visited upon the Philistines. Additionally, when Carmichael discusses the laws in Leviticus 15 concerning genital discharges, he links the uncleanness to various events in the historical books.[17]

It is not sufficient, however, to make a direct connection between a narrative paragraph and a ritual regulation based solely on the similarity of the thematic pattern of texts. On the one hand, repeated thematic patterns or key concepts might have been emphasized in a different compositional time period. On the other hand, these direct textual connections, apart from any consideration of their immediate textual contexts, might have resulted from scholars' subjective and open-ended judgment of the texts rather than objective literary analysis. On closer inspection, however, as Damrosch claims, the interweaving of the law and history in the Pentateuch is intended not to interrupt the fluency of the narratives, but to complete the laws that have been shaped and framed by the narratives.[18]

For this reason, some scholars approach the relationship between narratives and laws in the Pentateuch from a perspective of literary unity.[19] In other words, the immediate narrative context of the laws affects how the laws should

17. Carmichael, *Illuminating Leviticus*, 11–36.

18. "Such neglect, whether benign or hostile, distorts the central literary concern of the Priestly writers who shaped the final form of the Pentateuch, which was precisely the interweaving of law and history. Far from interrupting the narrative, the laws complete it, and the story exists for the sake of the laws that it frames." Damrosch, *Narrative Covenant*, 262. Damrosch notes that "on the one hand, the narrative focus is altered, and the very representation of history is affected, by the prominence of ritual/legal material (and ritual/legal perspectives) in the Priestly Pentateuch. At the same time, on the other hand, the presentation of the Law is in turn affected by the great body of narrative around it, and the laws themselves are typically presented in narrative form." Damrosch, *Narrative Covenant*, 262.

19. For instance, Sprinkle reflects this perspective in his provision of several examples that explain biblical laws in Sprinkle, *Biblical Law*, 57–66. Watts also states that "the narrative context of Pentateuchal law confirms that the Torah is intended to be read as a whole and in order. . . . The placement of law within narrative conforms (at least in part) the reading of law to the conventions of narratives." Watts, *Reading Law*, 29. Nanette Stahl believes that the combination of law and narrative in the Pentateuch is an instance of thematic polyphony in the Bible, and that it communicates depth and complexity in telling of the story, as well as some ambiguity. Stahl, *Law and Liminality*, 51–56. Averbeck also argues that the framework of narratives plays a crucial role when one studies the Sinaitic law. "I suggest that we reconsider the whole matter of the narrative framework surrounding the Sinaitic law and the best kinds of scholar[ly] methodology to use in seeking legitimate results." Averbeck, "Form Critical, Literary," 28.

be read and interpreted,[20] and vice versa.[21] Regarding the Sinai pericope from Exodus 19 to Numbers 10:10, God has established his relationship with the Israelites by showing his grace and mercy through the salvific act of the historical exodus. The later giving of the laws should be regarded as a means of maintaining and regulating the relationship that has been made within the Sinai pericope.[22] If one compares this passage with other Ancient Near Eastern (ANE) texts and certain covenant-making narratives in the Bible (e.g. Gen 31:44–54), it becomes clear that it can be regarded as a covenant-making narrative.[23] In this covenant-making framework, the laws also serve as an instrument by which the narrator communicates God's character to his people, the Israelites, since the laws are God's own words and thus an effective means to portray his character.[24] On the other hand, the laws themselves provide the

20. In the literary approach to the laws and narratives in the Pentateuch, some scholars adopt the synoptic/resumptive approach to a text. For example, Chirichigno adopts the resumptive approach to analyze the structure of Exodus 19–24, which results in the nonlinear temporal ordering of events. Chirichigno, "Narrative Structure," 478–79. Sprinkle agrees with the resumptive approach proposed by Chirichigno. Sprinkle, *Biblical Law*, 56–57. However, this approach is criticized by Averbeck, who argues that "the narrative framework of Exod[us] 19–24 is, by and large, sequential." Averbeck, "Form Critical, Literary," 24.

21. Sprinkle mentions that the legal context in the Pentateuch also affects the reading of narratives. Sprinkle, *Biblical Law*, 61–66.

22. Sprinkle, 49–50. "Israel's relationship with God originates *before* the giving of the law in the divine-human encounter between God and Israel at the exodus. . . . The law's context in the narrative of God's establishing a personal relationship with Israel explains the frequent use of first and second person personal pronouns, 'I-Thou' language, in the laws of Exod 20–23. This personal language thus shows the laws to be more than a list of 'do's and do not's.' They are part of God's personal message to his people meant to deepen their personal relationship with him."

23. "The covenant making narrative framework seems to be intact, the theophany encased within the covenant making narrative makes more sense as it stands than we have often realized, and the connections between the beginning and end of the pericope are substantial." Averbeck, "Form Critical, Literary," 28. Watts also concludes that the material from Exodus 25 through Numbers 9 employs the rhetoric of narrative and law to develop a dialectical tension between the idealistic divine-human communion and realistic warnings of its dissolution. "The persuasive intent behind this pattern aims to inspire compliance with the legislative program by describing ideal communion with God and to discourage noncompliance by detailing past and future threats." Watts, *Reading Law*, 55.

24. Sprinkle points out that both biblical and nonbiblical narrators can portray a character through the character's own words. Sprinkle, *Biblical Law*, 53. "The way a character is 'shown' is through his own words – his speech – and his actions (these are in the words of the narrators, of course). Biblical narrative makes extensive use of the speech and actions of characters to further the plot and to create characterization." Berlin, *Poetics and Interpretation*, 38–39. "Traits of both the speaker and the interlocutor are expressed through speech, or to be more precise, all speech reflects and exposes the speaker while it sometimes also brings to light qualities of the person being addressed (or reveals the speaker's opinion of that person)." Bar-Efrat, *Narrative Art in the Bible*, 64–65. Genette claims that this kind of direct/reported speech is a

divine authority and motivation for the Israelites to obey them.[25] After all, as Sprinkle has pointed out, "the laws of the Pentateuch at the least assume the narratives of the Pentateuch. . . . Perhaps greater attention to the relationship of laws and narratives will prove a fruitful avenue for future OT research."[26]

Moreover, within the Sinai pericope (Exod 19–Num 10:10) Knierim points out that there are two parts in the total narrative with respect to the locations where the revelation of YHWH was given: the revelation on Mount Sinai in Exodus 19–40 and the revelation in the tent of meeting from Leviticus 1:1–Numbers 10:10.[27] However, Smith further observes that there are three stages for the Israelites to the covenant-making between YHWH, who called them, and the Israelites: namely, setting up the tent of meeting, YHWH speaking to them from the tent of meeting, and preparation for moving with the tent of meeting.[28] The internal structural indicators are the inclusio framework of Leviticus 1:1 and Numbers 1:1. The specific formula וַיְדַבֵּר יְהוָה אֵלָיו מֵאֹהֶל מוֹעֵד and וַיְדַבֵּר יְהוָה אֶל־מֹשֶׁה בְּמִדְבַּר סִינַי בְּאֹהֶל מוֹעֵד appears only in these two verses, with the emphasis of the tent of meeting forming a pair of "bookends" for the book of Leviticus.[29] These "bookends" act as indicators, prompting us not only to recognize the book of Leviticus as an independent literary unit, but also to realize that the "Sinai-pericope aims at the book of Leviticus," which "is

constitutive element of narration. Genette, *Narrative Discourse*, 172–85; Genette, *Figures III*, 191–203. However, I cannot agree with Ruwe, who adopts Genette's observation and argues that the direct speeches in Leviticus are just a "mimetic form" of the presentation of speeches. Ruwe, "Structure of Book of Leviticus," 57.

25. Sprinkle, *Biblical Law*, 55. For a detailed discussion of the motivation of the laws in the Pentateuch, see Sonsino, *Motive Clauses in Hebrew*, 65–133; Cf. Rodd, *Glimpses of a Strange Land*, 109–25. Levinson concludes that "one of the features that distinguishes the biblical concept of revelation is that it is a legal revelation. The attribution of the ultimate authorship of a corpus of law to God and its designation as his personal will are unique in the Ancient Near East to the Hebrew Bible." However, he believes that "the divine attribution of the laws points finally to the divine voice of human exegesis." Levinson, "Right Chorale," 148, 150. This conclusion totally rejects the divine revelation in the Hebrew Bible. He further claims that the Bible deconstructs itself in this way by containing a colophon structure in Leviticus. He observes that the book of Leviticus concludes with a colophon (Lev 27:34), which is standard in Near Eastern ritual texts. Moreover, he regards the detailed repetition in Leviticus 26:46 as seeming to raise questions regarding the book's structure. Levinson, 150.

26. Sprinkle, *Biblical Law*, 67.

27. Knierim, "Composition of Pentateuch," 405.

28. Smith, "Literary Structure of Leviticus," 19.

29. Smith, 19.

the center of the Pentateuch."[30] Thus, in the following section, we will closely examine the relationship between law and narrative in the book of Leviticus.

The Relationship between Law and Narrative in Leviticus

In approaching the ritual texts in Leviticus, one finds that the genre(s) and contents of this book are prominent in the Sinai pericope. Since Leviticus bears a clearly defined objective that is fulfilled within its own texts, one can almost confirm that it should be dealt with as a separate book in the Pentateuch,[31] even though there is also a certain level of continuity among Exodus, Leviticus, and Numbers, especially within the Sinai pericope.

Mann astutely observes that in the Pentateuch, "there is a symbiotic relationship between narrative framework and the rules: the narrative converts the rules into the words, the speech, of Yahweh, and the speech tells us more about the person rendered by the narrative."[32] He further explains that the regulations cannot be understood correctly without their narrative framework, while the narratives are imperfect without the divine speeches with which they coexist.[33] It is true that one should explore the relationship between saying (the proclamation of ritual regulations) and doing (the narrations) in order to understand the meanings of rituals in Leviticus. Thus, before we devote our attention to the literary structure of Leviticus in view of the role of Leviticus 17, it is important to obtain a preliminary understanding of the relationship between narrative and law in Leviticus per se.

Leviticus is a good place to begin considering the literary relationship between narrative and law, which is a complex but harmonious interplay. In Leviticus, "law and history meet on a common ground composed of ritual, symbolic, and prophetic elements."[34] The initial chapters of Leviticus describe the regulation of sacrifices in an instructional way. However, as Levinson

30. Knierim, "Composition of Pentateuch," 405.

31. Regarding the consideration of Leviticus as a separate book, see footnote 29 in chapter 1, on page 7 of this book.

32. Mann, *Book of the Torah*, 116.

33. "Words and deeds belong together, and only together do they fully render the person of Yahweh as represented in the Pentateuchal narrative." Mann, 116. Rappaport concludes that "the complex relationship between the self-referential and the canonical streams of ritual's messages is best approached through further exploration of the relationship between saying and doing." Rappaport, *Ritual and Religion*, 107.

34. Damrosch, *Narrative Covenant*, 263.

observes, the ritual regulations can be analyzed in the same way as the narratives in terms of their stylistic features: voice of persona, repetition, point of view, literary structure, and so on.[35]

Repetition as a Literary Device

According to the critical interpretation, repetition in the law and narrative is a feature of multiple diachronic sources combined together later in history.[36] Other interpreters, however, have increasingly recognized repetition as a literary device that functions in Pentateuchal law much as it does in narrative or wisdom texts.[37] As one investigates the rhetorical and didactic function of laws and rituals, the element of repetition thus becomes conspicuous in the study of the literary structure of Leviticus. Since the Israelite laws were traditionally read in public, the repetition may serve not only to highlight the significant themes in the ritual,[38] but also to enhance the mnemonic force of the commandments.[39] Amid the repetitions in the composition of instructional ritual regulations, variation – such as that in Leviticus 1–3 – is also a prominent feature in the law codes, though it is rare to repeat the entire ritual.[40]

35. Levinson, "Right Chorale," 148. Regarding the narrative features of the rituals in Leviticus, see Lund, *Chiasmus in New Testament*, 51–59. Lund concludes that "the chiastic structures in the Law are not confined to the legal sections only but are found also in the narrative parts." Lund, 59.

36. Noth, for example, insists that the various blocks of legal material in the Pentateuch "were once independent units, subsisting in their own right, each having its own purpose and sphere of validity, and having been transmitted individually for its own sake in the first place." Noth, *Laws in Pentateuch*, 7; See Johnstone, "Reactivating Chronicles Analogy," 28; See also Blum, *Studien zur komposition*, 197–200.

37. "Recent redactional theories of the Pentateuch's composition . . . confront multiple repetitions with a single redactional layer. Such theories have therefore highlighted repetition as a literary strategy employed consciously by the Pentateuch's editors." Watts, *Reading Law*, 69. This idea and practice also appears in Carmichael, *Laws of Deuteronomy*, 255; Dozeman, *God on the Mountain*, 145–75.

38. "Repetition plays a decisive role in many forms of narrative literature, including the stories of the Hebrew Bible. But its presence is even more pronounced in Pentateuchal law, with distinct codes overlapping in their subject matter and re-presenting laws that are elsewhere found in narratives." Watts, *Reading Law*, 68.

39. Watts, 70–71.

40. Watts, 73.

Recurrence of Theme as a Rhetorical Device

Similar to the device of repetition in the law codes, the recurrence of certain significant themes is also a prominent feature of the Pentateuchal composition. Watts mentions the distinct twelvefold repetition of the Sabbath command in the Pentateuch.[41] This Sabbath theme appears so often within "different sources" identified by traditional critical interpretation of the Pentateuch, while also bearing a strong thematic consistency in terms of contents, that it must have been intentionally emphasized in the compositional structure.[42]

Drawing upon the theme of divine-human communion in the Pentateuchal laws, Watts demonstrates that a strong thematic relationship exists between the golden calf incident in Exodus 32–34 and the inauguration account in Leviticus 8–10, in that both warn of dangers that threaten divine-human communion.[43] First, the golden calf incident in Exodus 32–34 is placed between the instructions for building the tabernacle and the narrative account of building the tabernacle. Likewise, the inauguration account is located between the prescription of sacrifices and the actual operation of the priestly office in the tabernacle.[44] Second, both the golden calf incident and the inauguration account threaten Israel's worship of God, especially in its observance of rituals.[45] Third, both incidents threaten the existence of the people as a whole and require the vigilance of priests and people alike (Exod 34:11–16;

41. Watts, 68.

42. Watts, 69.

43. Watts, 54.

44. Mann makes a similar observation and claims that these two narrative accounts (Exod 32–34 and Lev 8–10) are placed between a certain structural framework. However, Watts emphasizes the structural framework is the instruction and the operation of the instruction, while Mann emphasizes two sets of lists. "Two narrative complexes find places between sets of lists: the story of the golden calf and its consequences (Exod 32–34, which itself incorporates another list, the 'ritual decalogue' of 34.10–26) appears between the building instructions and the account of their fulfillment (itself mostly narrative repetition of the earlier list of instructions), and the story of the inauguration of cultic worship in the Tabernacle (Lev 8–10) sits between the sacrificial rules and the purity regulations." Mann, *Book of the Torah*, 114–15. It seems to me that Mann focuses more on the immediate textual details, while Watts has a broader textual context in mind.

45. "Thus both sets of narratives emphasize that observant maintenance of the cult preserves the people's standing before God. . . . Divine sanctions play a major structural role at the end of Leviticus, repeating the idealistic promise of the lists but emphasizing even more the dangers highlighted by the narratives." Watts, *Reading Law*, 54.

Lev 10:8–11).[46] Fourth, both incidents are related to the medium of fire (Exod 32:24; Lev 8:1) and result in death as punishment (Exod 32:25–35; Lev 10:2). Watts suggests that Leviticus 26 also stands out in regard to the theme of divine-human communion, since it designates both blessings of observance and curses of disobedience, with the latter receiving more attention (Lev 26:14–39). However, Leviticus 26 is different from the golden calf incident because Leviticus 26 expresses that God's mercy will always be met through repentance, even in exile.[47]

In Sailhamer's view, the golden calf incident and the mention of sacrifices to the goat idols are embedded among several sections of laws and regulations and constitute two occurrences of the theme of idol worship. These two events play a crucial role in structural strategy of the Sinai pericope. Sailhamer observes an ever-increasing cycle of disobedience followed by the addition of more laws. He concludes that a clear covenant-making structure is present in this pericope. It includes the original covenant at Mount Sinai (Exod 19–24), the covenant renewal after the sin involving the golden calf (Exod 32–34), and the subsequent laws (Lev 1–16). It then incorporates the offering of sacrifices to goat demons outside the camp (Lev 17), the subsequent laws (Lev 18–25), and, finally, the covenant renewal (Lev 26).[48] Sailhamer mentions that, except for the larger portion of narrative in the Sinai pericope (Exod 19–34), the Pentateuch contains mostly smaller but strategically important narratives. Among these, he identifies only Exodus 32 and Leviticus 17:1–9 as narrative passages in the Sinai pericope.[49] I cannot agree with Sailhamer

46. Watts, 54. The golden calf incident "narrates the subversion of Israel's cult into idolatry even before its institutions have been constructed. The incident threatens the existence of the people as a whole (Exod. 32.9–14) and the less dire outcome nevertheless emphasizes the close connection between ritual observances and Israel's endurance as a people (e.g. in the 'ritual decalogue', 34.10–26)."

47. "The blessings and curses that conclude Leviticus thus encapsulate the rhetoric of ideals and threats emphasized by the preceding lists and stories respectively, but end by synthesizing this dialectic into a vision of YHWH's eternal faithfulness to the covenant. As a result, the idealism of the priestly legislation becomes more than a statement of obligations enforced by threats; it unveils a vision of hope grounded in YHWH's covenant commitment to Israel. . . . The divine sanctions of Leviticus 26 combine both elements of the dialectic and transcends them with a wider promise of God's covenant faithfulness. The priestly writers and editors thus used the rhetoric of list, story and divine sanction to persuade their readers and hearers of both the serious consequences of human actions and the constancy of divine mercy." Watts, *Reading Law*, 55.

48. Sailhamer, *Meaning of Pentateuch*, 44–48.

49. Sailhamer, 360.

on this point, since there are at least two more apparent narrative passages in Leviticus:[50] Leviticus 8–10 and 24:10–12.[51] Given the literary style and contents of Leviticus 17:1–9, however, it should be regarded as a ritual regulation instead of a narrative passage because it has the same introductory formula as the other ritual regulation speeches in Leviticus (וַיְדַבֵּר יְהוָה אֶל־מֹשֶׁה לֵּאמֹר׃).

Dynamics between Narrative and Ritual

The interweaving of introductory narratival speeches and rituals is one of the prominent features of the book of Leviticus.[52] Sherwood points out the distribution of the *wayyiqtol* verbs in Leviticus via the statistic graphics.[53] Compared with Numbers, many *wayyiqtol* verbal forms simply introduce the speeches in Leviticus. These occurrences thus become a distinctive feature in the structure of Leviticus.[54] This forms a narratival context in which the level of direct speech stands out compared to the narrative level of the text, which stays in the background. Many ritual commands and instructions are phrased in the form of divine speeches.[55] Sherwood identifies וַיְדַבֵּר יְהוָה אֶל־מֹשֶׁה, which occurs thirty-four times in Leviticus, as one clear structural element of the book.[56]

---

50. Aside from these two blocks of narrative and speech formulas (e.g. Lev 4:1, "וַיְדַבֵּר יְהוָה אֶל־מֹשֶׁה לֵּאמֹר׃"), there is probably only one verse in Leviticus that could be classified as a narrative statement: Leviticus 24:23, which is related to the narrative in 24:10–12.

51. Scholars who hold this view include Damrosch, Watts, and Douglas. Damrosch, *Narrative Covenant*, 278. "Thus the short story of the half-alien blasphemer (Lev 24:10–23) becomes a key transition (the Tabernacle's second 'screen') simply because it is a narrative in contrast to its instructional context." Watts, *Ritual and Rhetoric*, 21; See also Watts, *Reading Law*, 53, and Douglas, *Leviticus as Literature*, 227–51.

52. Fretheim points out that while there is less narrative in Leviticus, there is enough – including at least Leviticus 8–10 and Leviticus 24:10–23 – to maintain this feature. Moreover, inasmuch as it is part of the larger Sinai narrative and most chapters contain the speech formula at the beginning, Leviticus is a composition related to Israel's ongoing life, not just a law code or a compilation of static statutes. Fretheim, *Pentateuch*, 124. McEntire identifies a series of divine speeches in Leviticus 1–7 that affects the macro-structure of this section. McEntire, *Struggling with God*, 126–27.

53. Sherwood, *Leviticus, Numbers, Deuteronomy*, 8–10. Sherwood also shows the number of *wayyiqtol* verbs (188) in Leviticus in comparison to Genesis (2113), Numbers (755), and Deuteronomy (252). In Leviticus, the *wayyiqtol* form "is relatively scarce." Sherwood, 8.

54. Sherwood, 9.

55. Though the narrative texts of Leviticus seem fragmentary, "it cannot be denied that Leviticus is a narrative context." Ruwe, "Structure of Book of Leviticus," 57.

56. Sherwood, *Leviticus, Numbers, Deuteronomy*, 19. Although Sherwood mentions that there are thirty-five occurrences in total, his actual list contains only thirty-four. Nonetheless, based on my examination of the speech formula in Leviticus, we will include וַיְדַבֵּר יְהוָה אֶל־אַהֲרֹן

Nonetheless, according to my examination of the speech formula in Leviticus in terms of the structural framework, we shall include וַיְדַבֵּר יְהוָה אֶל־אַהֲרֹן in Leviticus 10:8 and וַיֹּאמֶר יְהוָה אֶל־מֹשֶׁה in Leviticus 21:1. There are thus a total of thirty-six occurrences of the speech formula in Leviticus.[57]

Bibb observes that the rituals in Leviticus are "narrativized,"[58] while the narratives are "ritualized."[59] From Bibb's perspective, "narrativized ritual"[60] and "ritualized narrative"[61] represent two interactive aspects of the same genre because, on the one hand, the ritual aspect could not survive as a totally independent text, while, on the other hand, the narrative bears significant ritual elements within its narration.[62] Bibb emphasizes, moreover, that integrating the analysis of both the ritual dynamics and the narrative framework in Leviticus is critical to the book's interpretation. He thus points out that not only the inset narratives in Leviticus – Leviticus 8–10, 16, and 24:10–23[63] – but

in Leviticus 10:8 and וַיֹּאמֶר יְהוָה אֶל־מֹשֶׁה in Leviticus 21:1, bringing the total number of occurrences of the speech formula in Leviticus to thirty-six.

57. Please refer to Appendix 1 of this book.

58. "They contain prescriptive instruction for how (and when, and why) the people should conduct their basic practices. Ritual prescription has been put into narrative, creating a 'narrativized ritual.' The ritual dimension of this text is *still* ritual, but now taking a different literary form, that of narrative description." Bibb, *Ritual Words*, 35.

59. Bibb, 35. "Therefore, the story encountered by the reader in Leviticus is a special kind of narrative, a ritualized narrative, and interpretation of this story must attend to its ritual dynamics, just as one might do with any ritual text."

60. Bibb, 34. "Leviticus is not a priestly manual, a descriptive account of ritual behavior, or a fictional narrative with literary purposes. Actually, to some degree it is all of these things, but none of them define the book. These various generic elements interact in the final mix of the book to form a genre called here 'narrrativized ritual.'" I agree with Bibb that the rituals in Leviticus can be regarded as "narrativized ritual" since it is evident that the ritual regulations in this book are not only purely descriptive accounts of ritual behavior or priestly instructions, but also form a clear description of ritual within a narrative framework. However, I disagree with Bibb's view of Leviticus as a fictional narrative because the close relationship between narratival framework and ritual in Leviticus makes it difficult to deny these events did happen in Israel's history.

61. Bibb, 34. On the other hand, Bibb claims that "Leviticus is primarily a descriptive narrative, but the rituals it narrates have a clear prescriptive intention. Thus, the writing and reading of Leviticus are ritualized, whereby the telling and experiencing of this mythic narrative has ritual-like qualities, mirroring its ritual content." However, his identification of the narrative in Leviticus as a mythic but not historical narrative should be carefully examined.

62. Bibb, 35. Bibb argues that "as literature, Leviticus reveals a novel combination of ritual and narrative. The dynamic interaction of 'list' and 'story' blend into a single genre, called here 'narrative ritual,' in which the ritual prescriptions are narrativized and the story-telling itself is ritualized." Bibb, *Ritual Words*, 33.

63. Similarly, C. R. Smith claims that "we may be even more confident that ch. 16 functions structurally like the two more obvious narratives when we observe that ch. 8–10; 16 and 24.10–

also the introductory narrative setting posited at the beginning of every ritual passage should be recognized as "ritualized narrative."[64] Even though Leviticus 16 is not always regarded as a narrative passage,[65] Bibb's acknowledgment of the coexistence of narrative and ritual in Leviticus and the weightiness of the narrative framework in regard to the structure of Leviticus should be taken into consideration if one is to take the interpretation of Leviticus seriously.

Regarding the relationship between narrative and ritual in Leviticus, Bibb argues that, after some legal texts were enacted to anticipate a coherent system of behaviors, the narrative broke the harmony of the divine-human relationship and exposed the weakness of the legal enactment. Further law-giving was therefore necessary in order to cope with the newly discovered perplexity.[66] At first thought, this explanation of the interaction between narrative and ritual seems quite practical and reasonable. According to Bibb, this approach reveals that the laws given by God fall short of wholeness because whenever the weakness of a given law is exposed, more regulations must be enacted to resolve the exposed ambiguity. In other words, if the weaknesses of the laws had not been exposed, there would be no further enactments. However, I would regard the laws given by God in the Pentateuch as a whole: no matter what happened in history or how God's people responded to the legislations, God would have discoursed these legal texts in accordance with his will under his covenant with his people in Sinai. The historical reality of discoursing more regulations after certain events shows us that God revealed his will to the Israelites at different stages, providing regulations according to their changing needs. This elaborate and inseparable dynamic between narrative and ritual in Leviticus should not diminish our sense of the wholeness of

23 relate to one another self-consciously." Smith, "Literary Structure of Leviticus," 23. See also Hartley, *Leviticus*, xxxi–xxxii. I would rather regard Leviticus 16 as functioning as a narrative framework but, strictly speaking, not a narrative itself, since it contains narratival description only in Leviticus 16:1 and 34b.

64. Bibb, *Ritual Words*, 35.

65. For example, Ruwe notes that the narrative level of the text of Leviticus is limited to Leviticus 8–10, Leviticus 21:24, 23:44, 24:10–23, the summaries in Leviticus 7:37–38, 26:46, 27:34, and the thirty-seven so-called divine speech formulae. Ruwe, "Structure of Book of Leviticus," 57.

66. "These narrative sections, moreover, reveal the social dynamics of participation, negotiation, and power implicit in the previous ritual texts." Bibb, *Ritual Words*, 73.

God's laws – instead, we can see it as a manifestation of God's wisdom and action in the reality of human history.[67]

Since the rituals in Leviticus are texts rather than live actions in our modern social context, the literary structure – including the narrative framework and rhetorical emphases – should gain a heavier weight.[68] We are searching out the meaning of texts, and should not overemphasize our participation in the ritual processes described in the texts.[69]

The Connection between Leviticus 1–16 and 17

With respect to the macrostructure of Leviticus, Shea claims that the book could be divided naturally into two subunits – Leviticus 1–16 and 17–27.[70] Nevertheless, some scholars include Leviticus 17 in a different subunit. This group includes R. Gane, who regards Leviticus 17 as an independent unit;[71] Zenger, Jüngling, and E. S. Gerstenberger, who regard Leviticus 16–17 as an

67. In fact, no law code is comprehensive in the sense of covering all possible issues. This is recognized for all codes of law, ancient and modern.

68. Bibb, *Ritual Words*, 74. "The central claim is that the ritualization process has impacted the literary and rhetorical nature of the book, which can be discerned in characterization, narrative framing, and subtle use of ambiguity."

69. Bibb, 75. Bibb puts too much weight on reader experience as he discusses how readers can understand the meaning of rituals. He writes, "the narrative assumes that readers are interested in the outcome of the story, and that they acknowledge the necessity of learning these rules for themselves. In this way, the reader is drawn into the rhetorical web constructed by the narrative. This interpretative engagement follows the same contours of ritualization experienced by the characters in the story. We see and feel ourselves as participants within the community, standing alongside the priests as we watch every stroke of the knife, measuring our level of comprehension as the voice of God filters into our hearing."

70. "It is apparent from any review of the commentary literature on Leviticus that the book is well organized. Apart from a few minor differences, the outlines of Leviticus printed by the Bible commentaries are similar. The book divides naturally into two halves – chapters 1–16 and 17–27." Shea, "Literary Form," 135. Also see Averbeck, "Leviticus," in VanGemeren, *NIDOTTE* 4:909. Most scholars include Leviticus 17 in the latter part of Leviticus – chapters 17–26/27. See Elliger, *Leviticus*, 14–20; Wenham, *Book of Leviticus*, 3–6; Kornfeld, *Neue Echter Bibel*, 10–12; Knierim, "Composition of Pentateuch," 405–6; Cazelles, "Le Pentateuque comme Torah," 66–67; Hartley, *Leviticus*, xxx–xxxv; Grabbe, *Leviticus*, 18–21; Fretheim, *Pentateuch*, 122; Budd, *Leviticus*, 237–41; Smith, "Literary Structure of Leviticus," 26; Gorman, *Divine Presence and Community*, 2–3; Watts, *Reading Law*, 53; Otto, "Innerbiblische Exegese," 138–82; Otto, "Scribal Scholarship," 174–76; McDermott, *Reading the Pentateuch*, 155–64; Nihan, "Holiness Code," 81–82; Cox, *Pentateuch*, 64–65; Tidball, *Message of Leviticus*, 6, 23–25; Nihan, "Torah," 188–90; Nihan, *Priestly Torah to Pentateuch*, 108–10; Kiuchi, *Leviticus*, 18–23; Boyce, *Leviticus and Numbers*, 59–109; Willis, *Leviticus*, xix–xxi.

71. Gane, *Leviticus, Numbers*, 35–36.

independent subunit in the structure of Leviticus;[72] W. G. Scroggie, E. Blum, Ska, and Levine, who regard Leviticus 11–27 as a subunit;[73] Dorsey, who regards Leviticus 11–18 as a subunit;[74] Douglas, who regards Leviticus 11–17 as a subunit;[75] and J. Walton, who regards Leviticus 1–17 as a subunit.[76] These differences of opinion pertaining to the relationship between Leviticus 17 and the rest of the book disclose the importance of the discussion concerning the role of Leviticus 17 in the literary structure of Leviticus.

The Narrative Context of Leviticus 1–7

Since the book of Exodus concludes with the completion of the tabernacle, it seems that Leviticus should commence with the anointing of the tabernacle and the inauguration of the priests in Leviticus 8–10. A direct continuation of the story from the book of Exodus is expected, but Leviticus begins instead with a seven-chapter discussion of sacrificial prescriptions.[77] Moreover, as Mann observes, since the text of the golden calf incident (Exod 32–34) appears right before the section on the completion of the construction of the tabernacle (Exod 35–40), it is obvious that Leviticus 1–7 is embedded in a threatening situation. The Israelites broke the covenant between God and themselves through false worship conducted by the priest Aaron, as well as an unauthorized altar of sacrifice (Exod 32:5–6) – both of which took place in the golden calf incident in Exodus 32–34.[78] The detailed description of sacrifices in Leviticus 1–7 prior to the inauguration of the priests in Leviticus 8–10 is

---

72. Zenger, "Buch Levitikus," 65–72; Jüngling, "Buch Levitikus," 1–45; Gerstenberger, *Leviticus*, 18–19.

73. Scroggie, *Know Your Bible*, 31–32; Blum, *Studien zur komposition*, 318–32; Ska, *Introduction*, 32–33; Ska, "Structure du Pentateuque," 346–49; Levine, "Leviticus: Its Literary History," 1–23.

74. Dorsey, *Literary Structure*, 78–81.

75. Douglas, "Poetic Structure in Leviticus," 252–55.

76. Walton, "Equilibrium and Sacred Compass," 301.

77. Damrosch, *Narrative Covenant*, 263. The beginning of Leviticus, which seems to be disconnected from the end of Exodus, could be regarded as a gap of continuity in the text. As Walsh correctly observes, amid narratives in the OT, gaps of continuity "refer to places where there seems to be no logical connection between one passage (such as a speech or even a whole scene) and the next." Walsh further claims that, from a literary perspective, defining the gap of discontinuity as a point at which two originally independent sources have been combined cannot be accepted, since it denies the coherence of the text as a meaningful literary unity. Walsh, *Old Testament Narrative*, 68.

78. Mann, *Book of the Torah*, 114–15.

therefore a necessity that finds its significance in the literary background of the book of Leviticus. It is because the Israelites now have the tabernacle set up (Exod 40) that they now need regulations for its functioning. This would fit the way the last verses of Exodus 40 lead into the first verse of Leviticus as well. On the other hand, even though the threatening situation of the golden calf incident occurs in a period of time before the completion of the tabernacle, according to the text as it stands, it also indirectly points to the importance of the instructions for worshiping God in his presence. As a result, one can see that the dominant organizing principle in the Sinai pericope is narrative or narratival speech, not the list of ritual regulations, even though the list comprises the majority of Leviticus.[79]

Moreover, as far as the structure of the Sinai covenant in Exodus 19–Numbers 10:10 is concerned, close observation of the structure of the speeches reveals similar verbal conjugation – (וַיִּקְרָא אֵלָיו יְהוָה in Exodus 19:3 and וַיִּקְרָא אֶל־מֹשֶׁה וַיְדַבֵּר יְהוָה in Lev 1:1). These are the only two occurrences of the verb קרא in the speeches given by Yahweh to Moses in the entire Sinai pericope. The placement of these two occurrences is prominent, since they introduce major sections in the Sinai pericope: Exodus 19:3 initiates the covenant making procedure between Yahweh and the Israelites, while Leviticus 1:1 launches the new assignment given by Yahweh to the Israelites after the completion of the tabernacle that was filled with the glory of Yahweh.[80] As Jonker astutely points out, when the verb קרא is used with Yahweh as its subject, it expresses a certain level of theological significance. He claims that

79. I thus do not agree with Watts's opinion about this. He regards list, not story, as the dominant organizing principle in the priestly legislation. According to Watts, in the Sinai pericope: "Three kinds of lists follow each other in succession: instructions for building the Tabernacle (Exod. 25–31), continued and partially repeated by the listlike narrative of the fulfillment of these instructions (chs. 35–40); laws and regulations, which themselves divide into three literary blocks consisting of sacrificial regulations (Lev. 1–7), purity rules (Lev. 11–16), and laws of the holy community (Lev. 17–27); and census lists and rules for religious personnel (Num. 1–9)." Watts, *Reading Law*, 53. As for the genre of list, Scolnic points out its importance:"lists became an essential element in the functioning of society" as primitive but useful memory tools. Moreover, Scolnic emphasizes that "in a sense, all Biblical lists are imbedded in an ongoing context." See Scolnic, *Theme and Context*, 1–23.

80. Niehaus recognizes that Exodus 3–Numbers 36 belongs to the Sinai covenant, with treaty elements in the narrative, and that the book of Leviticus basically belongs to the section of Exodus 25–Leviticus 27, which is assigned by Niehaus as further *torah* of the Sinai covenant. Niehaus, "Covenant and Narrative," 550–51.

the meaning of קרא is "to call someone to be in service of Yahweh."[81] This meaning emphasizes that Leviticus 1:1 not only reveals a continuity with Exodus, but also denotes the beginning of a brand-new assignment given by Yahweh to the Israelites (וַיִּקְרָא אֶל־מֹשֶׁה וַיְדַבֵּר יְהוָה אֵלָיו מֵאֹהֶל מוֹעֵד לֵאמֹר׃) in Exodus 40, Moses could not enter the tabernacle. In Leviticus 1:1, Yahweh calls Moses from the tabernacle.[82] With this introductory formula, it denotes a new assignment to Moses by Yahweh. It also strengthens the argument that Leviticus is a separate book with respect to its literary structure.[83]

Aside from the use of the word קרא in the Sinai pericope, speeches are mostly given using the word דבר.[84] The word אמר is only used twice, in Exodus 20:22 and 31:12–13. According to Lund, אמר is one of the most frequently used verbs of communication and declaration in the Hebrew Bible. Especially in narrative texts, אמר is widely used to introduce direct speech without any special theological reference. However, in the expression of Yahweh's speeches to Moses in the Sinai pericope, אמר occurs only two times.[85] As for דבר, it is the verb most frequently used to express the action of speaking in the context of Yahweh's speeches to Moses in the Sinai pericope.[86]

Cynthia Miller compares the usage and focus of אמר and דבר. She observes that "אמר almost always appears with a quotation or objective noun phrase that gives the content of the speech event," while "דבר may appear alone to represent a speech event without specification of the content." On the other hand, "דבר, then, focuses upon speech as social action; אמר is the

81. Jonker, "קרא," in VanGemeren, *NIDOTTE* 3:972.

82. Knierim remarks that Leviticus 1:1 is a decisive literary signal in terms of the macrostructure of the Sinai pericope, because it designates a shift in place from Mount Sinai to the tent of meeting. Knierim further suggests that "Lev 1:1 signals the highest level in the macrostructure of the Sinai-pericope. According to this structure, the total narrative consists of two parts: the revelation from the mountain (Exod 19:3–40:38), and the revelation from the 'tent of meeting' (Lev 1:1–Num 10:10)." Knierim, "Composition of Pentateuch," 405. Cynthia Miller also points out that "Lev 1:1 introduces a divine speech to Moses with instructions for sacrifice." Miller, *Representation of Speech*, 162.

83. I do not agree with Tidball's argument that Leviticus cannot be read as a separate book. Tidball, *Message of Leviticus*, 24–25. See footnote 29 in chapter 1, on page 7 of this book.

84. Exod 20:1; 25:1–2; 30:11, 17, 22, 34; 31:1; 33:1, 5; 40:1; Lev 1:1–2; 4:1; 5:14; 5:20 [Eng. 6:1]; 6:1–2 [6:8–9], 12 [6:19], 17–18 [6:24–25]; 7:22–23, 28–29; 8:1; 10:8; 11:1–2; 12:1–2; 13:1; 14:1, 33; 15:1–2; 17:1–2; 18:1–2; 19:1–2; 20:1–2; 21:1, 16–17; 22:1–3, 17–18, 26; 23:1–2, 9–10, 23–24, 26, 33–34; 24:1–2, 13; 25:1; 27:1–2; Num 1:1.

85. Lund, "אמר," in VanGemeren, *NIDOTTE* 1:444.

86. Ames, "דבר," in VanGemeren, *NIDOTTE* 1:912.

semantically unmarked verb, indexing only the fact of the speech event in order to introduce its content."[87] Furthermore, she points out that the use of דבר is particularly striking in Leviticus: the most frequent use of דבר in Leviticus is the frame with לאמל, and it occurs forty-five times in Leviticus.[88] Together with other various structures of דבר, Miller observes, all occurrences are related to the message of YHWH. In contrast, the occurrences of אמר in Leviticus introduce the speech of humans.[89] Miller thus concludes that

> these data suggest that within Leviticus the metapragmatic resources for the representation of speech have been manipulated for special discourse-pragmatic effect. The local oppositions that exist in this particular portion of the Pentateuch between דבר and אמר reflect a particular narrative trope for segmenting the narrative and for highlighting divine, as opposed to human, speech.[90]

The Literary Flow of Leviticus 1–16

The legislation commences with a subsection touching upon private burnt offerings (Lev 1), the accessory cereal offerings (Lev 2), and a class of sacrifices known as well-being offerings (Lev 3). These first three chapters show a consistent triadic form. Each of these offerings is in turn divided into three variants, which describe different offerings that can be made to fulfill each type of sacrifice. This tripled threefold structure gives these chapters a certain lyrical aspect. Each subsection even ends with a refrain consisting of some variation on the formulaic phrase אִשֵּׁה רֵיחַ־נִיחוֹחַ לַיהוָה.[91] Besides the

87. Miller, *Representation of Speech*, 373. For more discussions regarding אמר and דבר, see pp. 373–98.

88. Miller, 384.

89. Miller, 384. As for the multiple-verb frames with קרא, there are only two instances in Leviticus (Lev 1:1 and Lev 10:4). Even-Shoshan, *New Concordance*, 1028. In Leviticus 10:4, the frame is קרא אל . . . אמר אל, while in Leviticus 1:1, it is קרא אל . . . דבר אל. The former one denotes the speech of Moses by using אמר and the latter one introduces the speech of Yahweh by using דבר. For more discussion on the multiple-verb frames of קרא, see Miller, *Representation of Speech*, 331–40.

90. Miller, 384–85.

91. This formulaic phrase and its variants appear in Leviticus 1:9, 13, 17; 2:2, 9, 16; and 3:5, 11, 16. Regarding the meaning of אִשֶּׁה in ritual contexts in the OT, Averbeck concludes that it "refers more specifically to the parts of offerings that were (a) burned on the altar, (b) reserved for the priests from those offerings of which a portion was burned on the altar, or (c)

lyrical structure in Leviticus 1–3, the dramatic presentation goes beyond simple description and portrays these texts as a ritual drama by showing us the interaction between three major characters: the person who offers the sacrifice, the priest, and God.[92]

The next subsection (Lev 4:1–5:13) deals with the important subject of the sin offering. The categories of persons who will offer this particular sacrifice are described in descending order of rank, beginning with the priests (Lev 4:3–12), followed by the congregation as a whole (Lev 4:13–21), the tribal leaders (Lev 4:22–26), and, finally, the common people as individuals (Lev 4:27–35). In general, the sacrificial animals used by the first two categories were young bulls, whereas those offered by the latter two groups were he-goats and she-goats, respectively. The guilt offerings are the final class of sacrifices discussed (Lev 5:14–26 [Eng. 5:14–6:7]). The animals used in all three instances of guilt offerings were young or adult sheep.

The text now turns to priestly regulations regarding the handling of these same sacrifices (Lev 6:1–7:38 [Eng. 6:8–7:38]).[93] The sequence is the same, with the exception that the verses dealing with the well-being offerings appear last (Lev 7:11–36).[94] Leviticus 7:37–38 finalizes the first section of seven chapters dealing with sacrificial legislation.[95] On the one hand, because Leviticus 6–7 deals specifically with the responsibilities of the priests in different sacrifices, these two chapters anticipate Leviticus 8–10. On the other hand, since they look back on one special aspect of the sacrifices prescribed in Leviticus

reserved for the priests and their families from those offerings of which a portion was burned on the altar." Averbeck, "אִשֶּׁה," in VanGemeren, *NIDOTTE* 1:548.

92. Damrosch, *Narrative Covenant*, 264.

93. "The presentation of the variants in each form of sacrifice has been handled with great skill. . . . Thus the text dramatized the sense of orderly sequence at the heart of ritual. The singularity of the giving of the law at Sinai is extended, through the rituals inaugurated at Sinai itself, to a narrative order of varied repetition. . . . The emphasis on the different forms of sacrifice gives a place for narrative contingency within the ritual order." Damrosch, 265.

94. Shea observes that the section comprised of well-being offering regulations is divided into two subsections, Leviticus 7:11–21 and 28–34. However, I will argue that this whole section should be extended to Leviticus 7:11–36 in regard to the textual contents, because the two sections – Leviticus 7:22–27 and 35–36 – excluded by Shea are closely connected to their textual precursors. Therefore, one should regard Leviticus 7:11–34 as a unified section of teaching on the well-being offering. Shea, "Literary Form," 136.

95. Shea argues that the concluding statement of Leviticus 1–7 is comprised by Leviticus 7:35–38; however, I would regard Leviticus 7:37–38 as the conclusion of Leviticus 1–7 since Leviticus 7:35–36 is a summary statement of the previous text regarding the well-being offering. Shea, 136.

1–5, they are not repetitious in a manner that detracts from the purpose of the book. Rather, they add a new dimension to the subject under discussion and form a natural transition between Leviticus 1–5 and 8–10.[96]

In Leviticus 8–10, the phrase כַּאֲשֶׁר צִוָּה יְהוָה appears thirteen times as a refrain.[97] This phrase appears ninety-four times in the Pentateuch,[98] with fifty-six of these instances occurring in the Sinai pericope.[99] Outside the Pentateuch, this phrase occurs only twenty-two times in the OT: twenty times in the historical books and only twice in the prophetic books (Jer 13:5; 26:8).[100] In this regard, one can see that this is relatively significant for the Sinai pericope in the Pentateuch, since about half the phrase's OT occurrences occur in this passage. Moreover, more than one-fifth of the occurrences in the Sinai pericope appear in Leviticus 8–10. This phrase thus becomes the literary emphasis in Leviticus 8–10.

First, the repetitive phrase not only highlights the thematic unity of Leviticus 8–10 and its preceding text (Lev 1–7) but also points back to the previous instructions for clothing and consecrating the priest in Exodus 29. In addition, this repetition drums the theme of perfect compliance with divine instructions into the core of the message of Leviticus 8–10.

Second, the emphasis on this phrase emphasized in Leviticus 8–10 immediately recalls the similar accent in Exodus 39–40.[101] Moreover, these two passages are thematically matched: Leviticus 8–10 emphasizes the inauguration of the priests and the rules for the priestly service in the tabernacle, whereas Exodus 39–40 focuses on the clothes of the priests and the consecration of the

96. Shea, 137.

97. Leviticus 8:4–5, 9, 13, 17, 21, 29, 34, 36; 9:6–7, 10; 10:15. Even-Shoshan, *New Concordance*, 980.

98. Even-Shoshan, 980.

99. Even-Shoshan, 980. Exodus 34:4; 35:1, 4, 10, 29; 36:1, 5; 38:22; 39:1, 5, 7, 21, 26, 29, 31–32, 42–43; 40:16; Leviticus 7:36, 38; 8:4–5, 9, 13, 17, 21, 29, 34, 36; 9:6–7, 10; 10:15; 16:34; 17:2; 24:23; 27:34; Numbers 1:19, 54; 2:33–34; 3:42, 51; 4:49; 8:3, 20, 22; 9:5.

100. Even-Shoshan, 980.

101. Watts points out that the phrase recalls the passage in Exodus 35–40; however, I would argue that the similar passage is Exodus 39–40 (in which the phrase occurs eighteen times) and would forgo including Exodus 35–38 (in which the phrase occurs only seven times). Watts, *Ritual and Rhetoric*, 104. The phrase כַּאֲשֶׁר צִוָּה יְהוָה appears eighteen times in Exodus 39–40: Exodus 39:1, 5, 7, 21, 26, 29, 31–32, 42–43; 40:16 (כְּכֹל אֲשֶׁר צִוָּה יְהוָה), 19, 21, 23, 25, 27, 29, and 32. Even-Shoshan, 980.

tabernacle. Both passages highlight the personnel who serve before Yahweh and the importance of the consecration of the tabernacle.

Third, the account of Nadab and Abihu's death in Leviticus 10 reveals the danger of priestly service and the necessity of total compliance with divine instructions. After that incident, Yahweh's direct speech to Aaron in Leviticus 10:9–11 grants authority to the high priest, but also emphasizes the important responsibilities of the priests in their office before Yahweh, clearly hinting at the following section of regulations in Leviticus 11–15.[102]

In Leviticus 11–15, the personal laws pertaining to uncleanness deal with unclean animals (Lev 11), uncleanness arising from childbirth (Lev 12), unclean diseases (Lev 13), cleansing from such diseases (Lev 14), and unclean discharge (Lev 15). After coming into contact with unclean animals, a person was regarded as unclean until evening and was to cleanse himself or herself by washing his or her clothes (Lev 11:24–25, 27–28, 31–32, 39–40).[103] Purification from uncleanness in connection with childbirth or discharges required the sacrifices of burnt offerings and sin offerings (Lev 12:6–8; 15:14–15, 29–30).[104] However, purification from the skin disease known as leprosy required the full sacrificial spectrum: burnt offering, cereal offering, guilt offering, and sin offering, although the well-being offering was not mandated (Lev 14:10–32). This section of Leviticus can quite clearly be seen as a coherent whole. As Shea points out, "An important point to observe is that purification from uncleanness did not require a different kind of offering from that which was previously prescribed for sin. Sin offerings and burnt offerings were offered for both sin and the more serious kinds of uncleanness."[105] Shea further suggests that Leviticus 16, which details the Day of Atonement,

102. Though the literary characteristics of each section of the book of Leviticus are varied in detail, the themes of Leviticus are smoothly and naturally united by the flow of narration. I therefore disagree with Bibb's conclusion regarding the composition of Leviticus as a priestly manual with some descriptive elements "serving only a rhetorical or pedagogical role in telling." Bibb, *Ritual Words*, 34–35.

103. Shea concludes that those in this category should cleanse themselves by bathing and washing their clothes. Shea, "Literary Form," 137. In Leviticus 11, however, it is clear that the only cleansing required is the washing of clothes.

104. Some minor differences exist between these two categories of uncleanness. For uncleanness due to childbirth, there is no mention of cleansing by bathing or washing. For uncleanness caused by discharge, however, the affected person remains unclean until evening and must then bathe and cleanse his or her clothes.

105. Shea, "Literary Form," 138.

may be seen as a kind of summary and close of the sacrificial system in the book of Leviticus, as well as a special ritual for the cleansing of the sanctuary rather than for the individual's forgiveness.[106]

The Contextual Relationship between Leviticus 1–16 and 17

First, one of the distinct commonalities between Leviticus 1–16 and 17 is the emphasis on sacrifices to Yahweh. Leviticus 1–16 is the main passage in the Pentateuch in which God enacted through Moses the regulation of sacrifices for the Israelites, setting up a clear system of sacrifices in the tabernacle, the building of which had been completed at the end of Exodus. In this regard, Leviticus 17 is much more similar in content to Leviticus 16 than it is to Leviticus 18, which focuses on sexual relations.[107]

Second, after carefully observing the context, one should realize that the occurrences of the regulation of well-being offerings show a certain repetitive pattern between Leviticus 1–16 and 17, binding them together. The regulation of well-being offerings appears in only three places in the Pentateuch, and they are all in Leviticus—Leviticus 3:1–17; 7:11–27; and 17:3–16. Moreover, all of them include two essential elements in their structures: the prescription of the regulation of well-being offerings (Lev 3:1–16; 7:11–21; and 17:3–9), followed immediately by the prohibition of eating blood and fat (Lev 3:17; 7:22–27; and 17:10–16). This thematic pattern thus unites the content of Leviticus 1–16 and 17.

Third, the mention of כפר and שָׂעִיר connects Leviticus 17 with Leviticus 16. The verb כפר is used one hundred and one times in the OT, including sixty-one times in the Sinai pericope.[108] This shows that the concept of כפר is prominent in covenant-making in the Sinai pericope, especially when God first set up the regulation for the Israelites to approach him in the tabernacle. Furthermore, of the sixty-one pericope occurrences, forty-nine appear in the book of Leviticus, with forty-five of these forty-nine appearing in Leviticus 1–16.[109] כפר appears twice in Leviticus 17:11, and only twice in Leviticus 18–27. This distribution apparently signals another strong tie linking Leviticus

106. Shea, 132–33, 138.

107. Rendtorff, "Is It Possible?" 29.

108. Even-Shoshan, *New Concordance*, 560.

109. Even-Shoshan, 560. In the book of Leviticus, כפר occurs in Leviticus 1:4; 4:20, 26, 31, 35; 5:6, 10, 13, 16, 18, 26; 6:23; 7:7; 8:15, 34; 9:7 (twice); 10:17; 12:7, 8; 14:18, 19, 20, 21, 29,

17 with its precursor, Leviticus 1–16.[110] As for the word שָׂעִיר, it appears twenty-one times in Leviticus, with fourteen occurrences in Leviticus 16 (vv. 16:5, 7, 8, 9, 10, 15, 18, 20, 21[twice], 22[twice], 26, and 27) and one in Leviticus 17 (v. 7).[111] The commandment to send the שָׂעִיר to bring the sins to the wilderness in Leviticus 16 and the prohibition against offering sacrifices to the שָׂעִיר in the wilderness are closely related to each other.

Fourth, special literary marks are present in the beginning of the Sinai pericope, the beginning of Leviticus, and Numbers. These texts do not start simply with וַיְדַבֵּר יְהוָה אֶל־מֹשֶׁה, but are instead introduced with וַיִּקְרָא אֵלָיו יְהוָה מִן־הָהָר (Exod 19:3), וַיִּקְרָא אֶל־מֹשֶׁה (Lev 1:1), and וַיְדַבֵּר יְהוָה אֶל־מֹשֶׁה בְּמִדְבַּר סִינַי בְּאֹהֶל מוֹעֵד (Num 1:1). However, Leviticus 17 has no notable introduction, beginning, like other subunits in Leviticus, with וַיְדַבֵּר יְהוָה אֶל־מֹשֶׁה. This observation thus supports the observation of continuity between Leviticus 1–16 and 17, as Leviticus 17 does not seem to be an introductory passage for a new paragraph.

The Connection between Leviticus 18–27 and 17

Upon approaching the discussion of Leviticus 17–27, one must immediately acknowledge that some scholars from the historical-critical perspective regard this portion as a composition independent from the preceding chapters (Lev 1–16). This argument offers both advantages and disadvantages concerning the structural connection between Leviticus 18–27 and 17. Before we devote our attention to evaluating this debate, we will first examine the literary flow of Leviticus 18–27.

The Literary Flow of Leviticus 18–27

When readers seek to assess the literary flow of Leviticus 18–27, they are often dismayed, since this portion of Leviticus largely lacks a narrative form. In the absence of any clear literary structure, it is filled with an assortment

31, 53; 15:15, 30; 16:6, 10, 11, 16, 17 (twice), 18, 20, 24, 27, 30, 32, 33 (three times), 34; 17:11 (twice); 19:22; 23:28.

110. Rendtorff, "Is It Possible?", 29; Milgrom, *Leviticus 17–22*, 1472–84.

111. Even-Shoshan, *New Concordance*, 1194.

of regulations and ethical statements, so-called "miscellaneous laws."[112] Damrosch, for example, claims that readers "are presented not with a non-narrative but with an antinarrative."[113] However, even though some scholars assert that Leviticus 18–27 seems to have no clear literary structure or focus, they still regard this text as somehow filling the need or purpose for a law governing the total life of community.[114] Such scholars maintain that, without this segment, Leviticus 1–16 would be too narrowly focused on the sanctuary and ritual, as Patrick has noted.[115] However, as we examine the text more closely, we can trace its literary flow, which is a continuation of its textual precursor, Leviticus 1–17.

It is clear that Leviticus 18 is closely related to Leviticus 20 in regard to content. The prohibition of various Canaanite customs in Leviticus 18 recurs in Leviticus 20 with some variation, along with an emphasis on the punishment for violating such prohibitions. Leviticus 19 also enacts crucial laws pertaining particularly to the Israelites as they settled in the land of Canaan – the land Yahweh promised to give to them. Moreover, Leviticus 19 emphasizes the holiness of Yahweh and the covenantal relationship between Yahweh and the Israelites as a means of motivating them to obey the regulations. As has been mentioned, the prohibitions against following Canaanite customs in Leviticus 18–20 continue in Leviticus 21–22, but the focus in the latter case is on the circle of priests and their similar motivations to obey the

112. The wide range and diversity of laws in Leviticus 17–26 have perplexed scholars attempting to determine the purpose of this portion of laws. For example, Patrick notes that "like the other lawbooks, H contains rules on the place and procedures for sacrifice (Lev. 17) and a festival calendar (Lev. 23). Other cultic duties of the laity are scattered through the code. Unlike any other biblical lawbook, H contains sections on the priesthood (Lev. 21; 22). Both chapters are addressed to the priests rather than the people (21:1, 16; 22:1; 22:17 includes laity), suggesting that in fact these rules are out of place in a lawbook designed for the publication of the divine law to the community." Patrick, *Old Testament Law*, 153. For a discussion of Leviticus 17 as the introductory chapter to the H collection, performing a role similar to that of Exodus 20:22–26 and Deuteronomy 12 in other law codes that begin with the regulations of sacrifices, see Driver, *Introduction to Literature*, 48. Cf. Haran, "Holiness Code," 820.

113. Damrosch, *Narrative Covenant*, 279.

114. Damrosch, 279.

115. Patrick claims that "H contains law and exhortation on a wide range of religious, communal, and economic topics. As part of the Priestly Source, it fills the need for a law governing the total life of the community. Without it, Priestly Law would be too narrowly focused on the sanctuary and ritual." Patrick, *Old Testament Law*, 145.

prohibitions, on the holiness of Yahweh, and on Yahweh's sanctification of his people.[116]

After enacting the regulations for life in Canaan, especially those related to the holiness required by Yahweh, Leviticus 23–26 continues the reference to Yahweh's feasts that the Israelites should observe every year. The word שׁבת appears in every chapter of Leviticus 23–26, where it not only emphasizes Yahweh's exaltation and sovereignty among his people but also reminds readers of Yahweh's creation work – He is the Lord of all the earth. Everyone, including non-Israelites, shall honor his name (Lev 24:10–23). Some scholars doubt the rationale for the placement of Leviticus 24;[117] however, if we follow the focus on honoring and exalting Yahweh in Leviticus 23–26 through to the end of the book, we will see that Leviticus concludes with the very same focus, evident in the climax of honoring God among his people. Furthermore, the mention of Mount Sinai in Leviticus 25:1 (בְּהַר סִינַי) signals the highest embodiment of the spirit of שׁבת. On the other hand, the mention of Mount Sinai in the concluding statement in Leviticus 26:46 (בְּהַר סִינָי) and Leviticus 27:34 (בְּהַר סִינָי) provides closure to the enactment part of the Sinai pericope, while serving as an apt conclusion to the book of Leviticus.

The Literary Characteristics of Leviticus 18–27

Before we continue to explore the relationship of Leviticus 17 and 18–27, let us look in depth at the literary characteristics of chapters 18–27. The following are some prominent literary features of Leviticus 18–27.

The Exodus Theme

F. Crüsemann has pointed out the important roles played by references to the exodus event in Leviticus 18–26.[118] In these passages (Lev 18:3; 19:34, 36; 22:33; 23:43; 25:38, 42, 55; and 26:13, 45), the exodus is bound up with the categories of holiness, sanctification, and the lordship of Yahweh.[119] One

116. Shea claims that the theological core of Leviticus 17–25 is sanctification (Lev 19:2). Shea, "Literary Form," 132.

117. "The rationale for the placement of the intervening ch. 24 has previously eluded exegetes. Its rules for certain rituals within the Tent and an apparently unrelated account of an incident of blasphemy seem at odds with the surrounding chapters." Kiuchi, *Leviticus*, 23.

118. Crüsemann, "Exodus," 117–29.

119. Even-Shoshan, *New Concordance*, 701–2.

should notice that there is one reference to the exodus in Leviticus 11:45 and that this reference introduces the exodus theme, which is magnified into the exodus pattern in Leviticus 18–26. By means of the exodus, Israel is separated from other peoples (Lev 20:24b). The Israelites become Yahweh's people, and he becomes their God. Therefore, the exodus is also understood as an act of sanctification, a term that is interpreted to mean "set apart." The lordship of Yahweh through his deed is both the presupposition and the foundation for everything in the exodus pattern.

Repetitive Motive Clause and Keyword

Some repetitive motive clauses add thematic unity to lists of extremely diverse material in Leviticus 18–26.[120] For example, in the book of Leviticus, the תּוֹעֵבָה (abomination) clauses appear only in chapters 18 and 20 (Lev 18:22, 26–27, 29–30; and 20:13),[121] and they are all related to the sexual behaviors that violate God's design for his creation. Another refrain appears much more often in Leviticus: אֲנִי יְהוָה אֱלֹהֵיכֶם/ אָנֹכִי יְהוָה אֱלֹהֶיךָ/ אֲנִי יְהוָה/אֲנִי יְהוָה אֱלֹהֵיהֶם (I am the LORD their God/I am the LORD your God/I am the LORD/I am the LORD your [plural] God). This phrase appears sixty times in the Sinai pericope,[122] including fifty-two times in Leviticus. However, the phrase appears forty-nine times in Leviticus 18–26, thus seeming to provide motivation for, and unification of, this entire body of text.[123]

120. Watts, *Reading Law*, 67; Also see Gemser, "Importance of Motive Clause," 51, 54–55, 63.

121. Even-Shoshan, *New Concordance*, 1223–24.

122. Even-Shoshan, 441. Exodus 20:2, 5; 29:46 (two times); 31:13; Lev 11:44, 45; 18:2, 4, 5, 6, 21, 30; 19:2, 3, 4, 10, 12, 14, 16, 18, 25, 28, 30, 31, 32, 33, 34, 36; 20:7, 8, 24, 26; 21:8, 12, 15, 23; 22:2, 3, 8, 9, 16, 30, 31, 32, 33; 23:22, 43; 24:22; 25:17, 18, 55; 26:1, 2, 13, 44, 45; Numbers 3:13, 41, 45; and 10:10. For more discussion regarding this phrase, see Sonsino, *Motive Clauses in Hebrew*, 110.

123. "I am the LORD (your God)" appears regularly throughout Leviticus 18–26 (see 18:2, 4–6, 21, 30; 19:3–4, 10, 12, 14, 16, 18, 25, 28, 30–32, 34, 36–37; 20:7–8, 24; 21:8, 12, 15, 23; 22:2–3, 8–9, 16, 30–33; 23:22, 43; 24:22; 25:17, 38, 55; 26:1–2, 13, 44–45). Gemser claims that "the same applies to the Law of Holiness, where moreover all the stipulations are sanctioned by the motive refrain *kî ʾanî Jahwè ʾelôhēkèm* and its variations. This refrain can better be understood as a kind of antiphon to the recital of the laws by the priest at the assembly in the sanctuary . . . than as an insertion of a scribe and redactor." Gemser, "Importance of Motive Clause," 63. From the historical-critical point of view, the argument is made that these various repetitions in Leviticus 18–26 point to a combination of several individual, autonomous collections. This view is supported by Sonsino, Eissfeldt, Fohrer, Killian, Feucht, and others. I do not agree with this view, however, because these repetitions, especially the motive clauses, could also contribute to the unity of these chapters. See Sonsino, *Motive Clauses in Hebrew*, 90; Eissfeldt, *Old Testament:*

Regarding the usage of קדשׁ in Piel form, this term appears thirty-nine times in the Sinai pericope.[124] Of these, twenty-one occur in Exodus, fifteen in Leviticus, and three in Numbers.[125] Four of the occurrences in Exodus and eight of the instances in Leviticus refer to consecration of the Israelites rather than of the priests, various objects, or the tabernacle.[126] קדשׁ occurs as a refrain – אֲנִי יְהוָה מְקַדִּשְׁכֶם – in Leviticus 20–22 (Lev 20:8; 21:8, 15, 23; 22:9, 16, 32),[127] which emphasizes the separation of the Israelites from the nations by Yahweh, who calls them and sanctifies them.

In regard to the clause קְדֹשִׁים תִּהְיוּ כִּי קָדוֹשׁ אֲנִי יְהוָה אֱלֹהֵיכֶם in Leviticus 19:2, three more similar clauses occur in Leviticus, namely, וִהְיִיתֶם קְדֹשִׁים כִּי קָדוֹשׁ אָנִי (Lev 11:44–45), וִהְיִיתֶם לִי קְדֹשִׁים כִּי קָדוֹשׁ אֲנִי יְהוָה (Lev 20:26), and כִּי קָדוֹשׁ אֲנִי יְהוָה מְקַדִּשְׁכֶם (Lev 21:8).[128] Shea argues that one of the features that bind Leviticus 17–27 together is "the theological impetus for their observance that appears in the recurrent statements, 'You shall be holy; for I the LORD your God am holy' (Lev 19:2). Hence, the identification of this reasonably well-organized collection of laws as the Holiness Code."[129] However, since this formulaic statement already appears in Leviticus 11 and does not appear in the beginning chapters of the Holiness Code (Lev 17–18), one should not conclude that this statement is a distinct and sole characteristic of Leviticus 17–26. Instead, the formula occurs in literary contexts where the emphasis is on not being unclean, but where the concern is separation from other nations.[130] This formulaic statement appears to be based on its literary context. One could observe that the formula occurs in a literary context emphasizing

Introduction, 236; Fohrer, *Introduction to Old Testament*, 138; Kilian, *Literarkritische*, 164–76; Feucht, *Untersuchungen*, 62–73.

124. Even-Shoshan, *New Concordance*, 1002–3.

125. Even-Shoshan, 1002–3. Exodus 19:10, 14, 23; 20:8, 11, 12; 29:1, 21, 27, 33, 36, 37, 44; 30:25, 29, 30; 31:13; 40:9, 10, 11, 13; Leviticus 8:10, 11, 12, 15, 30; 16:19; 20:8; 21:8, 15, 23; 22:9, 16, 32; 25:10; Numbers 6:11; 7:1 (2 times).

126. Even-Shoshan, 1002–3. Exodus 19:10, 14; 20:12; 31:13; Leviticus 20:8; 21:8 (2 times), 15, 23; 22:9, 16, 32.

127. Even-Shoshan, 1002–3.

128. Even-Shoshan, 999–1000.

129. Even-Shoshan, 1002–3. קדשׁ appears 171 times as a verb and 477 times as a noun in the OT. Even-Shoshan, 1002–5; Also see Warning, *Literary Artistry*, 218.

130. Ska is aware of the limitation of this linguistic marker and points out that, "unfortunately, the linguistic markers that would have permitted singling out this section [Lev 17–26] are not clear." He observes that the fomulatic phrase in Leviticus 19:2 neither occurs in the beginning of Leviticus 17, nor appears for the first time. Ska, *Introduction*, 33.

the commandment to not be unclean; on the other hand, this is why this formulaic statement appears as a group in the subunits of the literary structure of Leviticus that emphasizes the concept of separation from other nations and the requirement of cleanness in the Mosaic covenant.[131]

Furthermore, almost one-fifth of the OT occurrences of the root קדשׁ appear in Leviticus. In Leviticus, the root appears thirty-one times in different verbal forms, and ninety-two times as a noun. Taken together, these facts reveal that the concept of "holiness" runs through the whole book of Leviticus, striking a particularly prominent note in Leviticus 18–26.[132]

Commandment to Keep the Sabbath

Watts mentions that the Sabbath commandment in Exodus, Leviticus, and Deuteronomy is motivated by reference to Yahweh's identity.[133] In Leviticus, the root שׁבת appears thirty-eight times, including thirty-three times in Leviticus 23–26 (Lev 23:3[three times], 11, 15[twice], 16, 24, 32[four times], 38, 39[twice]; 24:8; 25:2[twice], 4[three times], 5, 6, 8[twice]; 26:2, 34[three times], 35[three times], 43).[134] The frequent occurrence of this word, especially in Leviticus 23–26, is distinct.[135] It is closely related to God's cessation from his creation of the world, and it not only underscores the significance of the holy nature of time – which is inseparable from who God is and what he has done in history – but also refers to the observance of rules within the human heart. This is emphasized through the two basic requirements of the feasts: cessation from ordinary work and dedication of oneself to Yahweh by

131. Naudé claims that "their call to holiness was based on the fact that they had become God's possession by virtue of his separating them from the nations (Lev 20:26). Thus, holiness should characterize Israel in its distinctiveness in relation to the nations with regard to purity laws (Lev 11:44–45) or moral behavior (Lev 19)." Naudé, "קדשׁ," in VanGemeren, *NIDOTTE* 3:883.

132. Shea, "Literary Form," 138–39. קדשׁ appears 171 times as a verb and 477 times as a noun in the OT. Even-Shoshan, *New Concordance*, 1002–5; Also see Warning, *Literary Artistry*, 218.

133. See Leviticus 19:3, 30 and 26:2. Watts, *Reading Law*, 73.

134. Even-Shoshan, *New Concordance*, 1112–13. Besides the occurrences in Leviticus 23–26, this root appears only five times in the rest of the book: Leviticus 16:23, 31 [twice]; 19:3, and 19:30.

135. Budd, *Leviticus*, 319.

means of sacrifices and offerings.[136] The contribution of the Sabbath regulations to the structure of the Sinai pericope will be examined in a later section.

Person-Using

In Leviticus 18–27, chapters 18–19 and 23–24 are dominated by laws in the second-person. Laws in the third-person are also present in Leviticus 17, 20 (vv. 1–16), and 27. However, both types of laws are interspersed in sections that mix third-person casuistic formulations with second-person apodictic commands, such as Leviticus 20:17–22:33 and Leviticus 25.[137] The rhetorical force of the second-person legal address was recognized by A. Alt, who located the original setting of apodictic language in cultic liturgies, rather than in the legal settings suggested by casuistic laws.[138] The second-person addresses serve to remind the reader that this is Yahweh's personal message for Israel;[139] however, they also give commandments a sense of immediacy and urgency and distinguish themselves by their normative force.[140] Second-person addresses thus highlight the rhetorical function of law, a function that seeks to persuade hearers or readers of the urgency of practicing a law's teaching. In other words, they aim to instruct their audience in a way of life.[141]

Exhortations

Leviticus couches its exhortations – for example, חֻקַּת עוֹלָם תִּהְיֶה־זֹּאת לָהֶם לְדֹרֹתָם (Lev 17:7) – in the indicative, which makes them easier to distinguish, especially in Leviticus 17–26 (Lev 3:7; 7:36; 10:9; 16:29, 31, 34; 17:7; 18:4, 5, 26; 19:19, 37; 20:8, 22; 23:14, 21, 31, 41; 24:3; 25:18; and 26:43, 46.)[142] These exhortations make explicit the didactic purpose behind the law: the text aims to instruct its readers, and through second-person addresses and exhortations calls them to pay close attention to its contents.[143]

---

136. Kiuchi, *Leviticus*, 430. See also Boyce, *Leviticus and Numbers*, 87; Willis, *Leviticus*, 192–93.

137. Watts, *Reading Law*, 63.

138. Alt, "Origins of Israelite Law," 125.

139. Sprinkle, *Biblical Law*, 52.

140. Watts, *Reading Law*, 53–54.

141. Watts, 64.

142. Even-Shoshan, *New Concordance*, 394–95.

143. Watts, *Reading Law*, 64–65.

The Contextual Relationship between Leviticus 18–27 and 17

As we have seen, a certain level of connection exists between Leviticus 1–16 and 17. There is also a clear connection between Leviticus 17 and 18–27. First, in Leviticus 17 and 20, the same punishments ("cut off" or "put to death," from כרת) are attached to many different laws (Lev 17:4, 9–10, 14; 20:3, 5–6, 17–18). Besides the occurrences in Leviticus 17 and 20, this condemnation occurs in Leviticus 7:20, 21, 25, 27; 18:29; 19:8; 22:3; and 23:29.[144] If one investigates these occurrences closely, two main categories of deeds emerge that lead to this punishment: most of the verses are related to the holiness of sacrificial procedure (Lev 7:20–21, 25, 27; Lev 17:4, 9–10, 14; 19:8; 20:3, 5–6, 17–18; 22:3; 23:29); the other category pertains to the holiness of sexual behavior, especially when the Israelites are in the land of Canaan (Lev 18:29; 20:17–18). The relationship between Leviticus 7 and 17 in regard to the holiness of sacrificial procedure is obvious, and this theme of sacrifice connects Leviticus 1–7 and 17. This condemnation also shows a close relationship between Leviticus 17 and its subsequent chapters, especially Leviticus 18–22. As Watts points out, "the regular repetition of these sentences unifies diverse material by emphasizing identical consequences. Repetition thus serves to unify at the thematic level particularly the legal collections and the Pentateuch as a whole. It establishes emphases which by their frequent reappearance come to represent the whole. Repetition makes law memorable and persuasive."[145]

Second, as one closely examines the contents, receivers, audience, and verb usage for receiver and audience in each of the occurrences of the divine speeches in the book of Leviticus, it becomes clear that there is an explicit literary function revealed in the divine speeches in consideration of the macro-structure.[146] W. Warning offers the hypothesis that "Leviticus has

144. Even-Shoshan, *New Concordance*, 563–64.

145. Watts, *Reading Law*, 71.

146. Labuschagne is aware of the pattern of the divine speeches in the Pentateuch and proposes that the verbs used in the divine speeches are unmistakably significant elements for the structure of Leviticus. Labuschagne, "Pattern of Divine Speech," 268–96. However, Klostermann was probably the first scholar to point out the function of the divine speeches. He claimed, "Man kann im allgemeinen sofort deutlich sehen, daß diese Gesetzessammlung die Form einer Gottesrede gehabt hat." [In general, one can immediately see clearly that this collection of laws took the form of a divine speech.] Klostermann, *Pentateuch*, 374. Gerstenberger contends that "although this expression ['he spoke to Moses'] seems to occur at peculiarly asymmetrical intervals,. . . it nonetheless is clearly conceived as an element of division." Gerstenberger,

been artistically structured by means of the phrase וידבר/ויאמר יי אל משה (ואל אהרן) לאמר 'the Lord spoke/said to Moses (and Aaron):' and the phrase וידבר יי אל אהרן לאמר 'and the Lord spoke to Aaron:' (10:8), the only case in Leviticus where the Lord addresses Aaron directly."[147]

Now, let us turn our focus on the relationship between Leviticus 18–26 and 17 in consideration of the speech formulas. Table 1 shows the results of an exploration of the divine speeches in Leviticus 17–22. The second column reveals that nine speeches in Leviticus 17–22 were given by Yahweh through Moses alone. However, the fifth column (labeled "speech audience") contains two occurrences of a phrase – דַּבֵּר אֶל־אַהֲרֹן וְאֶל־בָּנָיו וְאֶל כָּל־בְּנֵי יִשְׂרָאֵל ("speak to Aaron, his sons, and the Israelites") – that stands out in the book of Leviticus and is found in Leviticus 17:1–2 and 22:17–18.[148] These are the only two occurrences that include all three "parties" as the addressees of Yahweh's speeches in Leviticus and in the Sinai pericope, which makes this feature significant. In his recent study on the structure of the book of Leviticus, A. Ruwe declares that even though Leviticus 17 does not contain the exodus theme or repetitive motive clause (אֲנִי יְהוָה) that is typical of other chapters in Leviticus 18–26, there is no doubt that, structurally, Leviticus 17 belongs with the subsequent chapters, Leviticus 18–26, because "the divine speech formula in 17:1–2 is exclusively identical with the one in 22:17–18."[149] Furthermore, in both Leviticus 17 and Leviticus 22:17–25, one finds content concerning the animals permitted in sacrifices,[150] as well as specific mention of the well-being offerings. Therefore, based on the speech observations in Table 1, I would like to present some thoughts on the structure of Leviticus 17–22.

Leviticus, 4. Budd believes that "it is very probable that the repetition of the divine word to Moses (Lev 4:1; 5:14; 6:1; 6:8; 6:19; 6:24; 7:22; 7:27) marks the beginning of new sections and is an indicator of the component parts in each collection." Budd, *Leviticus*, 41. Meier points out that "the repetition in marking Yahweh's speech in Numbers and Leviticus . . . functions as a structuring device for distinct cultic and legislation topics." Meier, *Speaking of Speaking*, 74, n.1.

147. Warning, *Literary Artistry*, 38. McEntire notices that there are seventeen divine speeches using an introductory formula in Leviticus 17–27:1. See Table 4.4 in McEntire, *Struggling with God*, 141.

148. Warning, 40–41. Warning singles out these two identical phrases in his table of introductory formulae and addressees.

149. Ruwe, "Structure of Book of Leviticus," 70, n.37.

150. Ruwe, 70, n.37. Ruwe points out the connection between these two passages by discussing the permitted animals.

As mentioned above, the book of Leviticus contains only two passages in which all three parties (Aaron, his sons, and the Israelites) appear together as the speech audience. Furthermore, the reference to the well-being sacrifices not only forms a close relationship between Leviticus 17 and 22, but also introduces the inclusio structure in Leviticus 17–22 (A: 17:1–2 אֶל־אַהֲרֹן וְאֶל־בָּנָיו וְאֶל כָּל־בְּנֵי יִשְׂרָאֵל). Upon observation of the speech audience, one can find a very neat and orderly structure in these chapters: following Leviticus 17, with its unique speech audience of the three parties, chapters 18–20 consistently adopt only one of the three parties – namely, the Israelites – as the audience of three speeches. Beginning with Leviticus 21, the speech audience switches to the other two parties, Aaron and/or his sons, and there are three sections of speech before the end of the inclusio framework (A': 22:17–18 אֶל־אַהֲרֹן וְאֶל־בָּנָיו וְאֶל כָּל־בְּנֵי יִשְׂרָאֵל) appears in Leviticus 22:17–18.

Table 1. Analysis of the Speech Formula in Leviticus 17–22

Verse	**Speech Giver**	**Verb Used (Receiver)**	**Speech Receiver**	**Speech Audience**	**Verb Used (Audience)**	**Length of Speech**
17:1–2	יְהוָה	וַיְדַבֵּר	אֶל־מֹשֶׁה	אֶל־אַהֲרֹן וְאֶל־בָּנָיו וְאֶל כָּל־בְּנֵי יִשְׂרָאֵל	דַּבֵּר	**Chapter 17** **17:3–9 Regulation of well-being offerings** **(17:10–16 Prohibition of eating fat and blood)**
18:1–2	יְהוָה	וַיְדַבֵּר	אֶל־מֹשֶׁה	**אֶל־בְּנֵי יִשְׂרָאֵל**	דַּבֵּר	**Chapter 18**
19:1–2	יְהוָה	וַיְדַבֵּר	אֶל־מֹשֶׁה	**אֶל־כָּל־עֲדַת בְּנֵי־יִשְׂרָאֵל**	דַּבֵּר	**Chapter 19** **(19:3, 30 Sabbath)**
20:1–2	יְהוָה	וַיְדַבֵּר	אֶל־מֹשֶׁה	**וְאֶל־בְּנֵי יִשְׂרָאֵל** (1st word in v.2)	תֹּאמַר (2nd word in v.2)	**Chapter 20**
21:1	יְהוָה	וַיֹּאמֶר	אֶל־מֹשֶׁה	**בְּנֵי אַהֲרֹן** (1st word in the sentence) אֲלֵהֶם (3rd word)	וְאָמַרְתָּ (2nd word)	**21:1–15**

21:16–17	יְהוָה	וַיְדַבֵּר	אֶל־מֹשֶׁה	**אֶל־אַהֲרֹן**	דַּבֵּר	**21:16–23** **21:24 – Narrative statement** וַיְדַבֵּר מֹשֶׁה אֶל־אַהֲרֹן וְאֶל־בָּנָיו וְאֶל־כָּל־בְּנֵי יִשְׂרָאֵל
22:1–3	יְהוָה	וַיְדַבֵּר	אֶל־מֹשֶׁה	**אֶל־אַהֲרֹן** **וְאֶל־בָּנָיו** אֲלֵהֶם	דַּבֵּר אֱמֹר	**22:1–16**
22:17–18	יְהוָה	וַיְדַבֵּר	אֶל־מֹשֶׁה	אֶל־אַהֲרֹן וְאֶל־בָּנָיו וְאֶל כָּל־בְּנֵי יִשְׂרָאֵל	דַּבֵּר	**22:17–25** **Regulation of well-being offerings**
22:26	יְהוָה	וַיְדַבֵּר	אֶל־מֹשֶׁה			**22:26–33**

Moreover, as one examines the texts closely, a small unit of inclusio becomes evident in these two subunits (Lev 18–20 and Lev 21–Lev 22:16). In Leviticus 18–20, both chapters 18 and 20 are addressed to the Israelites (אֶל־בְּנֵי יִשְׂרָאֵל); however, chapter 19 emphasizes the congregation of Israelites (אֶל־כָּל־עֲדַת בְּנֵי־יִשְׂרָאֵל) as the central addressee in these three chapters. This finding is also consistent with the observation regarding content made by Kiuchi in his commentary on Leviticus. Kiuchi notes that variations of various prohibitions of Canaanite customs occur in both Leviticus 18 and 20, even though the emphasis in Leviticus 20 is more on punishment for violation of such prohibitions.[151] As for Leviticus 19, it is not only the structural center of these three chapters, but also the theological pivot of this subunit because it speaks of holiness and commands the Israelites to be holy.[152]

Similarly, in Leviticus 21:1–22:16, Leviticus 21:1–15 addresses Aaron's sons while 22:1–16 is addressed to Aaron and his sons; Leviticus 21:16–23, the center of three addresses in this subunit, addresses Aaron alone. Both Leviticus 21:1–15 and 22:1–16 deal with holiness in outward behavior and the handling of offerings; however, at the center of this subunit, the address given to Aaron alone focuses on the qualification of being a priest before the holy God, which is the foundation of Leviticus 21:1–15 and 22:1–16. Also, after Leviticus 21:16–23, there is one verse of narrative statement in Leviticus

151. Kiuchi, *Leviticus*, 23.

152. Kiuchi, 23.

21:24 regarding obedience to the commandment of Yahweh that recaptures the total audience of three parties in narration.

Lastly, between these two subunits (Lev 18–20 and Lev 21:1–22:16), another observation emerges that is worthy of discussion here. In the transition point of these two subunits – the last address of Leviticus 18–20 (וְאֶל־בְּנֵי יִשְׂרָאֵל תֹּאמַר) and the first address of Leviticus 21:1–22:16 (אֱל־הַכֹּהֲנִים בְּנֵי אַהֲרֹן וְאָמַרְתָּ אֲלֵהֶם) – a syntactical emphasis on the change of audience is achieved through fronting the preposition and the object instead of placing the verb at the beginning of the sentence.[153] This emphasis of discontinuity signals and leads readers to expect the macrostructure of Leviticus 17–22 to form a closed related subunit in the book of Leviticus.[154]

A Proposed Structure of Leviticus Based on the Role of Leviticus 17

Before proposing the structure of Leviticus, we should present a summary of the scholarly debates. For this, see Table 2, a modification of Luciani's summary table.[155]

153. "The *affected* object can be put at the beginning for the sake of emphasis; in this case the order is usually O–V–S." Joüon, *Grammar of Biblical Hebrew*, 583.

154. Ruwe, "Structure of Book of Leviticus," 70. Ruwe argues that the divine speech formulae confirm that Leviticus 17:1–26:45 "is a fairly independent complex within 9:1–27:34." Moreover, Ruwe identifies 17:1–22:31 is the first unit and 23:1–25:55 is the second unit in this complex. Based on the appearance of the divine speech formulae in Leviticus 17–22, however, I disagree with Ruwe's observation that leaves Leviticus 22:32–33 out of the structure. In my observation of the texts, according to the divine speech formulae the best way to divide Leviticus 22 is as follows: vv. 1–16, 17–25, and 26–33, in which it is vv. 17–25 which has the same speech formula as the one in Leviticus 17:1–2.

155. Cf. Luciani, *Sainteté et pardon*, 2:239.

Table 2. The Structure of Leviticus Suggested by Scholars[156]

Ska Segal Staübli Levine Blum	1–10 Inauguration of the cults			11–27 Rules for the Israelites to live in the presence of Yahweh			
Wenham	1–7 Rules for sacrifices		8–10 The priests	11–16 Laws on purity and impurity		17–26 Laws on sanctification	
Kornfeld	1–5 Rules of sacrifices for the people	6–7 Rules of sacrifices for the priests	8–10 Priestly Laws	11–15 Purity Laws	16 The ritual for the Day of Atonement	17–26 Holiness Laws	27 Redemp-tion of vows and sanctuary offerings
Cazelles Gorman	1–7 Instructions of sacrifices		8–10 Nomi-nation and the inaugural service	11–16 Instructions on purity		17–26 Laws on sanctification	27 Appendix
Hartley Elliger Grabbe Budd	1–7 Regulations of sacrifices		8–10 Ordination and the sacrifices	11–15 Laws on purifi-cation rituals	16 Atonement	17–26 Laws on the chosen saints	27 Tithes and offerings

156. Ska, *Introduction*, 32–33; Ska, "Structure du Pentateuque," 346–49; Levine, "Leviticus: Its Literary History," 1–23; Dorsey, *Literary Structure*, 78–81; Douglas, "Poetic Structure in Leviticus," 252–55; Walton, "Equilibrium and Sacred Compass," 301; Gane, *Leviticus, Numbers*, 35–36; Elliger, *Leviticus*, 14–20; Wenham, *Book of Leviticus*, 3–6; Knierim, "Composition of Pentateuch," 405–6; Kornfeld, *Neue Echter Bibel*, 10–12; Shea, "Literary Form," 131–39; Cazelles, "Le Pentateuque comme Torah," 66–67; Hartley, *Leviticus*, xxx–xxxv; Grabbe, *Leviticus*, 18–21; Budd, *Leviticus*, 237–41; Smith, "Literary Structure of Leviticus," 22; Averbeck, "Leviticus," in VanGemeren, *NIDOTTE* 4:909; Gorman, *Divine Presence and Community*, 2–3; Nihan, "Holiness Code," 81–82; Nihan, *Priestly Torah to Pentateuch*, 108–10; Kiuchi, *Leviticus*, 18–23; Cox, *Pentateuch*, 64–65; Boyce, *Leviticus and Numbers*, 59–109; Willis, *Leviticus*, xix–xxi; Luciani, *Sainteté et pardon*, 1:325–28.

<table>
<tr><td>Zenger Jüngling</td><td colspan="2">1–7</td><td>8–10
Priestly holiness</td><td colspan="2">11–15
Purity</td><td colspan="2">16–17</td><td colspan="2">18–20
Holiness</td><td colspan="2">21–22
Priestly holiness</td><td colspan="5">23–27</td></tr>
<tr><td>Shea</td><td colspan="2">1–7
Legislations of cults</td><td>8–10
Priestly narrative</td><td colspan="2">11–15
Laws on the purity of the individual</td><td>16
The day of the expiation</td><td colspan="3">17–20
Laws on the morality of the individual</td><td colspan="2">21–22
Priestly legislations</td><td colspan="3">23–25
Religious legislations</td><td>26
Bless-ings and punish-ments</td><td>27
Conse-crations</td></tr>
<tr><td>Dorsey</td><td colspan="3">1–10
Laws on sacrifices</td><td colspan="5">11–18
Regulations of purity</td><td colspan="7">19–26
First section of holiness laws</td><td>27–Num 10:10
Second section of holiness laws</td></tr>
<tr><td>Smith</td><td colspan="2">1–7
Laws</td><td>8–10
Narrative</td><td colspan="2">11–15
Laws</td><td>16
Narrative</td><td colspan="6">17–24:9
Laws</td><td>24:10–23
Narrative</td><td colspan="3">25–27
Laws</td></tr>
<tr><td>Walton</td><td colspan="7">1–17
Balance of the sacred space</td><td colspan="4">18–22
Balance of the sacred status</td><td>23
Bal-ance of the sacred time</td><td colspan="4">24–27
Balance of the human being</td></tr>
<tr><td>Aver-beck</td><td colspan="2">1–7</td><td colspan="4">8–15/(16)</td><td>17</td><td colspan="2">18–20</td><td colspan="2">21–22</td><td colspan="4">23–26</td><td>27</td></tr>
<tr><td>Nihan</td><td colspan="3">1–10</td><td colspan="3">11–16</td><td colspan="10">17–26(27)</td></tr>
<tr><td>M. Douglas</td><td>1</td><td>2–7</td><td>8–10</td><td colspan="3">11–16</td><td>17</td><td colspan="2">18–20</td><td colspan="2">21–22</td><td>23–24:9</td><td>24: 10–23</td><td colspan="3">25–27</td></tr>
<tr><td>R. Knierim</td><td colspan="6">1–16
Concerning atonement</td><td colspan="10">17–27
Concerning societal life</td></tr>
<tr><td>Boyce</td><td colspan="2">1–7</td><td>8–10</td><td colspan="2">11–15</td><td>16</td><td colspan="10">17–27</td></tr>
<tr><td>Luciani</td><td colspan="2">1–7</td><td>8–10</td><td>11–12</td><td>13–15</td><td>16</td><td colspan="4">17–22:16</td><td>22:17–33</td><td colspan="2">23–24</td><td colspan="3">25–27</td></tr>
</table>

Since the presence of Yahweh among the Israelites is the sign of Yahweh's commitment and provision in his covenant with Israel, this becomes a prominent concept in the Sinai pericope. The presence of Yahweh now moves from Mount Sinai in Exodus to the sanctuary in Leviticus, and there is a very clear introduction of the different space where Yahweh speaks to Moses in Leviticus 1:1. This literary mark is sufficient to demonstrate that Leviticus has its own introduction as a separate book.[157] As Knierim asserts, "The mountain belonged to the past. The presence belonged to the sanctuary . . . And now, Yahweh could give the ultimately decisive instructions concerning the ongoing life of Israel . . . The Sinai pericope aims at the book of Leviticus. This book is the center of the Pentateuch."[158]

As we narrow our focus to the structure of Leviticus itself, I would like to present the following proposed structure in relation to the role of Leviticus 17. In my view, Leviticus as a book in the context of Sinai pericope is not just a collection of "manuals" as McEntire concludes.[159] Rather, the literary structure of Leviticus can be divided into the following four main subsections: chapters 1–7, 8–16, 17–22, and 23–27.

---

157. According to the textual-thematic approach, Blum argues that the macrostructure of the Sinai pericope can be divided into four parts. First, Exodus 25–40 is the constitution of the sanctuary and its equipment; second, Leviticus 1–10 is the foundation of the service; third, Leviticus 11–26 is the purity and sanctification of God's people; and fourth, Numbers 1–10 is the constitution of the "pure" camp. "Nach inhaltlich-thematischen Schwerpunkten gliedert sich die (priesterliche) Sinaiperikope im wesentlichen in vier Textbereiche: a) Ex 25–40: die Konstitution des Heiligtums und seiner Einrichtungen, b) Lev 1–10: die Stiftung des Gottesdienstes, c) Lev 11–26: Reinheit und Heiligung des Gottesvolkes, d) Nu 1–10: die Konstitution des »reinen« Lagers." Blum, *Studien zur komposition*, 300.

158. Knierim further claims, "These instructions have two foci: the provision of the atonement institution for the continuous liberation from the destructive burden of guilt and pollution (Leviticus 1–16), and the regulations for Israel's societal life as a 'holy' community (Leviticus 17–27)." Knierim, "Composition of Pentateuch," 405. Knierim offers the following outline of the Sinai pericope ("Composition of Pentateuch," 405–6).

I. The revelation from the mountain (Exod 19:3–40:38)

A. Preparation: the covenant–four ascent-descent cycles (Exod 19:3–24:8)

B. The goal: the sanctuary (Exod 24:9–40:38)

II. The revelation from the tent (Lev 1:1–Num 10:10)

A. Instruction of communal life (Lev 1:1–27:34)

i. Concerning atonement (Lev 1–16)

ii. Concerning societal life (Lev 17–27)

B. Preparation for the pilgrimage (Num 1:1–10:10)

159. McEntire, *Struggling with God*, 126.

Leviticus 1–7

The first subsection of the book of Leviticus consists of chapters 1–7. Several features mark this as a subsection. First, the receiver of Yahweh's speeches is always Moses alone, as is the case in the preceding section of the Sinai pericope, Exodus 19–40.[160] Second, Leviticus 7:28–38, in which Mount Sinai is mentioned, is recognizable as a conclusion to Leviticus 1–7. Third, this subsection contains two small, well-organized literary units: Leviticus 1–5 [Eng. Lev 1:1–6:7] and Leviticus 6–7 [Eng. Lev 6:8–7:38]. In these two units, the same five offerings or sacrifices are prescribed, but the order of the prescription is varied. In Leviticus 1–5, the order is burnt offerings, cereal offerings, well-being offerings, sin offerings, and guilt offerings. Regulation of well-being offerings is placed in the center, with emphasis on the prohibition of eating fat and blood. In Leviticus 6–7, the order is the same, except that well-being offerings are placed at the end rather than the center of the list. As in Leviticus 1–5, the prohibition of eating blood and fat is specified in Leviticus 7:22–27.

Fourth, though it seems redundant to have two small units prescribing the same five offerings in this subsection, there is a different emphasis in terms of the speech audience in these units: the Israelites in Leviticus 1–5, and mainly Aaron and his sons in Leviticus 6–7. This difference in audience, along with the similar content, contributes to the harmonious and well-organized structure of Leviticus 1–7.

Leviticus 8–16

The second subsection of Leviticus is Leviticus 8–16. It contains three small units: chapters 8–10, 11–15, and 16. First, Leviticus 8–10 focuses on the inauguration narration, with an emphasis on the glory of Yahweh as magnified at the end of chapter 9. A dramatic literary reversal appears in the dishonoring of his commands in Leviticus 10:1–7; and Leviticus 10:8–20 begins with the only occurrence of Aaron as the lone speech receiver in the Sinai pericope. After the inauguration ceremony and the death of Aaron's two sons, Yahweh

160. Refer to Appendix 1 of this book.

spoke to Aaron alone instead of Moses. The glory of Yahweh is a prominent theme in Leviticus 8–10.[161]

Second, the subunit of clean and unclean laws in Leviticus 11–15 occurs after the incident in Leviticus 10, and it is stated clearly in the speech of Yahweh to Aaron alone (Lev 10:10–11) that one of the major duties of Aaron and his sons as priests is to instruct the Israelites to distinguish the unclean and the clean. Furthermore, in the summary passages in Leviticus 11–15, the purpose of these clean and unclean laws is distinct: the Israelites are to distinguish the unclean and clean (Lev 11:46–47, 13:59, 14:54–57, and 15:31–33) so they will not die in their uncleanness. On the other hand, in Leviticus 11–15, the speeches are addressed to Moses and Aaron (Lev 11), to Moses (Lev 12), to Moses and Aaron (Lev 13), to Moses (Lev 14:1–32), and to Moses and Aaron (Lev 14:33–57 and Lev 15). Though the content of the purification regulations does not seem to specifically depend on the addressee, the alternation of speech receivers is nevertheless purposeful: such alternation not only introduces the priestly office of Aaron's family, but also signifies the importance of Aaron and his sons as the instructors of practical holiness in the daily life of the Israelites.

Third, Leviticus 16 commences with narration that mentions the death of Aaron's two sons as recorded in Leviticus 10:1–7. Moreover, the speech audience of Leviticus 16 is Aaron alone, since he is the only person permitted to enter the most holy place once every year on the Day of Atonement. Following the death of Aaron's two sons, Leviticus 11–15 and 16 deal with the issue of purification before Yahweh's presence among the Israelites. In Leviticus 16, the purification is effective not only for the priesthood and the whole congregation once a year (Lev 16:34), but also for the most holy place and the tabernacle.[162]

161. Damrosch claims that "Leviticus 10 forms a fitting conclusion to the first third of the book. Taken overall, Leviticus 1–10 serves as a narrative introduction to the symbolic order of moral laws and cultic regulations that make up the remaining two-thirds of the book: the laws of purity and atonement in chapters 11–16, and the group of ordinances known as the Holiness Code (chaps. 17–26, with an appendix in chap. 27)." Damrosch, *Narrative Covenant*, 278–79.

162. Shea notes that the theological essence of Leviticus 1–15 is justification (Lev 5:10). "Transgressions (Lev 1–7) and uncleanness (Lev 11–15) are the two major concerns discussed in the first limb [Lev 1–15] of the chiasm." Shea, "Literary Form," 132.

Leviticus 17–22

The third subsection of Leviticus contains chapters 17–22. Based on the strength of the previous discussion regarding the "contextual relationship between Leviticus 18–27 and 17," I will propose the following structure for Leviticus 17–22: Leviticus 17 (A) and Leviticus 22:17–25 (A') form the outer framework of the inclusio,[163] while Leviticus 18–20 (B) and Leviticus 21–22:16 (B') comprise the inward parallel sections, emphasizing the holiness of the Israelites and the priests, respectively. Leviticus 22:26–33 functions as a conclusion to Leviticus 17–22.[164] The following is a summarized framework of the literary structure of Leviticus 17–22.

- **A** Leviticus 17 (regulations regarding sacrifices with Aaron, his sons, and all the Israelites as the audiences)
  - **B** Leviticus 18–20 (the Israelites as the audience)
    - **B1** Leviticus 18 (the Israelites; prohibitions of Canaanite customs)
      - **B2** Leviticus 19 (the congregation of Israelites; holiness)

163. In Cazelles's view, Leviticus 17 serves as the introduction to the Holiness Code just as Deuteronomy 12 serves as the introduction to the Deuteronomic Code. Cazelles, "Le Pentateuque comme Torah," 66–67. Also see Moraldi, *Espiazione sacrificale*, 237–52. As for the regulation of altars, it is also noted that "Exod. 20.24 envisions multiple altars for the worship of Yahweh, Deut. 12.13–15 endorses sacrifice on only one altar but allows profane slaughter elsewhere, while Lev. 17 restricts all sacrifice and slaughter to the Tabernacle altar alone." Watts, *Reading Law*, 73.

164. Shea has promoted the understanding of Leviticus as a well-organized literary form by showing that it was written according to a chiasmic structure. In his perspective, Leviticus is naturally divided into two halves: chapters 1–15 and chapters 16–27. However, he argues that in terms of the literary device of chiasmus, Leviticus is divided into six sections. The first three sections – chapters 1–7 (cultic legislation), chapters 8–10 (priestly history), and chapters 11–15 (personal laws of uncleanness) – form an inverted chiasmus with the latter three sections – chapters 17–20 (personal moral laws), chapters 21–22 (priestly legislation), and chapters 23–25 (cultic legislation). Shea further concludes that chapter 16 is the pivotal point of this chiasmatic structure and that the last two chapters (26–27) are not included in this structure. Shea, "Literary Form," 131–32. Shea observes that "the fact that the Day of Atonement ritual lies at the literary center of Leviticus emphasizes its importance in the sanctuary system. Furthermore, this central position indicates its function as the capstone of the sacrificial rituals (presented in the first limb of the chiasm) and as the natural transition point to the subject of holy living (presented in the second limb)." Shea, 131–32. From my perspective, the structure of Leviticus 17–27 proposed by Shea is a comparatively loose structure that does not pay enough attention to literary characteristics.

B1' Leviticus 20 (the Israelites;[165] prohibitions of Canaanite customs)

B' Leviticus 21–22:16 (Aaron and his sons as the audiences)

B'1 Leviticus 21:1–15[166] (Aaron's sons; holiness in behaviors and dealings with offerings

B'2 Leviticus 21:16–23 (Aaron; qualification for being a priest before a holy God)

B'1' Leviticus 22:1–16 (Aaron and his sons; holiness in behaviors and dealing with offerings)

A' Leviticus 22:17–25 (regulations regarding sacrifices with Aaron, his sons and all the Israelites as the audiences)

C Leviticus 22:26–33 (Moses as the speech receiver with no audience)

Moreover, the parallel sections B and B' have their own inclusio structure, with the center emphasizing the fundamental requirements – the nature of holiness in Leviticus 19,[167] and the basic requirement of the priestly office in Leviticus 21:16–23.

Scholars often treat the three chapters of section B (Lev 18–20), as a cohesive unit, as McEntire has mentioned.[168] McEntire also mentions that there is an echo of Leviticus 18 in Leviticus 20 in terms of message, while Leviticus 19

165. Sherwood's analysis of the speaking formula in the book of Leviticus fails to recognize the audience of Leviticus 20:1–2, "וְאֶל־בְּנֵי יִשְׂרָאֵל" (Lev 20:2). The audience here is both obviously stated and emphasized by its placement at the beginning of the sentence. Sherwood, *Leviticus, Numbers, Deuteronomy*, 19.

166. Sherwood, 19. Sherwood only recognizes "וַיְדַבֵּר יְהוָה אֶל־מֹשֶׁה" as the key structuring element of Leviticus; as I have mentioned, however, "וַיֹּאמֶר יְהוָה אֶל־מֹשֶׁה" (Lev 21:1) is a major speaking formula within the structure of Leviticus as well.

167. Y. T. Radday declares Leviticus 19:18 to be "the summit of the entire Torah," because Leviticus, as the center of the Torah, culminates in chapter 19, the climax of the "Holiness Code." Radday, "Chiasmus in Hebrew Biblical," 89. Furthermore, Radday emphasizes the importance of the center of the chiasmatic structure by quoting Saadiah's assertion, "The best and most important is always found in the middle." Radday notes in his endnote 38 on page 114 that he found this in H. Graetz's book, but could not locate this in Saadiah's writings. See Graetz, *Structure of Jewish History*, 109. However, Graetz's mention of Saadiah's idea is in the context of an argument about faith and reason in regard to the creation and the creator, rather than in a discussion of the importance of the center of a chiasmatic structure. Therefore, Radday's quotation of Saadiah's assertion may be a misrepresentation of Saadiah's original intention. For Saadiah's argument, see Graetz, *Stucture of Jewish History*, 107–10.

168. McEntire, *Struggling with God*, 142.

seems like the pivot of this cohesive unit due to "the repeated punctuating remark, 'I am YHWH' (eight times) or 'I am YHWH your God' (eight times)."[169]

Moreover, the two chapters of section B' (Lev 21–22) share the same concern for the behaviors of the priests, dealing with the offerings and the qualification of the priests, the discussion of which is located at the center of this subunit (Lev 21:16–23). These two chapters are also closely linked with the previous subunit, chapters 18–20,[170] through the commands to holiness,[171] the repeated word קדשׁ,[172] and the use of the punctuating phrase אֲנִי יהוה, which appears in 22:9, 16, 27, 31, 32, and 33, as well as six times in chapter 19.

Kiuchi also suggests a structure for Leviticus 17–22: "The structure of chs. 17–22 is as follows: ch. 17 (introduction), ch. 18 (A), ch. 19 (B), ch. 20 (A'), chs. 21–22 (B')." We can see that although Kiuchi recognizes the inclusio structure of the subunit in Leviticus 18–20, he does not place much emphasis on it, especially on the relationship between Leviticus 17 and 18–22 and the literary interaction within Leviticus 21–22.[173]

Leviticus 23–27

The fourth subsection of Leviticus contains chapters 23–27, within which chapters 23–26 generally function as a covenant reconfirmation of the Sinai pericope due to their common emphasis on the idea of Sabbath.[174]

First, as discussed in the previous section titled "Commandment to Keep the Sabbath" on pages 51–52 of this book, this prominent feature emphasizes

---

169. McEntire, 142–43.

170. McEntire, 143. McEntire also discusses the close link between chapters 18–20 and 21–22.

171. The commands appear in 19:2, 20, 26, and 21:6, 8.

172. The word קדשׁ occurs twenty times in Leviticus 22, fourteen times as a noun and six times in a verbal form. This word also appears in 19:8, 24, 20:3 (noun), 7, and 8 (verbal). Even-Shoshan, *New Concordance*, 1002–5.

173. Kiuchi, *Leviticus*, 22–23.

174. Drawing upon scholars' observations of ANE treaty patterns, Hoffmeier addresses the biblical treaty patterns in terms of the Sinai legislation. In that structure, Leviticus 1–25 falls into the category of stipulations, while Leviticus 26:3–13 and Leviticus 26:14–33 belong to blessings and curses, respectively. In Hoffmeier's biblical treaty patterns, the following are brief classifications for the Sinai legislation: (1) Preamble/Title: Exodus 20:1–2a; (2) Historical Prologue: Exodus 20:2b; (3) Stipulations: Exodus 20:3–17, 22–26; 21:1–23; 25–31; Leviticus 1–25; (4) Deposition of Text: Exodus 25:16; (5) Public Reading: Exodus 24:7; (6) Witnesses Summoned: Exodus 24:4; (7) Blessings: Leviticus 26:3–13; and (8) Curses: Leviticus 26:14–33. Hoffmeier, *Ancient Israel in Sinai*, 183–88. Also see discussions on this in Kitchen and Lawrence, *Overall Historical Survey*, 125–32.

the Sabbath framework and reinforces the covenantal relationship between the creator, Yahweh, and his people, the Israelites, by commanding them not to do any work on the seventh day. In Timmer's conclusion to his research on the Sabbath's framework in Exodus 31–35, he maintains that "this sign's [the Sabbath's] particular significance was initially identified as involving Yahweh's commitment to sanctify Israel, both in terms of his relationship with her and as it concerns her moral behavior vis-à-vis his laws."[175] All the occurrences of "Sabbath" in Leviticus 16, 19, and 23–26 also clearly present Yahweh's commitment to sanctify Israel, as illustrated by the textual context of these passages.[176] Conversely, the mention of presenting an offering to Yahweh by fire right after the prohibition of work in several passages of Leviticus 23–26 also reminds the Israelites of Yahweh's covenant renewal with them after the golden calf incident in Exodus 34. Moreover, as Timmer argues in his conclusion,[177] the commandment that offering be made to Yahweh by fire on that day emphasizes the necessity of honoring Yahweh alone, and also functions as a guard against syncretism. With this emphasis on the Sabbath theme in mind, one may understand the consequences of defilement of Yahweh's name described in the narrative (Lev 24:10–12, 23) and its subsequent regulation (in Lev 25) as surrounded by the sanctification of Yahweh.

Second, the phrase בְּהַר סִינָי appears in the introductory formula in Leviticus 25:1, as well as in the concluding statements in 26:46 and 27:34, which are the last verses in Leviticus 26 and 27, respectively. These three occurrences of בְּהַר סִינָי in chapters 25–27 indicate a well-organized ending for the book of Leviticus. On the one hand, the content of blessings and curses in Leviticus 26 serves as the conclusion of Yahweh's covenant with the

175. Timmer, *Creation, Tabernacle, and Sabbath*, 176; See also Timmer, "Creation, Tabernacle and Sabbath," 258–59.

176. In Leviticus 19:3, 30, it is emphasized in the context of commands to fear YHWH and not follow the customs of the Canaanites. Leviticus 23–25 contains several occurrences of the word שבת and its regulation, and the Israelites are instructed to observe Sabbaths weekly, yearly, and once every several years. In Leviticus 26, the conclusion of the book, containing Moses's charge to the people to obey, the שבת theme recurs. These three occurrences of the שבת theme in Leviticus may also call our attention to the fact that they are all significantly related to an emphasis on covenant as a marking symbol in their respective literary contexts – that is, in relation to the avoidance of Canaanite customs, the observance of feasts, and the challenge of commitment to the covenantal relationship with YHWH.

177. Timmer, *Creation, Tabernacle, and Sabbath*, 176; Cf. Timmer, "Creation, Tabernacle and Sabbath," 259.

Israelites at Sinai. On the other hand, Leviticus 27 follows with an emphasis on the regulations of the vows to the Lord. This chapter, dealing with the promises of humans, shows the readers how a promise was to be fulfilled once it was made to the Lord. Kitchen points out that the blessings and curses in Leviticus 26 "duly end the main text in Lev. 26, plus colophon." He further asserts that Leviticus 27 "*ends things totally with an addendum to the laws, and its colophon*. Even such addenda are otherwise attested in the late 2nd millennium."[178] Even though I agree with Kitchen's view of 27:34 as the end-colophon,[179] I would argue that, as stated above, the content of Leviticus 27 is not just an addendum of the Sinai covenant. Chapters 26 and 27, which accent the significance of covenant promises in different ways, thus bring profound closure to the book of Leviticus and the Sinai covenant.[180]

Moreover, in terms of the place of Leviticus 27 in the book of Leviticus, Averbeck argues from the big picture of the Sinai pericope that there is a common pattern found at the beginnings and ends of the noncultic law collections in the Sinai pericope (namely, Exod 22:22–23:19; Lev 17–27; and Deut 12–26).[181] He points out that these three collections all begin with a major unit of cultic altar regulations (Exod 20:22–26; Lev 17; and Deut 12) and end with cultic regulations (Exod 23:14–19; Lev 27; and Deut 26). Averbeck therefore concludes that "it belongs to regular pattern of the cultic framing of the noncultic law collections."[182]

I agree with Averbeck's observations on these three units. These three are noncultic law collections;[183] nonetheless, the covenantal relationship between

---

178. Kitchen and Lawrence, *Treaty, Law and Covenant*, 127. (Emphasis original.)

179. Kitchen and Lawrence, 127.

180. This "double ending" soundly establishes the book of Leviticus as a unified, literary structure.

181. Averbeck explains this observation in a forthcoming article: Averbeck, "The Cult and Its Relationship, " 258–59.

182. Averbeck observes that "Just as the festival regulations in Exodus 23:14–19 conclude the laws in the Book of the Covenant and the firstfruits and third-year tithe festival regulations in Deuteronomy 26 conclude the core law section of Deuteronomy, so Leviticus 27 contains a series of diverse cultic regulations. . . . If, as it appears, Exod 20:22–26 corresponds to 23:14–19, Deut 12 to 26, and Lev 17 to 27, we have a regular pattern of the cultic framing of the three parallel non-cultic law collections in the Pentateuch." Averbeck, "The Cult and Its Relationship, " 258–59.

183. In these three noncultic law collections, not only the beginning and the end of cultic regulations presented in the texts respectively, Averbeck also mentions other important elements occurs as patterns in these three law collections. For example, the debt slave release laws in Exodus 21:2–11, Leviticus 25, and Deuteronomy 26; and the deliverance from slavery in Egypt

Yahweh and the Israelites in the Sinai pericope has put an emphasis on the worship of Yahweh, and this emphasis becomes the frame for these noncultic law collections.[184] From this point of view, we also could recognize that Leviticus 27 corresponds to Leviticus 17 and is not an appendix to the book of Leviticus, because it forms a structure for Leviticus 17–27.[185]

as the rationale for the Israelites to live it out in the community. Regarding these discussions, see Averbeck, "The Cult and Its Relationship, " 259–60.

184. Averbeck, "The Cult and Its Relationship, " 259

185. Averbeck, "The Cult and Its Relationship, " 259

CHAPTER 3

Restriction of the Place of Offering Well-being Offerings in Leviticus 17

As discussed in the previous chapter, Leviticus 17–22 forms a subunit due to its clear and tight syntactical coherence.[1] The subunit's literary structure can be summarized as follows:

A Leviticus 17 (Regulations regarding sacrifices addressed to Aaron, his sons, and all the Israelites; well-being offering is mentioned)

- **B** Leviticus 18–20 (Regulations addressed to the Israelites; warning not to behave according to the custom of the Canaanites)
- **B'** Leviticus 21–22:16 (Regulations addressed to Aaron and his sons; requirements for priests and the regulation of eating the most holy food and the holy food)

A' Leviticus 22:17–25 (Regulations regarding sacrifices addressed to Aaron, his sons and all the Israelites; well-being offering and burnt offering are mentioned)

C Leviticus 22:26–33 (Moses as speech receiver with no audience; an edible thank offering, which might be a well-being offering, is mentioned)

The framework of Leviticus 17–22, in which Leviticus 17 (A: 17:1–2 אֶל־אַהֲרֹן וְאֶל־בָּנָיו וְאֶל כָּל־בְּנֵי יִשְׂרָאֵל) and Leviticus 22:17–25 (A': 22:17–18

1. It is stated on pages 63–65 of this book.

(אֶל־אַהֲרֹן וְאֶל־בָּנָיו וְאֶל כָּל־בְּנֵי יִשְׂרָאֵל) form an outer inclusio with the same group of audiences shown above and – along with the final stand-alone description in Leviticus 22:26–33 – emphasize the well-being sacrifice, suggests that the well-being sacrifice is not only one of the crucial themes in Leviticus 17, but also a significant keynote of the message of Leviticus 17–22 as a whole.

This chapter seeks to explain the restriction, established in Leviticus 17, on where well-being offerings could be made. It will begin with a survey of this specific sacrifice as it is discussed in the OT and in near and simultaneous literature – the ancient Ugaritic sacrificial documents. Based on this understanding of well-being sacrifices, we will then launch our exploration of the reason for the restriction of the place of making well-being offerings, looking at both the immediate and broader literary contexts (Lev 17–22 and the Pentateuch, respectively.)

זִבְחֵי שְׁלָמִים (Well-Being Offerings) in the Old Testament

The word שְׁלָמִים/שֶׁלֶם ("well-being offering") appears in the OT once in the singular form (Amos 5:22) and eighty-six times in the plural form.[2] The well-being offering is referred to in the OT by the term שְׁלָמִים/שֶׁלֶם ("well-being") alone, by the term זֶבַח ("sacrifice") alone,[3] or by the combined term זֶבַח שְׁלָמִים ("sacrifice of well-being"), which is introduced in Leviticus 3:1. According to Modéus, these three terms can be understood to describe the same phenomenon. This argument is supported by the following facts. First, the terms appear together in some passages (e.g. Lev 7:11–38). Second, the relevant texts do not mention details that would distinguish among the sacrifices referred to by these terms. Third, none of the texts present the terms as if they have different meanings.[4]

2. Even-Shoshan, *New Concordance*, 1156–57. It is also mentioned in Averbeck, "שֶׁלֶם," in VanGemeren, *NIDOTTE* 4:136.

3. Goldingay mentions "A sacrifice (*zebaḥ*) is an act that involves killing something that is then shared by worshipers and Yhwh (see, e.g. Deut 27:7; 1 Sam 1:4–5). It is thus not 'very holy,' absolutely holy; ordinary people can join in eating it. But it is 'holy,' and all of it must be eaten on the day it is offered, or the next day; anything left until the third day must be burned, not eaten." Goldingay, *Israel's Life*, 141.

4. Modéus, *Sacrifice and Symbol*, 18-19.

The Term זֶבַח

In the Pentateuch, the term זֶבַח is used sixty-nine times in its singular and plural forms.[5] Of the twenty occurrences of the singular form by itself, all refer to well-being offerings. Some of these offerings are made for the reason of thanksgiving (Lev 7:12–13, 15–16) or during a feast such as the Passover (Exod 12:27; 23:18; 34:25[twice]). However, there are forty out of sixty-nine occurrences in which the term זֶבַח appears in combination with זֶבַח שְׁלָמִים. So while either זֶבַח alone or זֶבַח שְׁלָמִים can be used to refer to well-being sacrifices,[6] זֶבַח שְׁלָמִים is used more frequently for this purpose in Pentateuch.[7]

In Leviticus 1–2, the word עֹלָה is used for burnt offerings and the word מִנְחָה is employed for grain offerings, while in Leviticus 3 it is clear that the word זֶבַח is used only for well-being sacrifices. The usage of זֶבַח can also be observed in the regulations regarding five kinds of offerings that appear in Leviticus 1–7.[8] The burnt or עֹלָה offering is designated to be offered to the Lord as a whole by burning it in the fire; in the case of the grain offering, part is presented to the Lord in the fire, while the remainder may only be eaten by the priests. In this context, it is evident that the זֶבַח offering is completely different from the עֹלָה and מִנְחָה offerings. The word זֶבַח denotes "a sacrifice of slaughtered sheep, goat or cattle to create communion between the god to whom the sacrifice is made and the partners of the sacrifice, and the communion between the partners themselves."[9] In this sense, as Averbeck mentions, the זֶבַח offering at least conveys the meaning of gift and communion.[10]

5. Even-Shoshan, *New Concordance*, 322–23. It occurs 162 times in the OT.

6. Modéus, *Sacrifice and Symbol*, 19. Thus, Modéus in his book chose to employ שְׁלָמִים to cover both שְׁלָמִים and זֶבַח שְׁלָמִים.

7. Even-Shoshan, *New Concordance*, 322–23. However, De Vaux mentions that, aside from priestly rituals, "elsewhere the two terms rarely occur together. More often one finds *Zeḇaḥ* alone, or *šelāmîm* alone." De Vaux, *Studies in Old Testament*, 31. Kiuchi mentions that זֶבַח שְׁלָמִים is used mainly in legal parts of Leviticus and Numbers. Kiuchi, *Leviticus*, 77. Regarding the usage of שְׁלָמִים alone, see below.

8. Levine, *Leviticus*, 14. Levine points out that, despite the similarities shared between the burnt and the well-being offering and the grain and well-being offering, the major difference is that the offerer and his/her family and friends are invited to enjoy the feast of the offering.

9. "זֶבַח," *HALOT* 262.

10. Averbeck, "זבח," in VanGemeren, *NIDOTTE* 1:1070.

The Term שְׁלָמִים

The word שְׁלָמִים recalls the meaning of שָׁלוֹם, which embraces the idea of peace, communion, and fellowship in relationships. The regulation of שְׁלָמִים offerings in Leviticus 3:1–17 and 7:11–38 also embodies the spirit of fellowship and peace in a practical way by mandating that some portion of the sacrificial meat be shared and eaten among the offerer, family, and community. A שְׁלָמִים offering thus not only denotes peace between the offerer and God, but also gives expression to the well-being among the offerer, family, and the community. For this reason, both Averbeck and Goldingay prefer to translate שְׁלָמִים offering as "fellowship offering," which conveys the idea of community between the offerer and God and within the relationships surrounding the offerer.[11] In this study, however, I prefer to adopt the term "well-being offering" to translate שְׁלָמִים,[12] because this offering seems to make a great impression on the well-being between God and the offerer,[13] as well as the physical, psychological, and spiritual well-being shared among the offerer, his or her family, and the community. The שְׁלָמִים offering is often dedicated alongside another sacrifice, especially the עֹלָה offering, in celebration of important events in Israelite history.

Among eighty-seven references to the well-being offering in the OT, only one appears in the Poetic and Wisdom Literature. The term is used in

---

11. According to Averbeck, "The primary focus of this particular offering seems to be the communal celebration supplied by the meat of the offering. It was a fellowship or communion offering that indicated and enacted the fact that there was peace between God and his people and that the person, family, or community was, therefore, in a state of well-being." Averbeck, "שָׁלֵם," in VanGemeren, *NIDOTTE* 4:135. According to Goldingay, "The word *šĕlāmîm* could have various connotations, but it does recall *šālôm* and thus might suggest 'well-being' (NRSV) or 'fellowship' (TNIV). The latter is the more obvious implication as these sacrifices are occasions when families or the whole community eat together, and do so in fellowship with Yhwh. . . . Eating together before Yhwh brings into being or cements their relationship." Goldingay, *Israel's Life*, 141–42.

12. Levine, *Leviticus*, 14; Miller, *Religion of Ancient Israel*, 113. Levine asserts that "the translation of 'sacrifice of well-being' reflects one of these meanings, based on the rendering of *shalom* as 'well-being, wholeness.'" Miller states that "the translation 'offering of well-being' is a guess but consistent with etymology and the context in which the sacrifice functioned."

13. Goldingay, *Israel's Life*, 142. "Yhwh desires to be in the kind of fellowship with Israel that involves eating together, though people eat 'before' Yhwh not 'with' Yhwh, and once again Leviticus hardly implies that Yhwh ate the sacrifice. While the portions allocated to Yhwh are described as 'food' (Lev 3:11, 16), these portions were not very edible. . . . The priest offers the animal to Yhwh, and it thus belongs to Yhwh, so that what the offerers then eat is the food of God. The actual expression 'food of God' can also be used more generally of the offerings, though there too the fellowship offerings may be especially in mind."

Proverbs 7:14, which reads זִבְחֵי שְׁלָמִים עָלָי הַיּוֹם שִׁלַּמְתִּי נְדָרָי׃ ("Sacrifices of well-being were due from me. Today I have paid my vows"). These words are spoken by an adulteress to a youth she is attempting to lead astray. In this verse, it is stated that sacrificing the well-being offering is an act of paying a vow. This verse also demonstrates to us that after it was enacted in Leviticus, "well-being offering" became used in reference to a general category of expressing thanksgiving, voluntary, and vow-paying offerings in a later period of Israelite history. In the following sections, we will limit our focus to the eighty-six references to well-being offerings in the Pentateuch, historical books, and prophetic books.

זִבְחֵי שְׁלָמִים (Well-Being Offerings) in the Pentateuch

Most of the OT occurrences of the word שְׁלָמִים (fifty-four out of eighty-seven) appear in the Pentateuch. Of these, thirty appear in the book of Leviticus.

Leviticus

The regulation of שְׁלָמִים in the Levitical sacrificial system is discussed primarily in Leviticus 3 and 7. The ritual includes the presentation of a domestic animal – a male or female cow, sheep, or goat, but not a bird. The offerer follows the ceremony, which includes laying hands on the animal's head and slaughtering it, and the priest splashes its blood against the altar. Then the edible parts of the animals are divided into three different parts. The fat belongs to the Lord and must be burnt on the altar; the breast and the right thigh belong to the priests and can be eaten only by them; and the rest of the meat is given back to the offerer to be consumed by the offerer and the guests of the feast (Lev 3:1–17; 7:11–34).

The well-being offering plays a role in facilitating communion among God, the priests, and the offerer, and also between the offerer and those invited to partake in the meal following the well-being offering.[14] Following the initial discussion of the regulations for the well-being offering, the text turns

14. Rainey, "Order of Sacrifices," 498. The word שְׁלָמִים is mentioned in Leviticus 3:1, 3, 6, 9; 4:10, 26, 31, 35; 6:5; 7:11, 13, 14, 15, 18, 20, 21, 29 (twice), 32, 33, 34, and 37, for the description of its procedure, the responsibility of the priest, and the regulation in regard to eat the meat. Rainey mentions that well-being offerings represented the communal experience in which Yahweh, the priests, and the offerer – including the guests – had a share, and the ritual result was fellowship.

to the inauguration ceremony for the priests (Lev 8), and then moves on to a narration of the first sacrifices offered by Aaron and his sons.[15] However, both the responsibility of the priest and the regulations for eating the meat of well-being offerings are mentioned repeatedly in subsequent texts, including Leviticus 10:14–15; 19:5–8; and 23:19–20.[16]

The well-being offering is the only sacrifice to explicitly reflect theological significance of the relationship of communion between God and worshiper that was established through God's decision to make a covenant with the Israelites and dwell among them.[17] In the procedure for sacrificing well-being offerings, only the fat and blood,[18] which was proscribed in Leviticus 7:22–27, was given to the Lord as a food gift to him, while the priests received the breast and right thigh as a prebend of their office.[19] After presenting these portions, the worshiper and those among his or her family and friends who were in a state of ritual purity would share the rest of the meat as part of a communal meal before the Lord. Among all the sacrifices prescribed in the Levitical sacrificial system, well-being offerings are the only animal sacrifices that allowed people to eat the presented, identified, and consecrated flesh. The meat is not roasted as in the Passover sacrifice, but cooked in a pot (Lev 8:31). It is worth noting that whenever Leviticus describes a series of sacrifices, the well-being offering is the last to be offered. This signifies that one of the purposes of this offering is to conclude the series of sacrifices by connoting that all is well, both between the Lord and the offerer, and in the offerer's interpersonal relationships.

In addition, the motivations for offering a well-being offering are spelled out in Leviticus 7:12–16. The first possible motivation is a desire to give thanks (תּוֹדָה; vv. 12–15). Along with the animal for the well-being offering,

15. Even-Shoshan, *New Concordance*, 1156–57; Leviticus 9:4, 18, 22.

16. Even-Shoshan, 1156–57. The word שְׁלָמִים is mentioned in Leviticus 10:14; 17:5; 19:5; 22:21; 23:19.

17. De Vaux, *Studies in Old Testament*, 31. De Vaux asserts that the victim "is shared between God, the priest, and the offerer."

18. "All the fat belongs to Yahweh and people shall eat neither fat nor blood" (Lev 3:16–17; 7:23–25).

19. De Vaux, *Studies in Old Testament*, 35. However, in the Israelite history, "customs varied concerning the portion made over to the priests," De Vaux observes. For example, Samuel offered the thigh and the fat tail, which belonged to the priest and Yahweh in the Levitical ritual, to Saul after he had sacrificed in 1 Samuel 9:23–24; while in Deuteronomy 18:3, the priest should receive the shoulder, the jowls, and the inner parts.

the offerer would present four kinds of bread before the Lord (7:12–13) and one of each type of bread was presented to the priest as a "contribution to the LORD." All of the bread would later be eaten by either the priest or a family member or friend of the offerer in the sacred meal; none of the bread would be burnt on the altar. The highlight of a well-being offering was the sacred meal with meat from the sacrifice.[20] When the offerer was motivated by thanksgiving, the meat should be eaten over the first night after the sacrifice was offered (7:15). As its name reveals, a well-being offering motivated by thanksgiving was always given out of a sense of God's grace or deliverance.

The second motivation for a well-being offering is its use as a votive offering (נֶדֶר, 7:16). The well-being offering presented for a votive reason represented the fulfilment of a vow made to the Lord by a person in trouble. The final motivation for a well-being offering is the simple exercise of free will (נְדָבָה, 7:16). The emphasis of a freewill well-being offering is on spontaneity; it does not involve the repaying of a vow to the Lord. In terms of the respective emphasis of these last two kinds of well-being offerings, Kiuchi asserts that "while נֶדֶר refers to conditional self-dedication, נְדָבָה refers to unconditional self-dedication."[21] Even though these three motivations are distinct from each other, they have one characteristic in common: the will of the offerer.[22]

Both votive and freewill offerings were more flexible than thanksgiving offerings in that they could be eaten the day after the sacrifice (7:15–16).[23] The remainder of the meat was to be burnt, and whoever ate the meat beyond the prescribed timeframe would bear his or her own iniquity. Those who were unclean and ate the sacrificial meat of a well-being offering were to be cut off from the people (7:17–21).

The proclamation in Leviticus 17 that violators of the regulations for well-being offerings were to be cut off from the people has been exegeted in various

---

20. Gane, *Leviticus, Numbers*, 155.

21. Kiuchi, "Spirituality in Offering," 25.

22. Gorman, *Divine Presence and Community*, 50. Gorman asserts that the second and third kinds together are one part of the well-being offering according to the same time frame of eating these two sacrifices. However, the following scholars are some of those who deal with these as three different kinds of sacrifices. Hartley, *Leviticus*, 99; Gane, *Leviticus, Numbers*, 155; Kiuchi, *Leviticus*, 138–39; Baker, "Leviticus," 50; Milgrom, *Leviticus 1–16*, 220. Kiuchi mentions the will of the offerer in "Spirituality in Offering," Kiuchi, *Leviticus*, 138–39.

23. Gorman, *Divine Presence and Community*, 50. Gorman comments that the precise reason for the different time frame for eating the sacrifices here is not clearly stated in the Scriptures.

ways in rabbinic circles, though all agree that it is a penalty of God by its nature. The following are some major Jewish interpretations.[24]

First, it is related to the descendants of the violator: Rashi (*b. Šabb.* 25a) suggests that the penalty involves childlessness and premature death, while Ibn Ezra's understanding on Leviticus 17:14 leads him to assume it means that the descendants of the violator would be extirpated. If the violator already had descendants, it would be impossible to explain the punishment according to Rashi's perspective. Moreover, the premature death of the violator – supported by M. Tsevat and M. Weinfeld,[25] who claim that the penalty of כָּרֵת refers to a death penalty by divine intervention – is not well attested in the Hebrew Scriptures, especially in the regulations related to it in Leviticus. Nonetheless, Ibn Ezra's view covers a broader sense than Rashi's, as we will discuss below.

Second, Rabad and *Mo 'ed Qaṭ.* 28a suggest that the penalty was that the violator would die before a certain age (either sixty or fifty-two). The problem with this view is similar to the issue with Rashi's explanation. These precise views can hardly be derived from Scripture, however. On the one hand, the Hebrew Scriptures never mention the exact age of the violator who is to be cut off. On the other hand, these views fail to explain what would happen to someone who violated the regulation after the ages mentioned above.

Third, Maimonides claims that the violator could not enjoy the spiritual afterlife after his or her death (*Teshuva* 8.1),[26] meaning that this punishment ends the existence of the violator's soul. Maimonides's view will be discussed in depth in the section below (see pp. 78–79).

The punishment of כָּרֵת is recorded in Leviticus 7:20–21, 25, and 27: those who eat the well-being offering in the state of impurity and those who eat suet or blood must be cut off from the people. It is stated clearly in the regulations for well-being offerings that the suet and blood belong to God, while

24. Jewish views regarding the interpretation of the penalty of כָּרֵת in the Hebrew Scriptures are summarized from Milgrom, *Leviticus 1-16*, 457.

25. Tsevat, "Studies in Book of Samuel," 191–216. Tsevat's conclusion on the meaning of כָּרֵת penalty is based on his research and observation on 1 Samuel 2:27–36. Weinfeld, *Deuteronomy and Deuteronomic School*, 240–43.

26. The post-Rabbinic source, Maimonides, *Teshuva* 8.1 is cited in Milgrom, *Leviticus 1-16*, 457. However, the discussion on the reference of Teshuva 8.1 could be found in Henry M. Abramson, *Maimonides on Teshuvah: The Ways of Repentance*, 5th ed. (Brooklyn: Touro College, 2017), 198–200. Retrieved from https://touroscholar.touro.edu/lcas_books/1/?utm_source=touroscholar.touro.edu%2Flcas_books%2F1&utm_medium=PDF&utm_campaign=PDFCoverPages.

the rest of the sacrifice could be eaten by the offerer and his or her friends and families – but only those who were in a state of purity, since the offering itself was holy due to having been sacrificed to the holy Lord. Because violating any of these three terms represent an affront to the Lord himself, the punishment of כָּרַת is executed by God alone, not by humans, as the rabbinic views mentioned above.

As for the nature of the punishment of כָּרַת, the precise meaning of this word is no longer known to modern researchers. When we focus on the occurrences of the punishment of כָּרַת in Leviticus, it appears seventeen times in total (excluding two Hiphil occurrences which are not related to this punishment), and only in the Niphal or Hiphil stem of כָּרַת.[27] Fourteen of these occurrences are followed by a specific formula – כָּרַת followed by מִן and a social group from which the individual will be cut off – together they comprise more than half of the twenty-seven total occurrences of this formula in the OT.[28] This specific formula occurs predominantly in Leviticus 7 and 17, passages in which regulations for eating well-being offerings are stated. Because the meat people are going to share and eat is a holy sacrifice to the Lord, and the suet and blood have been designated to the Lord, whoever consumes the sacrifices in an impure state or consumes the parts that belong solely to the Lord will be an offender of the covenant between the Lord and his people. Thus, the offender will be cut off from his people who are the covenantal group with the Lord.

The occurrences of this formula in Leviticus 18, 19, 20, 22, and 23 are mainly related to prohibitions of Canaanite practices – especially religious practices (20:6; 22:3, cutting off from before God) and sexual relationships among family members (18:29; 20:17–18); the defilement of the holy thing (19:8); and not humbling oneself on the Day of Atonement (23:29). The common ground shared by these occurrences of the punishment is not specifically stated in the Scriptures. The punishment of "cutting off" from God's people

27. Even-Shoshan, *New Concordance*, 564. The punishment of כָּרַת appears in Niphal stem in Leviticus 7:20, 21, 25, 27; 17: 4, 9, 14; 18:29; 19:8; 20:17, 18; 22:3; 23:29 and in Hiphil stem in Leviticus 17:10; 20:3, 5, 6. In Leviticus 26:22 and 30, the Hiphil form of כָּרַת is used to denote the cutting of the cattle and the incense altar, respectively.

28. The fourteen occurrences exclude a variant in Leviticus 20:17, a fragment in Leviticus 17:14, and an exception in Leviticus 22:3 that do not bear the formula. Even-Shoshan, 564; Zimmerli, "Eigenart der prophetischen," 13–15.

is thus not distinct to discussion of well-being offerings. One can conclude, in general, that all of these occurrences involve offences against God in the form of disrespect.

We now must turn to the practice of the punishment of כָּרֵת. The first view we come across is that כָּרֵת refers to extirpation, the termination of the violator's line. Milgrom examines this view in detail.[29] First, Psalm 109:13 (יְהִי־אַחֲרִיתוֹ לְהַכְרִית בְּדוֹר אַחֵר יִמַּח שְׁמָם׃) contains a distinct parallel which is crucial for our attempt to identify the meaning of כָּרֵת. In this verse, "may his posterity be cut off" is parallel to "in a following generation let their name be blotted out." This could, therefore, refer to the extirpation of the violator's descendants. Second, in Ruth 4:10 (וְלֹא־יִכָּרֵת שֵׁם־הַמֵּת מֵעִם אֶחָיו וּמִשַּׁעַר מְקוֹמוֹ), Boaz redeemed Ruth in order to continue the line of her husband, and in this verse the extirpation of one's descendants is expressed as cutting off the name from the clan. Third, Malachi 2:12 (יַכְרֵת יְהוָה לָאִישׁ אֲשֶׁר יַעֲשֶׂנָּה עֵר וְעֹנֶה מֵאָהֳלֵי יַעֲקֹב) clearly speaks of the cutting off the line of the person from the tent of Jacob.[30] Moreover, when we examine the incidents in which offenders against God were put to death immediately, we find that none of them employs the term כָּרֵת to describe the punishment of sudden death.[31] Therefore, the punishment of כָּרֵת should not be interpreted as a reference to the immediate death of the violator in the OT context.

The other view of the meaning of כָּרֵת is that it refers to punishment executed on the violator after his or her death – the violator will not rejoin his or her ancestors to enjoy the spiritual life of the hereafter.[32] In contrast to the previous view, this interpretation sees the punishment of כָּרֵת as an individual punishment rather than a collective punishment that would affect the violator's descendants. Thus, "being cut off from his people" indicates that a person is cut off from family or clan. The Hebrew Scriptures contain

---

29. Milgrom, *Leviticus 1–16*, 457–60. Milgrom states that among the rabbinic exegetes, there are five major views to explain the exact nature of כָּרֵת: "childless and premature death," "death before the age of sixty," "death before the age of fifty-two," "being 'cut off' through the extirpation of descendants," and "at death, the soul too shall die and will not enjoy the spiritual life of the hereafter." Two of these possibilities will be discussed here due to the occurrences of the root כָּרֵת.

30. Milgrom, 459.

31. For example, see Nadah and Abihu in Leviticus 10; Dathan, Abiram, and Korah in Numbers 16; and other plagues in the wilderness in Exodus 11 and Numbers 11–14.

32. For more discussion, refer to Milgrom, *Leviticus 1–16*, 460.

several instances (Gen 15:15; 47:30; Num 20:24; 27:13; 31:2; Judg 2:10, etc.) of a standard statement, closely related to the Ancient Near Eastern (ANE) culture, that those who die are seen as going to be with their ancestors. In this light, those punished by being "cut off from their people" might be rendered unable to rejoin their ancestors after death.

It is difficult to determine which of these views accurately interprets the meaning of כָּרֵת in the OT. I would suggest that the view of extirpation has more scriptural evidence than the second view, which has only indirect scriptural support. It may be, however, that both meanings are true, and the punishment of כָּרֵת refers to both the extirpation of the descendants and the deprivation of fellowship with ancestors after death.[33]

Exodus

In addition to its use in Leviticus, the word שְׁלָמִים ("well-being offering") appears in Exodus, Numbers, and Deuteronomy. According to the canonical order of the Hebrew Scriptures, the first occurrence of this word appears in Exodus 20:24 in the discussion of regulations for the burnt and well-being offerings being sacrificed to the Lord on the altar of stones used before the construction of the tabernacle. Then, in Exodus 24:5, the Israelites follow these instructions in their offerings of burnt and well-being sacrifices on this altar. In the Sinai pericope, the combination of these two kinds of offerings, which occurs here for the first time after the instructions in Exodus 20:24, is crucial. It is not only obedience to the instructions in Exodus 20:24, but also the ceremony of the completion of the covenant between Yahweh and the Israelites. Enns points out that the nature of these two different offerings is significant: the burnt offering denotes consecration and the atonement for sin, which point to the commitment to Yahweh, while the well-being offering expresses fellowship with Yahweh and the sense of well-being in his people.[34] Furthermore, Enns also observes that the significance mentioned above regarding these two different offerings is also expressed in the following blood rituals of the well-being offering in this episode. Moses took half of the blood to sprinkle on the altar (Exod 24:6) and the other half he put in a bowl

33. Milgrom, 460. Milgrom supports the combination of two views in his interpretation of כָּרֵת.

34. Enns, *Exodus*, 490.

and sprinkled it on the people (Exod 24:8).[35] This is not only a ceremony of making covenant between Yahweh and his people; it also displays the meaning of atonement for the people and the fellowship between Yahweh and the Israelites.[36] After the blood ceremony of the covenant, the description of the leaders' eating and drinking becomes the expression of the covenantal meal that goes with the well-being offering in Exodus 24:5. In all, the ceremony of these two offerings in Exodus 24 sets the tune officially for the Sinai covenant.

The book of Exodus contains two further occurrences of the word שְׁלָמִים. In Exodus 29:28, the Lord commanded that the well-being offering must include certain portions for Aaron and his sons. Its use in Exodus 32:6 refers to the Israelites' offering of burnt and well-being sacrifices to the golden calf on an altar they built, thus sinning against the Lord . However, it describes the breaking of the covenant between Yahweh and the Israelites due to their offerings to the golden calf. Obviously, the covenantal meaning of the combination of the burnt and well-being offerings is once again emphasized in this event.

Numbers

The book of Numbers contains eighteen occurrences of the word שְׁלָמִים, thirteen of which appear in Numbers 7, which mentions the offerings made by each tribe at the dedication of the tabernacle.[37] On that day each of the twelve tribes offered several offerings to the Lord in a specific order: one silver plate, a silver sprinkling bowl with the grain offering and animals as the burnt offering, an animal as the sin offering, and finally several animals as the well-being offering.

The well-being offering is also mentioned in Numbers 6, which explains that Nazirites must sacrifice the burnt offering, the sin offering, and the well-being offering when their period of separation is over.[38] The remaining uses of שְׁלָמִים in the book of Numbers (Num 10:10; 15:8; and 29:39) relate to

---

35. Enns, 490. In terms of the covenantal meaning of the blood ceremony, see Propp, *Exodus 19–40*, 308–09.

36. Wells points to using blood to bind the agreement between two parties in the ANE context. Wells, "Exodus," 246.

37. Even-Shoshan, *New Concordance*, 1156; Numbers 7:17, 23, 29, 35, 41, 47, 53, 59, 65, 71, 77, 83, 88.

38. Even-Shoshan, 1156–57; Numbers 6:14, 17–18.

sacrifices made during feasts. In Numbers 10:10 and 15:8, it is mentioned together with the burnt offering.

Deuteronomy

The word שְׁלָמִים appears only once in the book of Deuteronomy, in Deuteronomy 27:7.[39] It appears here in a commandment that echoes the first occurrences of שְׁלָמִים in the Pentateuch, Exodus 20:4 and 24:5. Before they finished reannouncing the law of the Lord to the new generation of Israelites in the wilderness, Moses and the elders of Israel commanded the people to sacrifice both burnt offerings and well-being offerings on the altar of stones after entering the land which the Lord had promised them. This echo, coming as a concluding remark before the Israelites move into the Promised Land, reminds readers of the covenant formed between God and the Israelites on Mount Sinai.

Summary: שְׁלָמִים in the Pentateuch

To sum up, the use of the well-being offering in the Pentateuch reveals, first, that this offering emphasizes the covenantal relationship between God and his people, the Israelites. Except in the one case in which a well-being offering was offered to the golden calf (Exod 32), whenever the well-being offering is practiced it denotes either the significance of the covenant of God or the solemn dedication of the Israelites to their God. Second, the meal and fellowship shared between the offerer and other people that follow a well-being offering draws our attention to relational harmony on the horizontal axis, the relationship among peoples. Last but not the least, the well-being offering is always the last to be made when it appears as part of a series of offerings. Its placement at the end of a series of sacrifices not only allows the meal to take place immediately following this offering, but also signifies and accents the presence of well-being between the offerer and God and between the offerer

39. Even-Shoshan, 1156. Moreover, in Deuteronomy 12:5–6, 11, 17–18, and 26–27, the offerings of נֶדֶר and נְדָבָה, which belong to the well-being offerings, are mentioned: they should be offered at the place Yahweh will choose in the future when they enter Canaan. As Deuteronomy 12 is located at the beginning of the last noncultic law collection in the Sinai pericope (Deut 12–26), the mention of these well-being offerings not only points to the importance of worshiping Yahweh alone but also denotes the well-being relationship between Yahweh and the Israelites in the land of Canaan.

and other people. The well-being offering thus acts as a conclusion to the series of sacrifices prescribed in the Pentateuch.

זִבְחֵי שְׁלָמִים (Well-Being Offerings) in the Historical and Prophetic Books

The word שְׁלָמִים appears twenty-five times in the OT historical books.[40]

Joshua

This word occurs three times in the book of Joshua.[41] In the textual context, all three occurrences show that the Israelites offered burnt and well-being offerings to the Lord for the purpose of covenant renewal (Josh 8:31) and in confirmation of the eastern tribes not serving the idols (Josh 22:23) but serving solely the Lord (Josh 22:27).

Judges

The word שְׁלָמִים appears twice in the book of Judges at the critical moment when the Israelites encountered a hurdle and sought the Lord's guidance to preserve the Benjamites.[42] In these verses, both burnt and well-being sacrifices are mentioned together.

1–2 Samuel

There are six occurrences in 1–2 Samuel.[43] In 1 Samuel 10:8 and 13:9, burnt and well-being offerings are mentioned when Samuel instructs Saul to wait for him to offer these sacrifices in Gilgal and, later, Saul does not obey Samuel's instruction but makes the offerings by himself instead. In 1 Samuel 11:15, after the people confirmed Saul as the king of Israel, they dedicated the well-being offering in Gilgal. In 2 Samuel, David appears as the offerer of both the burnt and well-being offerings in all three instances. In 2 Samuel 6:17–18, David offered the sacrifices after he brought the ark of the Lord to his city, while in 2 Samuel 24:25, David made the sacrifices in order to stop the plague in Israel. We will discuss this instance in greater detail below in the discussion

40. Even-Shoshan, 1156–57.

41. Even-Shoshan; Joshua 8:31; 22:23, 27.

42. Even-Shoshan, 1156; Judges 20:26; 21:4.

43. Even-Shoshan, 1156–57; 1 Samuel 10:8; 11:15; 13:9; 2 Samuel 6:17, 18; 24:25.

in relation to its parallel texts in 1 Chronicles 21:26., in relation to its parallel texts in 1 Chronicles 21:26.

1–2 Kings

The well-being offering appears six times in the book of 1–2 Kings.[44] All five occurrences in 1 Kings related to well-being sacrifices made by King Solomon. In 1 Kings 3:15 and 9:25, he offered both the burnt and well-being offerings to the Lord, while in 1 Kings 8:63 and 8:64 (two times) he dedicated only the well-being offering to the Lord as the offering to dedicate the temple. The word's only appearance in 2 Kings occurs in a narrative comment that Ahaz, king of Judah, built an altar according to the altar of Damascus and offered the well-being offering along with other offerings on that altar (2 Kgs 16:13).

1–2 Chronicles

The word שְׁלָמִים appears eight times in 1–2 Chronicles.[45] The three occurrences in 1 Chronicles exactly parallel the three occurrences in the book of 2 Samuel. In 1 Chronicles 16:1–2, David offers both burnt and well-being sacrifices because the ark of the Lord was moved to his city, while in 1 Chronicles 21:26, he makes these two offerings in order to stop the plague in Israel. Hill points out that in 1 Chronicles 16:1–2, burnt offerings are made for the purpose of atonement for sin and demonstrating dedication to God, while the well-being offerings signify the completion of David's vow in 1 Chronicles 13:13 and thanksgiving offered on behalf of all the Israelites for the blessings of God in establishing David as king.[46]

Averbeck points out that, since the combined burnt and well-being offerings were brought from the solitary altar system to the sanctuary and appeared in the beginning of the Sinaitic covenant in Exodus 24, it might "be

44. Even-Shoshan, 1156; 1 Kings 3:15; 8:63, 64 (twice); 9:25; 2 Kings 16:13.

45. Even-Shoshan, 1156–571; 1 Chronicles 16:1, 2; 21:26; 2 Chronicles 7:7; 29:35; 30:22; 31:2; 33:16.

46. Hill, *1 and 2 Chronicles*, 237. As for the explanation of the meaning of combined burnt and well-being offerings here in 1 Chronicles 16:1–2, Knoppers does not specify their purposes in this narrative. He states the general purposes of these two different kinds of offerings in this text by noting that the burnt offerings have "propitiatory and expiatory functions, covering a wide range of motives, such as devotion, appeasement, and thanksgiving," and the common denominator of various well-being offerings "is rejoicing." Knoppers, *1 Chronicles 10–29*, 627.

associated with issues of atonement to some degree, but in a different way."[47] Averbeck goes a step further to explain that "atonement is not mentioned in Exod 24, but the parallel with the blood of the ordination peace offering in 29:19–21, 33 (cf. Lev 8:22–24, 30) and the guilt offering for cleansing the leper in Lev 14:12–18 (cf. vv. 25–29) suggests that it was intended in Exod 24 as well."[48]

Therefore, if we consider 1 Chronicles 21:26, the well-being offerings there make atonement to consecrate the Israelites so that they may be bound to Yahweh.[49] As Hill rightly observes, the offering of well-being sacrifices not only subjectively restored the fellowship between the people and Yahweh but also objectively achieved atonement for the people by means of the divinely ordained sacrificial ritual.[50]

In 2 Chronicles 7:7, King Solomon offers well-being sacrifices in the dedication of the temple. In 2 Chronicles 29:35 and 31:2, King Hezekiah sacrifices both burnt and well-being offerings to the Lord, while in 30:22, the Israelites dedicate well-being offerings to celebrate the Feast of Unleavened Bread during King Hezekiah's reign. Lastly, in 2 Chronicles 33:16, Manasseh, king of Judah, offers well-being offerings and thanksgiving offerings to the Lord on the altar he restored.

Ezekiel

The word שְׁלָמִים occurs six times in Ezekiel, the only prophetic book in which it appears.[51] Ezekiel 43:27 and 46:2 mention the responsibility of the priests to offer burnt and well-being offerings. Ezekiel 46:12 states that the king is to dedicate burnt and well-being offerings at the appointed feasts, while Ezekiel 45:15 and 45:17 report that the king of Israel should make several offerings, include well-being offerings, to the Lord for the Israelites. All of these occurrences appear in the context of instructions given to the priests and the king of Israel when the new temple is built.

47. Averbeck, "שֶׁלֶם," in VanGemeren, *NIDOTTE* 4:139.

48. Averbeck, 139–40.

49. For example, Averbeck points out that "the blood of the ordination peace offering made atonement to consecrate the priests." Averbeck, 140.

50. Hill, *1 and 2 Chronicles*, 295; Cf. Knoppers, *1 Chronicles 10–29*, 758–59.

51. Even-Shoshan, *New Concordance*, 1156–57; Ezekiel 43:27; 45:15, 17; 46:2, 12 (twice).

Summary: שְׁלָמִים in Historical and Prophetic Hebrew Literature

In the historical books, the usage of the well-being offering extends beyond its original use as a means of emphasizing the offerer's well-being with God and other people. In these books we see the well-being offering used in the process of seeking God's guidance (Judges), and to reconfirm and renew the relationship between God and his people (Joshua and 1–2 Samuel). In 1–2 Kings and 1–2 Chronicles, it appears that well-being offerings are usually related to dedication or covenantal renewal, and the offerers in these accounts are usually kings. Gradually, it seems, the focus of these offerings shifted from well-being in the relationship between God and an individual to well-being in the relationship between God and his people as a nation, represented by the kings. The only mentions of well-being offerings in the prophetic books occur in the book of Ezekiel, where the concept is developed under the vision of a new temple and the responsibility of offering well-being sacrifices falls on the priests and kings. In Ezekiel, the commandment to offer well-being sacrifices is emphasized by the cooperative action of these two categories of leaders.

Summary: שְׁלָמִים in the Hebrew Scriptures

As presented in the OT, well-being offerings fulfilled the following primary purposes. First, they emphasized the status of well-being in the offerer's relationships with God and other humans.[52] This meaning is accented by its placement at the end of a series of offerings to God. Because of this emphasis on the covenantal relationship between God and his people, God regarded the Israelites' well-being offering to the golden calf as the breaking of the covenant between himself and the people. The emphasis on the relationship between God and his people in the well-being offering has been reflected in Smith's interpretation of animal sacrifices in the ANE, which proposes that the main purpose of animal sacrifices is communion between gods and worshipers in ANE society.[53] Second, the well-being offering not only expressed the covenantal relationship between God and his people but also carried out the reconfirmation or renewal of the covenant between them. It thus appears in the accounts of the covenant renewal undertaken by David in order to stop

52. These two main ideas appear in Levy, *Tabernacle: Shadows of Messiah*, 112.

53. See pages 12–13 of this book for the communion theory of R. Smith. See also Selman, "Sacrifice in Ancient Near East," 96.

the plague from God in 2 Samuel 24:25 and 1 Chronicles 21:26. Third, the well-being offering manifests the people's willingness to seek God's guidance in their lives in the book of Judges. This also points to the people's dedication to the Lord through the well-being offerings. Finally, the well-being offering bears the concept of collective dedication, as the kings offered them to dedicate the temple to the Lord. The concept of collective dedication is amplified in Ezekiel's accounts of the sacrifices in the new temple. The well-being offering could be offered privately or publicly, as an individual expression of thanks or payment of a vow, or as part of a national dedication offered by the king of Israel.[54]

Ancient Near Eastern Parallels to זִבְחֵי שְׁלָמִים (Well-Being Offerings)

Del Olmo Lete points out that the Ugaritic liturgical texts demonstrate a wider sense of "fest/festival" in the offering rites,[55] and the festival component in the teachings on sacrifices also resides in the OT Scriptures. In the regulations governing Levitical sacrificial ritual, only animals sacrificed in well-being offerings were consumable by the worshiper and other members of the general community. The other four sacrifices, whether vegetable or animal, were to be either devoted solely to the Lord by fire or partially shared by the priests after the completion of the sacrificial procedure. The sacrificial meal shared after sacrificing the well-being offering was, however, only to be partaken of by ceremonially clean people (Lev 22:3), and the leftover meat had to be burnt after one or two days (Lev 7:15–18; 19:6; 22:30). The restriction of the meal to clean people signifies that the meat is holy (Hag 2:12; Jer 11:15), while the action of partaking of the meat at the end of the sacrificial procedure (1 Sam 9; 20:27) emphasizes the status of well-being among God, the offerer, family, and friends. This act of partaking in the sacrificial meal together reveals a confirmed obligation between the gods and the worshiper in ANE Semitic culture.[56]

---

54. Miller, *Religion of Ancient Israel*, 113

55. Olmo Lete, *Canaanite Religion*, 15. Smith also observes that the festive character of certain sacrifices is shared by most religions, not only the Semitic religions. Smith, *Lectures on Religion*, 254–55.

56. Selman, "Sacrifice in Ancient Near East," 96.

Parker mentions that "before the discovery of Ugarit, the native literature of ancient Syria-Palestine was unknown to us."[57] During that period of time, biblical scholars could only trace the biblical literature through critical analysis of the Bible itself and comparison with Egyptian, Mesopotamian, and Arabic culture and writings.[58] Beginning in 1929, however, the discovery of the Ugaritic tablets completely changed this situation. Among these Ugaritic documents, outlines of ritual and poetic narratives are genres that can play a significant role in advancing our understanding of biblical ritual documents. As Parker asserts, "Increasing understanding and appreciation of these has clarified the tradition to which the biblical writers were heirs."[59] Levine points out that the term *šelāmîm* is attested in Ugaritic documents dating from the second half of the second millennium BC.[60] We will therefore pay close attention to the description of the well-being offering in Ugaritic sacrificial documents as we seek to more fully understand the practice and meaning of the well-being offerings in the OT.

Ugaritic Sacrificial Documents

Ugaritic writing was not a direct ancestor of biblical literature. It does, however, present us with a fixed literary version of a large and widespread oral tradition that, as it was transmitted over the course of centuries, influenced and informed the authors of new literary compositions in the Hebrew community. According to Pardee, the Ugaritic sacrificial texts were composed within a relatively short period of time and reflected the precise situation at the time of writing: "it appears likely that the sacrificial texts reflect precise situations and that the vast majority of them date, therefore, to the last few years of the kingdom of Ugarit (i.e. to the years 1200–1185 [BCE] in round figures)."[61] Parker claims that "as different as the two literatures are, we can better appreciate the particular context, purposes, and achievement of each

57. Parker, "Ugaritic Literature Bible," 228.

58. Robertson Smith used Arabic sources, as did De Vaux and others. Smith, *Religion of Semites*; De Vaux, *Studies in Old Testament*, 42–51.

59. Parker, "Ugaritic Literature and Bible," 228.

60. Levine, *In the Presence*, 5. Based on this dating, Levine asserts that "as a term of sacrifice, *šělāmîm* has pre-biblical history in the Ugaritic texts. We need not, therefore, be bound to normative Hebrew idiom, and may be justified in giving precedence to cognate usage."

61. Pardee, *Ritual and Cult*, 2–3.

when we recognize the similar reservoir of poetic, narrative, and mythological forms and motifs on which both draw."[62] The Ugaritic sacrificial texts are among the best sources on the ANE background of the rituals in the Pentateuch. Grasping an idea of how similar offerings were described and interpreted in the Ugaritic documents will give us an excellent reference point from which to gain perspective on well-being offerings in the OT. While scholars have debated whether the Ugaritic ritual texts are prescriptive or descriptive in nature,[63] the following discussion adopts Pardee's proposal regarding the prescriptive character of Ugaritic ritual texts due to his careful observation of the documents' grammar, syntax, and structure.[64]

While additional ANE sources will be investigated as necessary,[65] our study of the well-being offerings in Leviticus 17 will draw primarily on Ugaritic documents such as *KTU* 1.40 (RS1.002) and *KTU* 1.109 (RS 24.253).[66] These fairly well-preserved texts are good representatives of the sacrificial feast that emphasizes the expiation of sin and the communion between humans and gods,[67] as well as the prescriptive sacrificial rituals for a single month.[68]

62. Parker, "Ugaritic Literature and Bible," 229.

63. Petersen, *Royal God*, 90. Petersen concludes that "the study of the Ugaritic ritual texts is extremely difficult. That is a fact known by anyone who has ever tried to tackle these often fragmentary and often almost incomprehensible texts." This characteristic of the texts adds a variable to the debate.

64. Pardee, *Ritual and Cult*, 25. Pardee affirms, "my definition of the vast majority of these texts as prescriptive in nature is based essentially on their grammatical and formal structure. Virtually all verbal forms are expressed imperfectively or imperatively rather than declaratively . . . and with rare apparent exceptions, the internal chronology of texts that are chronologically arranged is linear through a day, two days, a month, or two months." Del Olmo Lete agrees that the Ugaritic ritual texts are prescriptive or directive, as reflected in their basic syntactic structures. See Olmo Lete, *Canaanite Religion*, 10.

65. Merlo and Xella, "Ugaritic Cultic Texts," 293. The Ugaritic texts found at Ras Shamra regarding ¬*lmm* have also been discussed in De Vaux, *Studies in Old Testament*, 46–51. Wright contends that his main goal of Ugaritic ritual study is to examine how ritual functions within the narrative context of stories. Wright, *Ritual in Narrative*, 6.

66. Merlo and Xella, "Ugaritic Cultic Texts," 293; De Moor and Sanders, "Ugaritic Expiation Ritual," 283–300; Pardee, *Ritual and Cult*, 77–83; Clemens, *Sources for Ugaritic Ritual*, 1200.

67. See *KTU* 1.40 (RS1.002) in Pardee, *Ritual and Cult*, 77–79. Clemens notes that there is "a more explicit mechanism for restoring harmony in relation to ʾIlu and his entourage" in RS1.002. Clemens, *Sources for Ugaritic Ritual*, 83.

68. Refer to the introduction to *KTU* 1.109 (RS 24.253) in Pardee, *Ritual and Cult*, 25–27.

Individual Ugaritic Sacrificial Terms

The Ugaritic ritual texts use a series of technical terms to describe or record various actions of the cult. Merlo and Xella argue that "even if we are still very far from having resolved all the problems of interpretation, the meanings of some terms have now been determined with enough certainty."[69] In this section, therefore, we will discuss some crucial Ugaritic terms used in the sacrificial documents.[70]

dbḥ

This is a common word in Semitic vocabulary, with various meanings in its different religious contexts.[71] It usually appears in summary statements regarding Ugaritic sacrifices, functioning as a general term with reference to sacrifice, cultic celebration, and festival.[72] In Ugaritic, it is usually used as a noun to denote a shed blood sacrifice or a sacrificial meal.[73] Del Olmo Lete explains that this term was originally used to express the idea of "sacrifice of an animal victim" in both cultic and extracultic contexts, but later its semantic value gradually changed to express "ritual feast" or nonsacrificial "feast."[74] Its use is very similar to that of its Hebrew cognate, זֶבַח.[75] According to Merlo and Xella, *dbḥ* refers to a sacrificial activity including a sacrificial meal or banquet and other festival activities.[76]

---

69. Merlo and Xella, "Ugaritic Cultic Texts," 291.

70. Olmo Lete, "Sacrificial Vocabulary at Ugarit," 49. Olmo Lete suggests that if one would like to examine the whole semantic field of these words, many other contextual factors should be taken into account besides the sacrificial action (e.g. the sacrificial material, when and where the rite takes place, etc.).

71. Clemens, *Sources for Ugaritic Ritual*, 2.

72. Clemens, 22, 48; Olmo Lete, *Canaanite Religion*, 25-26.

73. Olmo Lete, "Sacrificial Vocabulary," 38. Olmo Lete asserts that cultic texts contain frequent examples of this word.

74. Olmo Lete, "Sacrificial Vocabulary," 38. Moreover, Clemens mentions that *dbḥ* occurs in a whole range of genres of Ugaritic documents, including administrative documents (*KTU* 1.91:2, 3, 14, etc.), letters (RS 2.40:16, etc.), and so on. Clemens, *Sources for Ugaritic Ritual*, 70-71.

75. Selman, "Sacrifice in Ancient Near East," 97; Cf. De Vaux, *Studies in Old Testament*, 47. See also "*dbḥ*," in Olmo Lete and Sanmartin, *Dictionary of Ugaritic Language*, 262; "זֶבַד," *HALOT*, 262. Olmo Lete and Sanmartin argue that this word refers to a sacrifice or a sacrificial banquet, but Merlo and Xella assert that it is not semantically connected with זֶבַח. Merlo and Xella, "Ugaritic Cultic Texts," 292.

76. Merlo and Xella, 292. Merlo and Xella verify that the meaning "feast" "is abundantly confirmed by the use of the term in the ritual texts. It is a sacrificial meal, that is, a sacred banquet, as has been proved by several terms which are parallel or actually synonymous to

*ṯ*ʿ

Clemens asserts that this word has been treated intermittently and eccentrically because there is no thorough discussion solely devoted to this sacrifice. Because of the diverse usages of this form and the possible cognates found in both ritual and administrative texts, the interpretation of the word *ṯ*ʿ is abstruse.[77] According to Merlo and Xella, however, "significantly, the terms *dbḥ* and *ṯ*ʿ denote the inner cultic sphere in which the Ugaritic *homo religiosus* has committed sin."[78] Del Olmo Lete and Sanmartín suggest that *ṯ*ʿ conveys the meaning of "offering," which is parallel to the words *dbḥ* and *nkt*.[79]

šrp

This Ugaritic word appears to refer to a certain type of sacrifice. It is usually accompanied by the word "fire," which suggests that *šrp* could be used to refer to a burnt offering in Ugaritic.[80] In the OT, the verb שָׂרַף is closely related to the burnt offering, עֹלָה. Clemens comments that this term "tends to receive coverage in comparative investigations of burnt offerings in other environments."[81] Del Olmo Lete and Sanmartín assert that the meaning of *šrp* in Ugaritic is "burnt sacrifice," which is also affirmed by Merlo and Xella.[82] However, del Olmo Lete points out that, strictly speaking, Ugaritic *šrp* does not have the meaning of complete burning of the victim, but denotes a type of offering in which the fire is used in a special way to offer some of its parts.[83] In terms of the contents of *šrp* offering, Clemens concludes that although there may be a nonbloody interpretation of the contents of *šrp* offering, it was "regularly composed of meat."[84] Clemens also mentions that *šrp* is treated as

---

it *dǵt*, *mṣd*, *ṯrm*, and *ʿšrt*. However, the meaning of the word sometimes seems to be more generic (precisely 'feast' in general), since *dbḥ* sometimes includes not only foodstuffs . . . but also objects, clothes or metals." For example, we can see the idea of "meal" in this word in *KTU* 1.41:20–22 (RS 1.003). Pardee, *Les textes rituels*, 178.

77. Clemens, *Sources for Ugaritic Ritual*, 49.

78. Merlo and Xella, "Ugaritic Cultic Texts," 293.

79. See "*ṯ*ʿ," in Olmo Lete and Sanmartin, *Dictionary of Ugaritic Language*, 892; Olmo Lete, "Sacrificial Vocabulary," 41. For instance, Olmo Lete gives an example in *KTU* 1.40:23.

80. Selman, "Sacrifice in Ancient Near East," 98.

81. Clemens, *Sources for Ugaritic Ritual*, 49; De Vaux, *Studies in Old Testament*, 47.

82. See "*šrp*," in Olmo Lete and Sanmartin, *Dictionary of Ugaritic Language*, 844; Merlo and Xella, "Ugaritic Cultic Texts," 293.

83. Olmo Lete, *Canaanite Religion*, 27.

84. Clemens, *Sources for Ugaritic Ritual*, 20.

an adjunct of *šlmm* in scholarly discussions, so there are few studies devoted solely to this word.[85]

šlmm

šlmm is the plural form of *šlm*, meaning "peace, health, well-being and prosperity."[86] Though Selman mentions that the meaning of *šlmm* as a Ugaritic sacrificial term is not assured, del Olmo Lete and Sanmartín assert that, when it is used in the ritual text, its meaning is "communion victim/sacrifice" or "peace offering."[87] Clemens mentions as well that even though this word also appears in the poetic narrative genre – in *Kirta*, for example – as well as in ritual texts, its meaning is consistent.[88] The Ugaritic word *šlm* is cognate with the word שָׁלוֹם in Hebrew, and they both appear in ritual texts as a plural noun to denote the well-being sacrifice.[89] In Ugaritic texts, *šlmm* usually describes an offering of animal victims, as it does in the OT, and it is often used with the verb *lḥm* ("to eat"). Moreover, both *šlmm* and the Levitical well-being offering are eaten by the worshipers.[90] In Ugaritic, this word often appears in combination with *šrp* in the phrase *šrp w šlmm* (the burnt offering and the well-being offering).[91] This usage is closely related to the Hebrew ritual texts in the OT.

There are also, however, some differences between this Ugaritic ritual and the Hebrew well-being offering. For example, in Ugaritic the *šlmm* sacrifices

85. Clemens, 49.

86. See "*šlm* (I)," in Olmo Lete and Sanmartin, *Dictionary of Ugaritic Language*, 818.

87. Selman, "Sacrifice in Ancient Near East," 98. Selman makes this comment basing on the following factors. "(a) the variety of meaning of words formed from the root *šlm* in Semitic language; (b) the existence of a deity Salim in Ugarit; (c) the unlikelihood of the singular form of the word (*šlm*) having a sacrificial meaning; and (d) the lack of any explanation of *šlmm* in the ritual texts themselves." See "*šlm* (II)," in Olmo Lete and Sanmartin, *Dictionary of Ugaritic Language*, 819; Olmo Lete, "Sacrificial Vocabulary," 44.

88. Clemens, *Sources for Ugaritic Ritual*, 73.

89. De Vaux, *Studies in Old Testament*, 47. De Vaux also mentions that these two words are correspondent to each other.

90. *KTU* 1.115 (RS 24.260:9–10), for example, is a relatively short text (only fourteen lines) covering a royal ritual for a single day. The well-being offering mentioned in line 9 may be eaten by all people after the ceremony. Pardee, *Ritual and Cult*, 66–67; Selman, "Sacrifice in Ancient Near East," 98.

91. Merlo and Xella, "Ugaritic Cultic Texts," 293. Merlo and Xella conclude that in Ugaritic rituals, *šrp* and *šlmm* almost always occur together. In those texts, *šrp* is related to a burnt victim while *šlmm* denotes a communal meals of the offerers.

were sometimes related to an ancestor cult, and this association is completely alien to the well-being offering in the OT.[92] Second, in the OT, the well-being offering occurs in connection with a blood ritual, and the priests could share part of the sacrificial meat. Selman asserts that neither of these practices is found in the Ugaritic *šlmm* sacrifices.[93] While Merlo and Xella identify *šlmm* sacrifices as blood rituals related to "the act of 'immolation' (*nkt*) or 'slaughter' (*qll*) of the victim,"[94] in *KTU* 1.41 and *KTU* 1.87:2 ,the *šlmm* sacrifice includes wine and flour, indicating that it is not necessarily a shed blood sacrifice.[95] Therefore, the uniqueness of the connection between well-being offerings and blood rituals in the OT does not exist in the Ugaritic *šlmm* sacrifices. Another difference is that in Ugaritic, we do not have exact the same expression of the combination of the words *šlmm* and *dbḥ* even though we could find these two words appear in the same paragraph of a document, while the equivalent words appear as a combined term, זֶבַח שְׁלָמִים, in Hebrew.[96]

nkt

This word appears repeatedly in *KTU* 1.40. Clemens suggests it is "a general term for 'slaughter' but used parallel to both *dbḥ* and *ṯ* ʿ."[97] Del Olmo Lete also notes that this word parallels *dbḥ* and *ṯ* ʿ, while Merlo and Xella suggest that *nkt* means "immolation."[98]

kbd

Clemens asserts that in ritual texts such as *KTU* 1.41:39 (RS 1.003) and *KTU* 1.87:[42] (RS 18.056), this word is "held to reflect a meaning 'honorific

92. Selman, "Sacrifice in Ancient Near East," 98.

93. Selman, 98.

94. Merlo and Xella, "Ugaritic Cultic Texts," 293-94.

95. Pardee, *Les textes rituels*, 180.

96. Selman, "Sacrifice in Ancient Near East," 98. Regarding *šlmm* and *dbḥ*, which appear in the same paragraph of a document, see an example in *KTU* 1.162, Olmo Lete, *Canaanite Religion*, 74.

97. Clemens, *Sources for Ugaritic Ritual*, 56.

98. Olmo Lete, "Sacrificial Vocabulary," 40; Merlo and Xella, "Ugaritic Cultic Texts," 294.

(gift).'"[99] This word is cognate with the OT Hebrew word, כָּבֵד, which means "heavy or honor."[100]

The Classification of Ugaritic Ritual Actions

Merlo and Xella suggest that most Ugaritic ritual actions could be classified into several major subdivisions: blood sacrifices, bloodless sacrificial offerings, processions, enthronements-investitures, and cultic meals.[101] As we examine the sacrificial rituals in the Ugaritic documents in relation to the well-being offerings in the OT, we will look particularly at the blood sacrifices and the cultic meals.

The Ritual Blood Sacrifice

The first category represents ritual actions involving blood. In Ugaritic ritual texts, *šrp* and *šlmm* belong to this category. As mentioned in the discussion of Ugaritic sacrificial terminology above, *šrp* is obviously connected with the action of "burning" the victim, as the root *šrp* shows. Based on etymology and comparison with Hebrew שְׁלָמִים, the second term, *šlmm*, should perhaps be translated "communion sacrifice" or "peace sacrifice." In Ugaritic documents, the burnt offering (*šrp*) is often paired with the peace offering (*šlmm*); these similarities of content and terminology seem to indicate that the meaning of these texts is similar to that of the sacrificial documents in Leviticus.[102] In *KTU* 1.115 = RS 24.260: 9–10, the phrase *š l'il bt . šlmm kl l ylḥm bh* ("a ram to the god of (royal) house as a *šlmm* offering; all eat it") may suggest that *šlmm* is a communal meal attended by the offerers.[103]

The Communal Meals

Communal meals – which include the consumption of drinks and food, especially meat, and frequently acquire religious significance – can also be

99. Clemens, *Sources for Ugaritic Ritual*, 60; Cf. Olmo Lete, "Sacrificial Vocabulary," 43-44.

100. See "*k-b-d*," in Olmo Lete and Sanmartin, *Dictionary of Ugaritic Language*, 424. The verb *k-b-d* in Ugaritic means "to honor, to pay homage to, welcome" which is similar to the meaning of the Hebrew word כָּבֵד.

101. Merlo and Xella, "Ugaritic Cultic Texts," 293. In addition to rites involving blood, the Ugaritic texts mention bloodless ritual actions documented in several texts, for example, *KTU* 1.41. Since this category is not the focus of this book, I will not discuss it in detail. See Merlo and Xella, "Ugaritic Cultic Texts," 294.

102. Weinfeld, *Place of the Law*, 44.

103. Merlo and Xella, "Ugaritic Cultic Texts," 293.

discussed among Ugaritic ritual actions. This common scene can be found in several Ugaritic poetic narratives, including *KTU* 1.17 VI: 1–8; *KTU* 1.15 II: 1–10; and *KTU* 1.17 I: 1–13, which depict "banquets offered to the deities in the epic literature."[104] Although three basic scenes – the banquet preparation, invitation, and the meal itself – that accompany banquet themes in Ugaritic poetic narratives do not appear in these two ritual texts (*KTU* 1.40 [RS1.002] and *KTU* 1.109 [RS 24.253]), other crucial terms and concepts related to communal meals do appear in them. On the one hand, both texts mention offerings of animals, including well-being offerings.[105] Moreover, Pardee concludes from *KTU* 1.109 that the deities all benefited from well-being sacrifices.[106] On the other hand, *KTU* 1.40 mentions different groups of sacrifice-offerers and different animals used for various situations.[107] Pardee points out that "the main kind of sacrifice in the premier liturgy was DBḤ, that is to say, the feast. The liturgy would have started with this feast, continued by offering, and terminated by the sacrifice of the donkey and sealing the peace that is concomitant of this sacrifice."[108] In conclusion, despite the differences in descriptions of communal meals between ritual texts and poetic narratives, it is clear that the concept of feasting is present in both ritual texts discussed here.

The Sacrificial Material in the Rites

Merlo and Xella mention that the Ugaritic blood rites involve the sacrifice of animals and are substantially similar to other known religious traditions in the ANE.[109] The animals offered most frequently are bovides (ox, bull, cow, etc.), ovines (ram or sheep, etc.), and birds (dove or domestic dove, etc.). Nonetheless, other kinds of animals, such as donkeys (*ʿr*) and fish (*dg*) also occasionally appear in the offerings.[110]

104. Clemens, *Sources for Ugaritic Ritual*, 77. On the Ugaritic texts of *KTU* 1.15 and 1.17, also see Parker, *Ugaritic Narrative Poetry*, 23–30, 51–63.

105. Lloyd, "Banquet Theme," 189–90; Merlo and Xella, "Ugaritic Cultic Texts," 296.

106. Pardee, *Les textes rituels*, 1:613–14. See also the text in Pardee, *Ritual and Cult*, 29–31.

107. Pardee, 77–83.

108. Pardee, *Les textes rituels*, 142.

109. Merlo and Xella, "Ugaritic Cultic Texts," 296.

110. Merlo and Xella, 296.

The Translation and Structure of KTU 1.40 (RS1.002)[111]

The following is the text of *KTU* 1.40 with my own English translation.

Table 3. Translation of *KTU* 1.40 (RS1.002)

KTU 1.40	English Translation
Obverse Section ? (I or II) 1. [. . .]⸢*w*⸣ *n*⸢*py*⸣[. . .] 2. [. . .] *npy* . *ʾu*[*grt*. . .] 3. [. . .]*y* . *ʾu l p* . [. . .] 4. [. . .]⸢*ǵ*⸣*br* . *ʾu* ⸢*l*⸣ [*p*. . .] 5. [. . .]⸢--⸣[. . .]	Obverse Section ? (I or II) . . . and well-being. . . . . . well-being for U[garit . . .] . . . whether (be it) according to the statement . . . ⸢Ḫ⸣apiru, whether (be it) according to the statement . . . . . . ⸢--⸣. . . . .
Section II 6. [*ṯʿ nṯʿ*]⸢*y*⸣ 7. [*d*]*r* . *b*⸢*n*⸣ ⸢*ʾi*⸣[l] 8. [ ]	Section II . . . the offering that we offer . . . the circle of the sons of god . . . . . .
Section III 9. [ ]⸢.⸣ *w npy* 10. [ ]*y* . *ʾugr*⸢*t*⸣ 11. [*qṭ*]*y* 12. [ ]⸢-⸣ 13. [ ] 14. [ ] 15. [*ndb*]*ḥ* 16. [ ]⸢ *yṯ*⸣ [*šʾi*] 17. [*mpḫ*]⸢*r*⸣*t* . [*bn* . *ʾil* *ṯkmn w šn*]*m hn š*	Section III . . . and well-being . . . well-being for Ugari⸢t⸣ . . . Qaṭ]ien . . . . we sacrifice . . . ⸢foreman⸣ a ram . . . . . . the assembly of [the sons of god, *Ṯukamuna-wa-Šuna]ma*: Here is the ram.
Section IV 18. [*w n*]*py* . *g*⸢*r*⸣[. *ḥmyt* . *ʾugrt* . *w np*]*y* 19. [ ]⸢-⸣. *w n*⸢*p*⸣[*y*]⸢-⸣. *ʾu tḫṭ*⸢*ʾi*⸣[*n* . *ʾu l p* . *qṭy*]	Section IV . . . and well-being of the foreigner (line 35–36) [(within) the walls of Ugarit, and well-being of . . . and well-being of]; whether you have si[nned, whether (be it) according to the statement of the Qaṭien].
20. *ʾu l p* . *ddmy* . *ʾu l* ⸢*p*⸣ [. *ḫry* . *ʾu*] ⸢*l*⸣ *p* . *ḫty* . *ʾu l p* [. *ʾalty* . *ʾu l p* .] *ǵbr*	Whether (be it) according to the statement (/ custom) of Didima. Whether (be it) according to ⸢the statement of⸣ [Hurrian. Whether (be it)] ⸢according to⸣ the statement of Hittite. Whether (be it) according to the statement of [ʾAlashian. Whether (be it) according to the statement of] Ḫapiru.

111. As for the explanation of signs please refer to the Abbreviations.

KTU 1.40	English Translation
21. *ʾu l p . ḫbtkn . ʾu l* ⸢*p*⸣ *. md*[*llk*]*n . ʾu l p . q*[*rzbl*]	Whether (be it) according to the statement of your pillagers. Whether (be it) according to ⸢the statement of⸣ your oppressors. Whether (be it) according to the statement of Q[RZBL].
22. *ʾu tḫṭʾin . b ʾapkn . ʾu b* ⸢*q*⸣*ṣrt . npš* [*kn . ʾu b qṭt*]	Whether you sin in your anger, in the shortness of your soul, in repugnance(s) . . . (connects to the first word of next line)
23. *tqṭṭn ʾu tḫṭʾin . l bḥ*⸢*m*⸣ *w l ṯʿ . db*[*ḥn . ndb*]⸢*ḥ*⸣	you have felt. Whether you sin in connection with the sacrifices or in connection with the offering. The sacrifice that we sacrifice,
24. *hw . tʿ . ntʿy . hw . nkt . n*⸢*k*⸣*t*[112] *. ytšʾi*[*. l ʾab . bn ʾil*]	This is the offering we offer. This is the victim we immolate. May it rise to the father of the sons of god.
25. *ytšʾi . l dr . bn . ʾil . l .* ⸢*m*⸣*pḫrt . bn* ⸢*ʾi*⸣[*l . l ṯkmn . w š*]*nm hn š*	May it rise to the circle of the sons of god, to the assembly of the sons of god [, to *Ṯukamuna-wa-Šu]nama*. Here is the ram.
Section V 26. *w . šqrb . ʿr . mšr mšr* [.] ⸢*b*⸣*n . ʾugrt .* ⸢*w*⸣ [*npy*] *ʾugr*	Section V And offer/bring near a donkey of justification, of justification, sons of Ugarit! ⸢And⸣ [well-being] for Ugarit.
27. *w npy . ymʾan . w npy . ʿrmt* ⸢*. w*⸣ *npy .* ⸢-⸣[ ]	And well-being of YMʾAN, and well-being of ʿRMT, ⸢and⸣ well being of [ ],
28. *w npy . nqmd . u šn . ypkm . ʾu l p . q*[*ṭy . ʾu l p . ddm*]*y*	and well-being of Niqmaddu. Whether your beauty/dignity (is) marred, whether (be it) according to the statement of the Qa[ṭien, whether (be it) according to the statement of the *Didim]a*,
29. *ʾu l p . ḫry . ʾu l p . ḫ*⸢*t*⸣*y . ʾu l p . ʾalty . ʾu* ⸢*l*⸣ [*p ǵbr .*] ⸢*ʾu*⸣ *l p*	Whether (be it) according to the statement of Hurrian. Whether (be it) according to the statement of Hit⸢ti⸣te. Whether (be it) according to the statement of ʾAlashian. Whether (be it) ⸢according to⸣ [the statement of Ḫapiru.] ⸢Whether (be it)⸣ according to the statement of
30. *ḫbtkm . ʾu l p . m*⸢*d*⸣[*l*]*lkm . ʾu l p . qrzbl . ʾu* ⸢*šn*⸣ [.] *ypkm*	your pillagers. Whether (be it) according to the statement of your oppressors. Whether (be it) according to the statement of QRZBL. Whether your beauty/dignity (is) ⸢marred⸣,

112. "NKT denotes basic 'slaughtering' and corresponds to the use of the West-Semitic verb *qatālu* and the Akkadian verb *dâku*, both meaning 'to kill' and both used in the Mari donkey-sacrifice texts." Pardee, *Ritual and Cult*, 112, n.115.

KTU 1.40	English Translation
31. *ʾu b ʾapkm . ʾu b q[ṣ]⸢r⸣t . npškm . ʾu b qṭt . tqṭṭ*	whether in your anger, or in the shortness of your soul, or in repugnance(s) you have felt.
32. *ʾu šn . ypkm . l d[b]ḥm . w l . ṯʿ . dbḥn . ndbḥ . hw . ṯʿ nṯʿy*	Whether your beauty/dignity is marred in connection with the sacrifices or in connection with the offering. The sacrifice that we sacrifice. This is the offering we offer.
33. *hw . nkt . nkt . ⸢y⸣[t]šʾi . l ʾab . bn . ʾil . ytšʾi . l dr*	This is the victim we immolate. May it rise to the father of the sons of god. May it rise to the circle of
34. *bn ʾil . l ṯkmn [. w] šnm . hn . ʿr*	the sons of god, to *Ṯukamuna-[wa]-Šunama.* Here is the donkey.
Section VI 35. *w . ṯb . l mspr . m[š]⸢r⸣ mšr . bt . ʾugrt . w npy ⸢.⸣ gr*	Section VI Now go back to the narrative/recitation of justification: Justification of the daughter of Ugarit. And well-being of foreigner
36. *ḥmyt . ʾugrt . w [np]y ⸢. ʾa⸣ṯt . ʾu šn . ypkn . ʾu l p ⸢.⸣ qṭy*	(within) the walls of Ugarit, and well-being of women/woman. Whether your beauty/dignity (is) marred, whether (be it) according to the statement of the Qaṭien,
37. *ʾu l p . ddmy . ʾu l [p . ḫ]ry . ʾu l p . ḫty . ʾu l p . ʾalṯy*	whether (be it) according to the statement of the *Didima*, Whether (be it) according to [the statement of Hu]rrian. Whether (be it) according to the statement of Hittite. Whether (be it) according to the statement of ʾAlashian.
38. *ʾu l p [.]ǵbr . ʾu l p . ⸢ḫ⸣[bt]⸢kn . ʾu l⸣ p . mdllkn . ʾu l p ⸢.⸣ qrz⸢bl⸣*	Whether (be it) according to the statement of your pillagers. Whether (be it) according to the statement of your oppressors. Whether (be it) according to the statement of QRZ[BL].
39. *l šn ypkn . b ʾap⸢k⸣[n . ʾu b q]⸢ṣ⸣rt . npškn ⸢.⸣ ʾu b q⸢ṭt⸣*	Whether your beauty/dignity (is) marred in your anger, or in the shortness of your soul, or in repugnance(s)
40. *tqṭṭn . ʾu šn y⸢p⸣[kn . l dbḥm .] w l ṯʿ dbḥn*	you have felt. Whether your beauty/dignity is marred [in connection with the sacrifices] or in connection with the offering. The sacrifice
41. *ndbḥ . hw . ṯʿ n[ṯʿy . hw . nkt . n]⸢k⸣t . ⸢yt⸣[š]⸢ʾi .⸣ l ʾab bn ʾil*	that we sacrifice. This is the offering we offer. This is the victim we immolate. May it rise to the father of the sons of god.
Reverse 42. *ytšʾi . l ⸢d⸣[r . bn ʾil . l] mpḫrt . bn ʾil* 43. *l ṯkm⸢n⸣ [. w šnm .] hn ⸢ʿr⸣*	Reverse May it rise to the circle of the sons of god, to the assembly of the sons of god, to *Ṯukamuna-wa-Šuna]ma.* Here is ⸢the donkey⸣.

The structure of *KTU* 1.40 is neatly done. Pardee discusses the primary structure of this text in his book.[113] However, because of the fragments in Sections I to III, I would like to propose the following brief structure of Sections IV to VI.

Table 4. Structure of *KTU* 1.40 (RS1.002)

	Section IV (lines 18–25)	**Section V (lines 26–34)**	**Section VI (lines 35–43)**
Introduction	•Well-being of. . . •The foreigner (18–19a)	•A donkey of justification for sons of Ugarit •Well-being of Ugarit and . . . (26–28a)	•Justification for daughter of Ugarit •Well-being of the foreigner and women (35–36a)
Condition I (the Shortness of Conducts)	Whether you have sinned according to nine groups of people (19b–21)	Whether your dignity is marred according to nine groups of people (28b–30a)	Whether your dignity is marred according to nine groups of people (36b–38)
Condition II (the Shortness of Personal Character)	Sin in . . . •Anger •Shortness •Repugnance (22–23a)	Your dignity is marred in . . . •Anger •Shortness •Repugnance (30b–31)	Your dignity is marred in . . . •Anger •Shortness •Repugnance (39–40a)
Condition III (the Shortness in Terms of Sacrifices)	Sin in connection with sacrifices and offering (23b)	Your dignity is marred in connection with sacrifices and offering (32a)	Your dignity is marred in connection with sacrifices and offering (40b)
Declaration and Prayer	•Blood sacrifice •Prayer (23c–25a)	•Blood sacrifice •Prayer (32b–34a)	•Blood sacrifice •Prayer (40c–43a)
Sacrificial Announcement	Here is the ram. (25b)	Here is the donkey. (34b)	Here is the donkey. (43b)

This structure provides us with some preliminary ideas about the blood ritual actions in Ugaritic ritual texts. First, the sacrifices concern both the Ugaritic people and foreigners (*gr*).[114] Similarly, in Leviticus we find that aliens (גֵּר)

113. Pardee, *Les textes rituels*, 99–100, 102.

114. Pardee, 142. Pardee points out this observation as well in his conclusion of the study of *KTU* 1.40.

among the Israelites are instructed to meet the same sacrificial requirements (Lev 16:29; 17:8, 12–13, 15; 22:18).

Second, the Ugaritic sacrifices involve both males and females. While Leviticus does not detail separate purification rituals for men and women at the Day of Atonement, Leviticus 15 describes purification rituals for both men and women when they face the problem of discharge.

Third, Pardee observes that sections IV to VI contain similar, repetitive passages. They are introduced by the formulas "*ʾu l p*" ("whether according to the statement"), and address three main domains of life: social, moral, and worship. This structure, Pardee believes, suggests that "the objective of this rite was to ensure the welfare of the city and its inhabitants and visitors in these three areas."[115] Turning to the book of Leviticus, especially its discussion of sacrificial rituals, we find these same three domains addressed in descriptions of the sacrifices. For instance, the guilt and sin offerings belong to the moral domain; the burnt and grain offerings may indicate the worship domain; and the well-being offering may belong to the social domain of sacrifices.

Fourth, although this Ugaritic ritual mentions that different animals or items must be sacrificed to atone for different conditions, it does not provide details about the procedures of this ritual.[116] This is different from the sacrificial texts in Leviticus, in which detailed procedures are prescribed to the people. Lastly, the usage of donkey in this justification ritual differs significantly from any practice in Leviticus, for donkeys do not belong to the category of sacrificial animals in the commandment of the Lord.

115. Pardee, 142.

116. Pardee, *Ritual and Cult*, 26. "It is clear that the primary act of the Ugaritic cult was the offering of bloody sacrifice and other offerings to deities. Not stated, however, are (1) the details of how the offerings were performed, (2) from whose assets they originated and whose assets they became, and (3) the function of each offering and sacrificial category, that is, the 'theology' of the cult. Most such details may only be deduced from the structure of the texts and from comparisons with other cultures."

The Translation and Structure of KTU 1.109 (RS 24.253)

Table 5. Translation of KTU 1.109 (RS 24.253)

KTU 1.109 (RS 24.253)	English Translation
Obverse	**Obverse**
1. *b ʾarbʿt . ʿšr[t]*	On the fourteenth [the day of the month],[117]
2. *yrtḥṣ . mlk . ⌜b⌝[rr]*	the king will wash himself clean.
3. *b ym . mlʾat*	On the day of fullness/full moon
4. *tqln . ʾalpm*	two bulls fall
5. *yrḫ . ʿšrt . l bʿ[l . ṣpn]*	(for) the Moon god/ *Yariḫu*, a banquet offering for Ba[al in the north.]
6. *dqtm . w ynt . qr[t]*	Two ewes and a dove of city/a domestic dove[118]
7. *w mtntm . ⌜w⌝ š l rm⌜š⌝*	and two kidneys ⌜and⌝ a ram for RM⌜Š⌝.
8. *w kbd . w š . l šlm ⌜k⌝bd*	A liver and a ram for Šalimu, a liver of
9. *ʾalp . w š l bʿl ṣpn*	a bull and a ram for Baal in the north.
10. *dqt l ṣpn . šrp . w šlmm*	An ewe for Ṣapunu as a burnt offering. And as a peace offering:
11. *kmm . w b bt . bʿl . ʾugrt*	Ditto. And in the temple/house of Baal of Ugarit,
12. *kkdm . w npš . ʾilʾib*	two livers and a piece of offal: for *ʾiluʾibi*
13. *gdlt . ʾil š . bʿl š . ʿnt*	a cow, for El a ram, for Baal a ram, for ʿAnatu
14. *ṣpn . ʾalp . w š . pdry š*	in the north[119] a bull and a ram, for Pidray a ram
15. *šrp . w šlmm ʾilʾib š*	as a burnt offering. And as a peace offering for *ʾiluʾibi* a ram,
16. *bʿl ʾugrt š . bʿl ḫlb š*	for Baal of Ugarit a ram, for Baal of Aleppo a ram,
17. *yrḫ š . ʿnt ṣpn . ʾalp*	for *Yariḫu* a ram, for ʿAnatu in the north a cattle
18. *w š . pdry š . ddmš . š*	and a ram, for Pidray a ram, for Dadmiš a ram
19. *w b ʾurbt . ʾilʾib š*	And in the opening for *ʾiluʾibi* a ram,
Lower Edge	Lower Edge
20. *bʿl . ʾalp w š*	for Baal a bull and a ram,

117. Pardee, 30.

118. Olmo Lete and Sanmartin, *Dictionary of Ugaritic Language*, 2:712.

119. Pardee, *Ritual and Cult*, 31. Pardee translates this as "ʿAnatu of Ṣapunu."

KTU 1.109 (RS 24.253)	**English Translation**
Reverse	**Reverse**
21. *dgn . š . ʾil tʿḏr* 22. *bʿl š . ʿnt š . ršp š* 23. *šlmm .*	for Dagan a ram, for the helper gods of Baal a ram, for ʿAnatu a ram, for Rašap a ram, as a peace offering.
24. *w šnpt . ʾil š* 25. *l ʿnt ḫlš . tn šm* 26. *l gtrm . ǵšb šm ʾal*	And as a ŠNPT offering:[120] or El a ram. For ʿAnatu-ḪLŠ two rams, for Gaṯarūma the left ǴṢB of
27. *d ʾalpm . w ʾalp* ⸢*w*⸣ *š* 28. *šrp . w šlmm kmm*	which (is) two bulls and a bull ⸢and⸣ a ram as a burnt offering. And a peace offering: ditto.
29. *l bʿl . ṣpn b ʿrʿr* 30. *pʿamt ṯlṯm . š l qẓrt*	For Baal in the north with the tamarisk thirty times; a ram for the *Qẓrt*/incense-burner of
31. ṯlḥn . *bʿlt . bhtm*	the table of Lady of the Palace
32. *ʿlm*⸢ .⸣ *ʿlm . gdlt . l bʿl*	Next: an offspring of a cow for Baal[121]
33. *ṣpn . ḫlb* ⸢. *w kb*⸣*d .*⸢ *d*⸣[*q*]⸢*t*⸣	in the north Aleppo,[122] and a liver (of?) an ewe
34. *l ṣpn*⸢ .--(-)⸣ [.] ⸢*b*⸣ *ʿl . ʾu*⸢*g*⸣[*rt. . .*]	for Ṣapunu . . . . . . Baal of Ugarit. . .
35. *ʾilʾib . g*⸢*dlt .*⸣ *b* ⸢*ʿl*⸣[. . .] 36. *ʾugr*⸢*t*⸣ [-?] [ ]⸢*nt ṣ*⸣*pn* [. . .]	for *ʾiluʾibi* a cow, for Ba⸢al⸣. . . Ugari⸢t⸣. . .[ ]⸢Anatu in the n⸣orth (refer to line 17). . .
37. ⸢ ⸣*šl*⸢-⸣[. . .]	⸢ ⸣ŠL⸢-⸣. . .[123]

My observations regarding the structure of this text are summarized in the following table.[124]

120. Pardee, 31. Pardee translates this as "presentation-offering."

121. Pardee, 31. Pardee translates it as "on the day after next: a cow for. . ."

122. Pardee, 31. In line 16, Pardee translates *ḫlb* into "Aleppo." However, here he doesn't translate it.

123. Pardee, 100, n.9. Pardee notes that this may read "as a peace [offering], but the presence of a wedge, which appears to be " " before this formula is unexplained."

124. See also the similar structure suggested by Pardee, *Les textes rituels*, 606.

Table 6. Structure of KTU 1.109 (RS 24.253)

Lines	Kind of Offering	Offerings and Deities	Day/ Place
3–5	"Fall, *ql*"	Two cattle for *Yariḫu*	Full moon
5–8	"banquet offering, *ʿšrt*"	for Baal in the north: two ewes and a domestic dove two kidneys and a ram for RM⸢Š⸣ a liver and a ram for Šalimu	
8–10	"burnt offering, *šrp*"	a liver of a cattle and a ram for Baal in the north An ewe for Ṣapunu	
10–11	"peace offering, *šlmm*"	Ditto. (a liver of a cattle and a ram for Baal in the north An ewe for Ṣapunu)	
11–15	"burnt offering, *šrp*"	Two livers and a piece of offal: for *ʾiluʾib* a cow, for El a ram, for Baal a ram, for ʿAnatu in the north a cattle and a ram, for Pidray a ram	In the temple of Baal of Ugarit
15–18	"peace offering, *šlmm*"	for *ʾiluʾib* a ram, for Baal of Ugarit a ram, for Baal of Aleppo a ram, for *Yariḫu* a ram, for ʿAnatu in the north a cattle and a ram, for Pidray a ram, for Dadmiš a ram	
19–23	"peace offering, *šlmm*"	for *ʾiluʾib* a ram, for Baal a cattle and a ram, for Dagan a ram, for the helper gods of Baal a ram, for ʿAnatu a ram, for Rašap a ram,	In the opening
24	"ŠNPT offering"	for El a ram.	
25–28	"burnt offering, *šrp*"	For ʿAnatu-ḤLŠ two rams, for Gaṯarūma the left ǴṢB of which (is) two cattle and a cattle and a ram	

Lines	Kind of Offering	Offerings and Deities	Day/ Place
28–31	"peace offering, *šlmm*"	Ditto. (For ʿAnatu-ḤLŠ two rams, for Gaṯarūma the left ǴṢB of which (is) two cattle and a cattle and a ram) For Baal in the north with the tamarisk thirty times a ram for the *Qẓrt*/incense-burner of the table of Lady of the Palace	
32–34	--	an offspring of a cow for Baal in the north Aleppo, and a liver (of?) an ewe for Ṣapunu . . . Baal of Ugarit . . .	Next
35–37	ŠL. . .?? "peace offering, *šlmm*"	for *ʾiluʾibi* a cow, for Baal . . . Ugarit . . . ʿAnatu in the north . . .	

When burnt and peace offerings are combined, we find that most of the cases in this text follow this sequence. Many similar descriptions appear in biblical texts ranging from Exodus, the historical books, to the prophetic books. Second, the kidneys, liver, or innards of an animal are the major offerings of blood rituals in Ugarit and in Israel as well. Third, although this Ugaritic ritual gives us the list of the sacrificial animals, it says nothing about the procedures in details. This is different from the sacrificial texts in Leviticus.

Observation and Summary

Our review of Ugaritic sacrificial terms, two sacrificial documents (*KTU* 1.40 and *KTU* 1.109), and some Ugaritic poetic narratives reveals several points of comparison between the OT and the Ugaritic sacrificial documents.

First, both the Ugaritic poetic narratives and the OT employ the concept of a banquet in the sacrificial setting. However, in the OT, it is the offerer and his or her family and guests who partake of the meat from the animal sacrificed as a well-being offering, as the sacrifice was never regarded as food for Yahweh,[125]

125. Miller, *Religion of Ancient Israel*, 128. When לֶחֶם is used for the offerings to YHWH, there are two general categories in the Levitical ritual system. First, in Leviticus 2, there is unleavened bread offered to YHWH; some of it is burnt on the altar, but some is designated for the consumption by the priests. Both are called the אִשֶּׁה offerings to YHWH. Second, the priests are to place twelve loaves of memorial showbread on the table of the sanctuary weekly.

while in the Ugaritic poetic narratives *KTU* 1.17 VI: 1–8, *KTU* 1.15 II: 1–10, and *KTU* 1.17 I: 1–13, the banquet is offered to the deities to eat and drink,[126] even though the offerers are invited by the deities to eat and drink as well.[127] Furthermore, Lloyd claims that eating and drinking are common activities in religious feasts, so it is impossible to trace a direct connection between the appearances of the banquet theme in the Ugaritic documents and the OT.[128] Moreover, Nicholson claims that the similarity of the banquet theme is superficial, since there is an obvious divergence in regard to the purpose of the banquet. In the Ugaritic texts, the banquets are held by the gods El and Baal "for other gods in order to honour one another or to celebrate the erection of a temple."[129] In contrast, in the OT, the eating and drinking reveal the covenantal relationship between the offerer, his family and guests, and the only God, Yahweh. As Nelson concludes, "the Hebrew Bible is always careful to note that human worshipers dine *before* Yahweh, not actually *with* Yahweh (Exod 18:12)."[130] In this relationship, the people join the banquet to experience well-being in their lives.

Second, the formula of preparation and the formula of feasting in the Ugaritic texts, which include the list of sacrifices for the gods, indicate that the gods enjoyed a high social status in Ugaritic society.[131] In the OT, however, these kinds of formulae are not present. Instead, some parts of the

---

Even though these twelve loaves of showbread are also called an offering made by fire (Lev 24:5–9), the incense is burned in their stead (Lev 24:7, 9) and they are eaten by the Aaronic priests (Lev 24:9). Therefore, the showbread seems to be a symbolic offering to YHWH and is used as food by the priests. For more detailed discussions see Wells, "Exodus," 249; O'Connell, "לֶחֶם," in VanGemeren, *NIDOTTE* 2:791; Milgrom, *Leviticus 23–27*, 2093–94; Propp, *Exodus 19–40*, 507–8. On the understanding of אִשֶּׁה offerings in terms of a general word for "gift" or "present," see detailed discussions in Averbeck, "אִשֶּׁה," in VanGemeren, *NIDOTTE* 1:540–49. Some scholars observe that, on the one hand, the twelve loaves of bread probably represent the twelve tribes of Israel according to the rabbinic tradition (for example, *b. Menaḥ* 94b), while on the other hand, the showbread is perhaps a continual reminder of the covenant made between God and the Israelites. See Milgrom, *Leviticus 23–27*, 2094; Enns, *Exodus*, 513–14.

126. Lloyd, "Banquet Theme," 187.

127. Olmo Lete, *Canaanite Religion*, 26.

128. Lloyd, "Banquet Theme," 187.

129. Nicholson, "Origin of Tradition," 158.

130. Nelson, *Raising Up a Faithful Priest*, 68. Italics by the author.

131. Lloyd, "Banquet Theme," 188. Pardee explains that the Ugaritic ritual texts "are characterized by their laconic formulations, by the occasionally bewildering reversal of the order of mention of the sacrifice and its divine recipient, and by the use of standard terms for offerings and for sacrificial categories." Pardee, *Ritual and Cult*, 26.

well-being offering were designated to be offered by fire to Yahweh alone, while the offerer and other participants ate the remaining meat from the sacrificial animals. There was a distinctive boundary between the offerers and the offering recipient, Yahweh.

Third, Weinfeld points out that there is a significant difference between the Israelite festival texts and the sacrificial documents in Ugarit when it comes to the role of the kings. In the Israelite festival texts, the kings do not play any role, while in the Ugaritic documents the kings appear as the leaders of the ceremonies in the festivals.[132] However, in the historical books we see that sometimes the king of Israel carried out the duty of offering sacrifices (e.g. 2 Sam 6:18; 1 Kgs 3:15; Ezek 45:17). Cogan points out that "the active participation of the king in the cultic ritual does not make him a priest."[133] As de Vaux observes, the king – sanctified by anointing and adopted by YHWH – holds a sacred office with the power to perform religious functions.[134] However, when we examine the occasions when the kings do perform the sacrifices, it is clear that all of them were exceptional.[135] In short, then, the ordinary conduct of worship was left to the priests, while on solemn occasions the king could act as the religious head of the people.[136]

Fourth, it has been revealed in *KTU* 1.40 that Ugaritic blood sacrifices, which included well-being offerings, were made for Ugaritic people and foreigners, males and females, and for worship, social, and moral purposes. In comparison, the OT does contain a provision that includes foreigners within the scope of this sacrifice, but does not specifically mention sacrifices for both males and females. Moreover, the OT and the Ugaritic documents indicate different purposes for the well-being sacrifices. *KTU* 1.40 describes well-being offerings being used to deal with shortcomings in morality, character, or worship practices, something that is not found in the OT. Sin and guilt offerings were two specific types of sacrifice designated to deal with sin and guilt among the Israelites. The well-being offering was different from the

132. Weinfeld, *Place of the Law*, 57.

133. Cogan, *1 Kings*, 289.

134. De Vaux, *Ancient Israel*, 113.

135. De Vaux, 114. We can see, for example, the transference of the Ark and the dedication of an altar or a sanctuary.

136. De Vaux, 114.

sin and guilt offerings, and could be made for one of three reasons: to give thanks, to repay a vow to the Lord, or as an act of free will.

Fifth, even though the sacrificial animal, a donkey, mentioned in *KTU* 1.40 is not an acceptable animal sacrifice in the OT, the combination of burnt offering and well-being offering appears in both Ugaritic and OT, and the blood and inner parts of the sacrificial animals are prominent parts of the sacrifices in both the Ugaritic and the OT documents.

Sixth, while the Ugaritic documents contain only lists of sacrifices, the OT includes detailed procedural instructions for each prescribed sacrifice. Moreover, while Ugaritic well-being offerings involved the sacrifice of animal victims, de Vaux observes that the contact of the animal's blood with the altar, which is the most important element in the Israelite rites, is missing from the Ugaritic documents.[137]

Based on a comparison of burnt offerings and well-being offerings in the OT and counterpart cultures – including evidence from the Ugaritic documents found at the Ras Shamra[138] – De Vaux proposed a hypothesis in the conclusion to his discussion of "Holocausts and Communion Sacrifices." He suggested that "the Canaanites borrowed the holocaust and communion sacrifice from a pre-Semitic civilization, and the Ras Shamra texts indicate that they were in possession of these cultic forms before the Israelites were settled in Palestine."[139] He further proposed that the Israelites borrowed the holocaust and communion sacrifices from the Canaanites when they possessed the land of Canaan.[140] When it comes to well-being offerings, however, the summaries above demonstrate that while there are some "similarities" between the OT and the Ugaritic documents, there are also unmistakable differences.[141] Moreover, the hypothesis of borrowing is based on the estimated writing dates of the documents, and since the dates of the OT documents are disputed by scholars it is hard to have any degree of certainty of the dates

137. De Vaux, *Studies in Old Testament*, 48; also see Selman, "Sacrifice in Ancient Near East," 98–99.

138. Regarding mixed ritual sacrifices in Ugaritic documents, see the discussion in Olmo Lete, *Canaanite Religion*, 101–10.

139. De Vaux, *Studies in Old Testament*, 50.

140. De Vaux, 50.

141. The main difference is that the Ugaritic texts are prescriptive, unlike many of the OT descriptive texts. Olmo Lete, *Canaanite Religion*, 10.

specific sections were written as we have realized that the OT books were formed through a historical process. As de Vaux wrote at the end of his hypothesis, based on the lack of blood rites in the Canaanite sacrifices, "this is no servile borrowing, and the Israelite sacrifices preserved their originality."[142]

Examination of the "Central Altar" Debate in the OT Canonical Texts

The first chapter of this book provided a brief introduction to the "central altar" debate, which has emerged primarily from Wellhausen's discussion of the historical place of P.[143] In Wellhausen's conclusion, especially in his observation on Leviticus 17, he asserted that, in Deuteronomy, sacrifices offered outside of Jerusalem were still offered to YHWH, while in Leviticus 17 sacrifices could only be offered at the tabernacle, and whoever made offerings elsewhere were simply offering them to devils. Wellhausen believed that the latter idea of making offerings exclusively in front of the tabernacle was impossible before the so-called Deuteronomic reformation under Josiah.[144] He therefore asserted that the contextual setting of Leviticus 17 is a fictional concept which primarily serves as the ground for central worship in Jerusalem later in the history of the kingdom of Judah.[145] Wellhausen claimed that "in that book [Deuteronomy] the unity of the cultus is *commanded*; in the Priestly Code it is *presupposed*. Everywhere it is tacitly assumed as a fundamental postulate, but nowhere does it find actual expression."[146]

In this section, I will conduct a preliminary investigation of the "altar centralization" issue, focusing particularly on the exegesis of Exodus 20:24–26, Leviticus 17:1–7, and Deuteronomy 12:2–5 in their literary and historical contexts. I will then revisit Wellhausen's claim and address its evaluation by other OT scholars.

142. De Vaux, *Studies in Old Testament*, 51.

143. Please refer to pages 18–20 of this book.

144. Wellhausen, *Prolegomena*, 50–51.

145. Wellhausen, 47–49.

146. Wellhausen, 35. Italics by the author. Here, Wellhausen made a note that "except in Lev. xvii; but the small body of legislation contained in Lev. xvii. xxvi. is the translation from Deuteronomy to the Priestly Code."

Observations on Exodus 20:24–26, Leviticus 17:1–7, and Deuteronomy 12:2–5

The conservative view regarding the authorship of the book of Deuteronomy is that Moses wrote the major part of it (excluding passages such as the record of his death in Deuteronomy 34) long before the time of Josiah. In this view, "the place" mentioned in Deuteronomy 12:5 would originally have been wherever the tabernacle was pitched, while after Solomon built the temple in Jerusalem, it became "the place." The problem with this traditional view is that the OT contains numerous cases in which other altars – such as those prescribed in Exodus 20 – seem to have been legitimately used for burnt offerings and sacrifices after the occupation of the land (e.g. Judg 6:26; 13:19–20; 21:4; 1 Sam 7:17; 14:35; 2 Sam 24:25; 1 Kgs 18:30–38; 1 Chr 21:26).[147] It is well known that the altar of earth law in Exodus 20:24–26 is hard to reconcile with references to the other altars in the Bible (Exod 27:1–8 [bronze altar]; Lev 17:3–9; Deut 12). Although there are a variety of ways to approach this problem, one way to explain the differences among these laws is based on their occurrences at different points in the narratives.

Exodus 20:24–26

Before the exodus, no explicit regulations about altars were recorded. Moreover, in later history well-being offerings for the purpose of obtaining meat to eat were available even for the ceremonially unclean (1 Sam 14:31–35), whereas the unclean were not permitted to eat meat from the tabernacle's altar (Lev 7:20) or other formally consecrated food (1 Sam 21:4). I have made several observations on this altar law in Exodus 20:24–26.[148] First, as far as history is concerned, it is clear that this altar law was enacted earlier rather than later in Israelite history, since it was spoken to the people, not the

147. "In light of this, some have argued simply that 'Israel failed to fulfill the command of Moses' on two occasions when they should have done so: during the rest in the land that followed the successful campaigns of Joshua (Joshua 22:4; 23:1), and then David (2 Sam 7:1; 1 Kgs 5:3–4 [17–18]) . . . The problem with this view is that the Lord seems to sanction the use of the solitary altars at least for the period from Joshua to David." Averback, "מִזְבֵּחַ," in VanGemeren, *NIDOTTE*, 2:894.

148. "The difference of material (Exod 20:22–26 – stones and Exod 27 – bronze) probably proposes to show the preeminence of the tabernacle's altar." Sprinkle, *Biblical Law*, 60. However, "stone had great significance in the nomadic cult." Heger, *Three Biblical Altar Laws*, 87.

priests.[149] This custom is reflected in the patriarchal narratives;[150] however, pilgrimage to distant shrines was a prominent feature of later Semitic heathenism, not its early period.[151] Second, in this pericope, it is stated that Yahweh will "come" to his worshipers in the context of a local altar (v. 24). This means that Yahweh is not dwelling at the local altar; nonetheless, he will be present at an altar described in Exodus 20:24–26 if such an altar is erected at a suitable place and sacrifices offered on it. It may be built anywhere, but building one in a right place is accompanied by a promise of Yahweh's presence and blessing. This kind of altar is different from the one in the tent of meeting or, later, the temple, because it is not a place of Yahweh's permanent presence. Moreover, many passages (e.g. Gen 18:21–22; 28; Num 23; Judg 13:20; 1 Kgs 18:24; 38; Mic 1:3, etc.) describe Yahweh's descent to the worshipers or response to the offerings.[152] Thus, even though the simple altars described in the Exodus pericope speak about local modes of worship – which is distinct from the elaborate cultic system of the ark, the tent of meeting, and the temple described elsewhere – as Pitkänen has pointed out, "the local and central modes of worship can fundamentally be seen to be rather complementary than contradictory to each other."[153]

Leviticus 17:1–7

In the wilderness, however, the ancient tabernacle's altar is underscored by a temporary measure limiting all sacrificial slaughter to the tabernacle (Lev 17:4–7).[154] This measure is meant to counteract the temptation of idolatrous goat-demon worship in the desert.

149. Noth comments that "the law [in Exod. 20.24–26] itself is of course old, as it presupposes very simple conditions." Noth, *Exodus*, 176. See also Wenham's comments in Wenham, "Deuteronomy and Central Sanctuary," 105.

150. Heger, *Three Biblical Altar Laws*, 77. "We observe in the biblical narratives of the Patriarchs that they erected some sort of worship artifact whenever they reached some critical point in their migrations, and/or had a vision of an encounter with the Deity."

151. Smith, *Religion of Semites*, 80.

152. These are pointed out in Levine, "*Lpny* YHWH," 199–203.

153. See Pitkänen, *Central Sanctuary and Centralization*, 66.

154. Weinfeld, *Place of the Law*, 19. "The Tabernacle constitutes an ancient tribal institution that accompanies Israel from its beginning, as expressed in the words of Nathan the prophet: 'From the day I brought the people of Israel out of Egypt to this I have not dwelled in a house, but have moved about in Tent and Tabernacle (באהל ומשכן)' (2 Sam 7:6)." For a detailed disputation about whether this law requires that every domesticated animal should be slaughtered at the altar of the "central sanctuary" or if it only requires that every ritual sacrifice

The explicit mention of the place of slaughtering as either in the "camp" or "outside the camp" (Lev 17:3–4) clearly refers to a situation that fits the wanderings in the desert,[155] since one should understand the restriction of worship to the site of the tabernacle as belonging to the time in which the tribes were dwelling in "camp."[156] In the following narratives in the OT, especially in the historical books, "the camp" gradually disappeared from the scene of Israelite history, and the city became more prominent after they had settled down in Canaan.[157] All of this fits perfectly with Weinfeld's conclusion that "the basic law of Lev 17 can by no means be considered a product of post-deuteronomic times. If this law were composed after the centralization of the cult, its effect would have been to ban the eating of meat for the majority of the people, who were unable to bring their animals to Jerusalem for sacrificial slaughter."[158]

A. Dillmann refutes Wellhausen's late dating of the Pentateuchal sources on the grounds that if a law-code were composed in the postexilic period, it would answer the needs of that time by addressing, for example, the functions of Levites as singers, gatekeepers, and musicians, or the crucial issue of that time, the prohibition of intermarriage. These issues are all absent from Leviticus. On the other hand, it is well-known that the literature of the exilic and postexilic period – the book of Jeremiah, for example – has been strongly influenced by Deuteronomy. We find no trace of Deuteronomy in Leviticus; on the contrary, we find priestly phrases in Deuteronomy. This points to the priority of the Priestly laws over Deuteronomy rather than vice versa.[159]

---

should be performed there, see Hartley, *Leviticus*, 269–71; Miller, *Religion of Ancient Israel*, 124–25. The wording and descriptions in Leviticus 17:4, 8–9 strongly favor the interpretation that this law concerns a sacrificial slaughtering. As long as God had set up the whole Levitical sacrificial system at that time, and all the Israelites dwelt around the tabernacle during the wandering period, it stands to reason that those sacrifices should be done in the tabernacle through the priests.

155. "The law of Lev 17 has been given for a wilderness setting. First, self-evidently, the narrative context suggests this. Also, the mention of the tent of meeting (vv. 4, 5, 6) and the words על־פני השדה are fully compatible with the wilderness context, even though they could be used in other contexts as well." Pitkänen, *Central Sanctuary and Centralization*, 91.

156. Weinfeld, *Place of the Law*, 21.

157. Weinfeld, 21.

158. Weinfeld, 21–22.

159. Dillmann, *Bücher Numeri*, 668–70, cited in Weinfeld, *Place of the Law*, 66–67. This perspective is also seen in Weinfeld, *Deuteronomy and Deuteronomic School*, 179–81.

Although the basic content of Leviticus 17 is ancient, we must admit that it was later applied to a new reality after the establishment of the monarchy. The Law of the Tabernacle first became valid for the Shiloh Tabernacle, while it was used later to legitimize the centralization of the cult in Jerusalem.[160] As Weinfeld asserts, "the Tabernacle of Shiloh is not then a retrojection of the temple of Jerusalem, but a predecessor and prototype of it. As indicated above, both Jer 7:12 and Ps 78:60 consider the temple of Jerusalem as the successor of the Shiloh Tabernacle."[161] Moreover, the phrase "this shall be to them a law for all time throughout the ages" (Lev 17:7) facilitated the application of an ancient law to the new enterprise of centralization sponsored by Hezekiah (2 Kgs 18:4, 22).[162]

Deuteronomy 12:2–5

Deuteronomy 12:5 is a key verse for the theory that Deuteronomy 12 calls for the centralization of Israel's worship at a single sanctuary (i.e. Jerusalem) and the consequent linking of Deuteronomy to Josiah's seventh-century reform, of which cult centralization is said to be a major feature.[163] Averbeck observes that in Wellhausen's theory, the "polemical and reforming attitude towards

160. Milgrom observes that P "presumes a central but not a single sanctuary." Milgrom, *Leviticus 1–16*, 34. According to Pitkänen, "Bringing everything to a central sanctuary is an ideal for which the cultic laws have been geared, but there is no need to think that it was ever envisaged the Priestly material that the ideal could actually be attained in the land." Pitkänen, *Central Sanctuary and Centralization*, 94.

161. Weinfeld, *Place of the Law*, 20.

162. Weinfeld, 23. Weinfeld comments that "Haran quite plausibly suggested that the centralization of cult in Hezekianic times was based on Lev 17. But contrary to Haran's suggestion, this does not mean that the very law of Lev 17 was contrived in the days of Hezekiah." However, see Haran, *Temples and Temple Service*, 146–47.

163. As for the history of the discussion of Deuteronomy 12 in the issue of central sanctuary, please refer to the summary in Wenham, "Deuteronomy and Central Sanctuary," n.146. See Wright, *Deuteronomy*, 7–8. However, as Wright observes, "the historical figure of Moses is clearly so central to the book and, without denying the very obvious likelihood of editorial updating of the material for subsequent generations, there seem to be no compelling reasons why a substantially Mosaic legacy should not underlie the book. . . . The constantly future orientation of the book virtually guarantees that ongoing relevance and address to later generations and centuries. But the book presents itself to us as the exhortations of Moses to Israel on the verge of the original settlement in Canaan, and it seems best, when expounding the text, to respect the integrity of that explicit context rather than to find explanations and meanings that depend upon the assumption that particular texts were actually pursuing a subliminal agenda related to issues of much later eras."

existing usage," as in Deuteronomy 12:8, "signals a major shift in the altar law: the multiplicity of (legitimate) altars is now eliminated."[164]

However, when we consider this regulation in the historical setting claimed by the text itself, we may realize that it occurs at the moment when the Israelites concluded their wandering journey in the wilderness and prepared to enter Canaan, the land given to them by God.[165] In the juncture of the transition from a nomadic life to settling down, their ways of worshiping God needed to be adapted accordingly. First, in Deuteronomy 12, the modification would reflect a need to assign a place for the public worship of offering sacrifices. De Vaux observes that, when the Israelites entered the Promised Land of Canaan and scattered to many cities, the result of this dispersion would be that the public sacrifices became predominant and family or personal sacrifices would be reduced to a minimum.[166] Second, since the centralized slaughtering practices prescribed in Leviticus 17 would become impossible for the Israelites, Deuteronomy 12 permits nonsacrificial slaughtering in one's own town.[167] Weinfeld points out that while Deuteronomy 12 echoes Leviticus 17 in its prohibition of eating blood due to the life in the blood, Deuteronomy 12:15 specifies that hunted animals (such as gazelle and deer) could be eaten by the ritually impure as well as those in a state of purity. The author also allows both pure and impure individuals to consume the meat of domestic animals (such as cows and sheep, which are used as sacrifices to the Lord in Leviticus 17) that have been killed for nonsacrificial purposes. In terms of this regulation, the consistency between Leviticus 17

164. Averback, "מִזְבֵּחַ," in VanGemeren, *NIDOTTE*, 2:893; See Wellhausen, *Prolegomena*, 33.

165. "Particularly in *Deuteronomy* and the Holiness Code the community addressed in the laws is emphatically distinguished from the 'Canaanites,' who are tied to 'other gods.' In the original form of the deuteronomic law the emphatic prohibition occurs at once, near the beginning, forbidding any relationships with 'those peoples' and their cults (Deut. XII.29ff.)." Noth, *Laws in Pentateuch*, 21–22.

166. De Vaux, *Studies in Old Testament*, 36.

167. De Vaux, 36; See Deuteronomy 12:15, 21. Both Leviticus 17 and Deuteronomy 12 deal with the shedding of blood outside the purpose of expiation; the blood of hunted animals in Leviticus 17 (v.13; cf. Gen 4:10; Job 16:18; Isa 26:21; Ezek 24:6–8) and the profane slaughter in Deuteronomy 12 (vv. 16, 24) per se. Vogt observes that there is a connection between the nonsacrificial ritual and Yahweh's blessings expressed in Deuteronomy 12:15; therefore, he asserts that "Deuteronomy 12 centralizes *sacrifice* to the central sanctuary, but *worship* is decentralized. Whenever the people slaughter animals for food and engage in the manipulation of the blood, they (however briefly) are demonstrating their allegiance to Yahweh and his purposes and plans for Israel, the nations and the whole of creation." Vogt, "Centralization and Decentralization," 131.

and Deuteronomy 12 is that animals slaughtered under profane conditions could be eaten in a state of impurity. Further, the blood of such animals has no sacrificial meaning of atonement, and should be poured on the ground instead of being poured out beside the altar of the Lord.[168] A closer look at the law of Deuteronomy 12 thus shows that its innovations were built upon the old reality reflected in Leviticus 17.[169]

With regard to the "place" chosen by the Lord in Deuteronomy 12:5 and the "high places" of pagan worship mentioned in later prophetic and historical texts, Christopher Wright provides several masterly arguments. First, Deuteronomy 12 cannot represent the alleged program of cult centralization from the time of Josiah because Josiah's program was the most sustained attempt in Israel's history to remove the בָּמוֹת, while Deuteronomy never uses the word בָּמוֹת at all.[170] Nelson does not see centralization as a means of royal political control but as a means of ensuring that covenant loyalty is lived out, which could eliminate apostasy. Moreover, Nelson argues that the texts of Deuteronomy demonstrate that the emphasis on centralization does not represent royal or priest power grab – on the contrary, Deuteronomy 17:14–20, the law concerning the king, insists on weakening the royal center.[171]

168. "By mentioning 'gazelle and deer' the author wants to make clear that just as until now only hunted game such as gazelle and deer could be eaten in a state of impurity (since their blood was not brought to the altar [Lev 17:13]), so from now on domestic animals too, when slaughtered as profane, could be eaten in a state of impurity." Weinfeld, *Place of the Law*, 22.

169. "Moreover, there are good grounds for seeing Deuteronomy as dependent on the Priestly material." Pitkänen, *Central Sanctuary and Centralization*, 108. According to Weinfeld, "One can still trace the background of Lev 17 in this new ordinance. In Deut 12:15 we read: 'the pure and impure alike may consume it as of the gazelle and deer (בצבי וכאיל).' What is the meaning of the *gazelle and the deer*, in the context of this law and why is it specified here? The answer is that with the reference to hunting animals such as gazelle and deer the author undoubtedly alludes to Lev 17 which distinguishes between cattle and sheep, which are fit for sacred slaughtering and game which is not. By mentioning 'gazelle and deer' the author wants to make clear that just as until now only hunted game such as gazelle and deer could be eaten in a state of impurity (since their blood was not brought to the altar [Lev 17:13]), so from now on domestic animals too, when slaughtered as profane, could be eaten in a state of impurity. On the other hand, Deuteronomy follows his predecessor in Lev 17 and prohibits the consumption of blood (12:16, 23). Furthermore, it quotes the old law." Weinfeld, *Place of the Law*, 22. For evaluation of the views of Weinfeld and Von Rod, see Vogt, *Deuteronomic Theology*, 58–70.

170. Wright, *Deuteronomy*, 168. "It is noticeable, however, that the technical term *b^{1}môt* (usually translated 'high places,' but probably meaning 'local shrines'), which is the repeated target of condemnation in the later prophetic and historical texts, is *not* used here [Deut 12:2] or anywhere at all in Deut."

171. Nelson, *Deuteronomy*, 149.

Second, Wright points out that the text does not demand a single place instead of many places of Israelite worship, but an exclusive place for the worship of Yahweh as opposed to the places of Canaanite worship.[172] Moreover, the place is not named in this text, meaning that the passage could have been applied to several central but temporary sanctuaries (e.g. Shiloh) during the period of time between the settlement and before Jerusalem permanently filled the role.[173] If Deuteronomy had indeed intended to centralize all worship on a single site, and that site is assumed to be Jerusalem, then the instructions for building an altar on Mt. Ebal (27:1–8) contradict that whole agenda and are thus inexplicable in terms of the theory.[174]

Third, with regard to grammatical usage, the singular "the place" in Deuteronomy 12:5 can also be understood in a generic sense – that is, applied to a class or category.[175] Furthermore, if the plurality of Canaanite shrines can be collectively called "that place" (הַמָּקוֹם הַהוּא) in verse 3, then "the place" of verse 5 could admit a generic or a distributive sense and need not be limited exclusively to a *sole* sanctuary.[176]

---

172. Wright, *Deuteronomy*, 169. "The text is primary concerned with the purity and exclusiveness of Israel's worship and its distinctiveness from *Canaanite* religion rather than with the centralization of Israelite worship as such."

173. Wright. "While the natural reading of the text certainly points to a specific central sanctuary, it is not necessarily implying a *sole* sanctuary for all Israel. There is an emphasis on the unity of Israel's faith and worship, but that unity is to be founded on the legitimacy of being chosen by Yahweh and bearing Yahweh's name, not necessarily on the numerical singularity of the place of worship." Regarding the preference for several central places in the Israelite history, see Niehaus, "Central Sanctuary," 10–17; Thompson, *Deuteronomy*, 116–17.

174. Wright, *Deuteronomy*, 169.

175. Wright, 169–70. "Even if the author had in mind a particular central place of worship, that would not necessarily exclude other legitimate sanctuaries. The use of generic or collective singular nouns to denote a whole class of people is a marked feature of Deut., e.g. the common use of 'the alien,' 'the widow,' 'the orphan.'"

176. Wright, 170. "It is often overlooked that a generic sense of *hamm¹qôm*, 'the place,' is actually present in the immediate context. Frequently commentaries contrast **the place** (sg.) of v. 5 with **the places** (pl.) of v.2 and argue from that to a policy of total centralization on a single sanctuary. However, they ignore the fact that the last two words of v. 3 are *hamm¹qôm hahû'*, 'that place' (sg.; the NIV again shows its preference for plurals with **those places**). The word is just as *singular* as in v. 5, and yet it clearly refers generically to the plurality of *Canaanite* shrines that the Israelites were to destroy."

A Proposal on This Restriction

After examining the texts in the previous sections, I would like to propose the following reconstruction of the altar centralization issue in the Pentateuch. Before the tabernacle was built, the Israelites were permitted to make sacrifices on the altars of stone, according to the text of Exodus 20. After the tabernacle was built, the Israelites began living in a portable camp around the tabernacle in the wilderness; the instructions stated in Leviticus became relevant at this point, as they aimed to prevent people from making pagan sacrifices to the goat. Under these wilderness conditions, the requirement to bring all the sacrifices to be killed at the entrance of the tabernacle was both crucial and achievable.

When Israel came to the land of Canaan, altars of stone were again permitted and built (Deut 26:4–8; Josh 8:30–35). Deuteronomy 12:5, however, anticipates a day when all sacrifice would be limited to the one "place that Yahweh your God will choose." Although altars after the description of Exodus 20: 24–26 continued to be allowed in Moses's day and for a number of generations after that, 1 Kings 3:2 sees this as temporary: "The people, however, were still sacrificing at the high places, because a temple had not yet been built for the name of Yahweh." The narrator of this text does not condemn the people for sacrificing on the high places as such, but it does foresee a day, after the temple is built, when sacrifice at the high places would cease. This prediction came true through Josiah's reforms around 621 BC (2 Kgs 23:15, 19–20).[177]

Driver, Levinson, and Block consider that the permission for a multiplicity of altars given in Exodus 20:24–25 was later countermanded in the law of Deuteronomy 12:2–4 due to the changed setting and environment that the Israelites faced in the land of Canaanites.[178] The law of Deuteronomy thus inaugurated a new era in the Israelite history in order to maintain the necessary purity of worship to Yahweh. Noth points out that, according to their canonical position, the laws in Leviticus and Deuteronomy are addressed to the community that had been brought up out of Egypt.[179]

---

177. Sprinkle, *Biblical Law*, 60–61.

178. Driver, *Critical and Exegetical Commentary*, 138; Levinson, *Deuteronomy and Hermeneutics*, 31–34; Block, *Deuteronomy*, 304–5.

179. Noth, *Laws in Pentateuch*, 25.

Academics have, however, produced alternative explanations of this issue, which can be discussed in terms of two main trends.[180] Some scholars – including, for example, Steinberg – maintain that Deuteronomic centralization served to advance the interests of the monarchy by allowing kings to exercise greater control over the people.[181] Lundbom concludes that, as far as we can tell from the context of world affairs, including archaeological discoveries, the centralization promoted in Deuteronomy 12 reflects the reform of Josiah.[182]

Block does not agree with the association of the centralization of worship in Deuteronomy 12 with the religious reforms of Josiah (2 Kgs 23). Instead, he argues that the place formula in Deuteronomy 12 is meant to emphasize not the place of worship itself but rather God's sovereignty and authority to choose the place for his own worship.[183] Block points to "the fulfillment of the place formula in a succession of locations: Shechem, Shiloh, Bethel, and ultimately Jerusalem" to support his point.[184] Moreover, if the reforms of Josiah formed the historical background of the composition of Deuteronomy, it is odd not only that the temple and Jerusalem go completely unmentioned in the book, but also that "the reference to Yahweh choosing the place 'from among all the tribes' (12:5, 14) makes no sense in later times."[185] The conclusion is that we can understand that the God who inspired Moses to write Deuteronomy 12 had Jerusalem in mind as the ultimate reference point for this text, and we should not "read later highly developed Zion theology into Moses' vague reference to the place that Yahweh would choose."[186]

180. Levinson mentions that there are two diverging approaches to the law corpus in the scholarly discussion. "One approach has maintained that the legal corpus represents pre-exilic legislation designed to implement a broad-based cultic, judicial, and administrative program. The other has emphasized the theoretical and impractical nature of the legal corpus, either in terms of Levitical homily or as utopian theological reflection dating to the exilic or postexilic period." Levinson, *Deuteronomy and Hermeneutics*, 51–52.

181. Steinberg, "Deuteronomic Law Code," 372–73. Haran also holds a similar perspective to regard the centralization of the cult as the perspective in the monarchal reforms of either King Josiah or King Hezekiah. Haran, *Temples and Temple Service*, 132–48.

182. Lundbom, *Deuteronomy*, 442–47.

183. Block, *Deuteronomy*, 311.

184. Block, 311. In Lundbom's view, the place chosen by Yahweh could also have been Shechem, Shiloh, Bethel, or some other place through history besides Jerusalem. Lundbom, *Deuteronomy*, 426. See also McConville, *Deuteronomy*, 35.

185. Block, *Deuteronomy*, 311.

186. Block, 311.

McConville also concludes that it is a misconception to view the altar centralization in Deuteronomy as an outcome of Josiah's reform, a situation in which the centralization must happen in Jerusalem. After all, "from the perspective of Josiah's time, the law must naturally be understood in relation to Jerusalem; but the OT knows that it could in principle have applied to other places too (Josh 9:27; Jer 7:12)."[187] McConville also observes that the view that centralization in Deuteronomy originates from Josiah's reform presupposes the enhancement of the interests of a particular sanctuary, priestly class, or royal administration. He asserts, however, that this presupposition aligns better with other ANE way of thinking than with the emphasis on the covenant with the Israelites in Deuteronomy.[188] In the monarchic period, the kings appeared to lead the festive celebrations and sacrifices (1 Kgs 12:32; 13:1, 2 Chr 29–30, 35; cf. 1 Sam 13:9; 14:34–35; 2 Sam 6:17–18, etc.), as was the case in the Hittite and Ugaritic festivals. Weinfeld infers that "if we miss them in the laws it is because of their pre-monarchic background."[189]

Other scholars, on the other hand, believe that, since centralized worship was never practiced strictly during the Israelite monarchy, this regulation of centralization must have originated after the exile as the leaders urged the people to repent from their past wrongdoings. R. E. Clements declares that the centralization did not occur in the reign of King Josiah – 2 Kgs 22–23 set a false trail leading in this direction – but rather resulted from the realities of exile after the destruction of the temple in 587 BC.[190] Clements asserts that, in light of the ruin of the temple in Jerusalem, the version of centralization in Deuteronomy commanded the Israelites not to transfer their loyalty to other gods. The chosen place was to be the only place where they could make sacrifices, because at that time people might think about making sacrifices to the Lord elsewhere during the Babylonian exile.[191]

187. McConville, *Deuteronomy*, 217.

188. McConville, 33–36, 216. "From samples of the content of the Old Testament laws, how little they could have been intended as state law, and how inappropriate they would be for those (always larger) areas with a completely 'Canaanite' population, which were included in the states actually established by the Israelite people; and also how they quite definitely centre on a cultic or 'theological' standpoint, and take the existing institution of the sacral confederacy of the twelve tribes of Israel as their accepted background." Noth, *Laws in Pentateuch*, 59–60.

189. Weinfeld, *Place of the Law*, 57.

190. Clements, "Deuteronomic Law of Centralisation," 5–25.

191. Clements, 16–20.

According to Hoppe, even though Jerusalem had a significant role in Judah and Israel, before the exile it never became the sole place for the Israelites to worship Yahweh. It was only after the exile that Jerusalem became the focus of the prophets who urged the people to submit obediently to the insistence that Jerusalem should be the only place for them to worship the Lord.[192] Hoppe summarized his thesis as following: "Deuteronomy's cult centralization is a reflection of exilic situation and is an attempt to make virtue out of necessity."[193]

Despite these counterarguments,[194] McConville advances a hypothesis that embraces all related features in this issue. He suggests that "Deuteronomy, or at least a form of it, is the document of a real political and religious constitution of Israel from the pre-monarchical period."[195] Moreover, after McConville reconstructs the setting of Deuteronomy in his hypothesis, he concludes that it "is quite different from both the royal, 'statist' interpretation, and the exilic utopian one."[196] He further argues that the message in Deuteronomy not only does not promote a royal reform, but also stands "against any royal hegemony over the people of Yahweh on the model of ANE monarchies."[197] Lastly, McConville asserts that the message of Deuteronomy "is to hold its hearers to practical obedience" in space and time "while proffering a vision that is never quite realized." It bears an eschatological sense but is not the utopian one that might spring from the exile.[198]

As McConville observes, of the three Pentateuchal texts containing altar laws, the Deuteronomy version is stricter than what appears in Exodus, but more tolerant than the law in Leviticus.[199] If we trace this development chrono-

192. Hoppe, "Jerusalem in Deuteronomistic History," 110.

193. Hoppe, 107.

194. In terms of the observations on his argumentation of this hypothesis in detail, please refer to McConville, *Deuteronomy*, 34–36.

195. McConville, 34.

196. McConville, 35.

197. McConville, 35. As Weinfeld concluded in this observation that "Julius Wellhausen's heroic attempt to depict the 'Law of Judaism,' manifested in the priestly stratum of the Pentateuch, as originating in the Second Temple theocracy and the antithesis to classical prophecy, is ultimately a failure. It is based on biased, foregone conclusions, argument from silence and misunderstandings, and is refuted by the findings of subsequent scholarship." Weinfeld, *Place of the Law*, 74.

198. McConville, 36. "It is true that one can hardly distinguish in the narrative of Joshua between authentic facts and later reconstruction, but it seems clear on the basis of all the sources that the tradition that the Israelites moved around in a camp (where the Tabernacle was stationed) cannot be seen as fiction." Weinfeld, *Place of the Law*, 20.

199. McConville, 212.

logically according to the historical narrative provided by the Pentateuch itself, we see that the series of altar laws begins with the most lenient in Exodus, then moves to the strictest commandment in Leviticus, and finally comes to the comparatively moderate one in Deuteronomy. It is because of its strictness that some scholars see the law in Leviticus as the latest in the series either in the Josiah reformation or in the later time in exile. However, as stated above, we need not rearrange the sequence of the altar regulations in these texts according to level of strictness. Instead, we shall take the contexts in which the specific regulation was instructed into account in order to get an understanding appurtenant to the texts respectively. For instance, Levinson rightly points out that if we examine Deuteronomy 12 in detail, grammatically and hermeneutically,[200] we will realize that the double movement of Deuteronomy – cultic centralization and local secularization – operates both synchronically and diachronically. In doing so, a distinct lexicon, for example, is used to distinguish "between action במקום 'in the place' and action בשעריך 'in your city-gates' – which is to say, between the central and the local spheres, or between cultic and secular activity."[201]

In Deuteronomy, we see the loosening of regulations on killing animals for consumption because the Israelites had arrived at another era in their history in which people would settle down in the Promised Land and be unable to partake of sacrificial meals at a sanctuary close at hand (Deut 12:15). All this fits perfectly with Averbeck's conclusion that "both systems [the multiplicity of altars in Exodus 20:24–26 and the altar centralization in Deut 12:5] could and, in fact, did legitimately function side by side during many periods of preexilic Israelite history. Wellhausen's 'two wholly distinct worlds' were not really wholly distinct, but to the degree that they were, their distinctiveness was sociological, not chronological."[202] Vogt makes a similar argument:

> Deut 12 emphasizes the supremacy of Yahweh by his choice of where and how he is to be worshiped. A careful reading of the text in its context shows that the number of altars is not the main

---

200. For a detailed hermeneutical and exegetical examination of Deuteronomy 12, see Levinson, *Deuteronomy and Hermeneutics*, 23–52.

201. Levinson, 51.

202. Averbeck, "Sacrifices and Offerings," 731–32. See also the claim of Pitkänen, who concludes that no matter in "JE" (e.g. Exod 20:24–26), D (e.g. Deut 12, in which the worship was centralized under favorite circumstances), and P (e.g. Lev 17, in which central sanctuary was emphasized), local altars were allowed. Pitkänen, *Central Sanctuary and Centralization*, 110; Cf. Von Rad, *Deuteronomy*, 90–91.

> point of Deut 12, so there is no conflict with Exod 20:24–25. The primary emphasis is on Yahweh's sovereignty and the contrast between proper Yahweh worship and the false worship of Canaanite gods. Choosing Yahweh means a fundamental rejection of the Canaanite gods and Canaanite worship practices.[203]

The above line of interpretation does not resolve all difficulties, but it does make it possible to explain the differences among the altar laws on the basis of their placement in the framework of the Bible's narrative chronology. It thus shows the fruitfulness, hermeneutically, of taking narrative into consideration when interpreting the law.[204] Based on this approach, we proceed to the interpretation of the prohibition of eating blood in relation to the significance of blood atonement in chapter 4.

203. Vogt, *Deuteronomic Theology*, 203.

204. Averbeck, "Sacrifices and Offerings," 731. Averbeck also arrives at this conclusion: "The notion that the Exodus 20:24–26 law of the solitary altar contradicts the Deuteronomy 12 centralization law is based on a misunderstanding of the intent of Deuteronomy 12 and a diachronic fallacy."

CHAPTER 4

The Prohibition of Eating Blood in Leviticus 17

Goldingay asserts that God's original plan was that human beings should not eat meat and that this was set out clearly in the OT before the flood in Noah's time, as it is stated in Genesis 1:29.[1] It is apparently after the disobedience of humanity that God allowed people to eat meat, with the condition of draining the blood before eating an animal (Gen 9:2–4). He further explains that in Leviticus 17:10–12, after the regulation of well-being offerings is prescribed, God reveals that the life of the animal is in the blood of the meat; therefore, the blood of the meat is designated to belong to God, the source of the life, and should be used as the means of expiation. Goldingay concludes that the prohibition of consuming blood in Leviticus 17:10–12, which follows a passage regarding the regulation of well-being offerings, is related to the eating of meat in the context of the well-being offering. Because God allows the offerer, with family and friends, to share the feast after sacrificing the well-being offering – the only sacrifice offered to him that can be shared by offerers and their guests – it is necessary to explain the use of blood in this process.[2]

1. Goldingay, *Israel's Life*, 142.

2. Goldingay. "The blood symbolized the life of the animal, the life that humanity shares with animals and that comes from God and belongs to God. . . . Leviticus 17:10–12 thus not only prohibits the consuming of blood but also notes that this same blood is the means of expiation for the lives of the people eating. Its regulation would affect only the fellowship sacrifice, because this is the one sacrifice that the offerer chiefly eats, and it is thus the one when the question of consuming the blood might arise. When Leviticus 17:10–12 adds to the explicit regulation for the fellowship sacrifice that the offering of the blood on this occasion make expiation for the offerers, perhaps the wrong for which it is making expiation is the wrong inherent in killing an animal with Yhwh's life in it."

McEntire notes that the message of Leviticus 17 is focused on improper sacrifices and improper ways of killing animals and that its major concern is the prohibition of blood consumption due to the fact that the life of the flesh is in the blood (17:11, 14).[3] This prohibition agrees with the regulation set forth in Genesis 9:4, and is further developed in Deuteronomy 12:23–25.[4] In Leviticus 17, it is stated that since the life is in the blood and its purpose is atonement, any blood not used for that purpose should be poured out on the ground.[5] As Snaith mentions, in sacrifices where the blood and the fat are brought to the altar, they are not offered as food for Yahweh – rather, these parts, which could not be consumed by the people, belong solely to Yahweh.[6]

The Nature and Function of Blood in the OT Ritual System

Before we make an effort to understand the prohibition of eating blood in its literary context, we need to clarify the nature and function of blood in the OT ritual system. Clearly, blood plays a significant role in OT rituals, especially

3. McEntire, *Struggling with God*, 142. McEntire further argues that this concept in some sense goes against the tradition in Genesis 2:7 where "the breath of life" is the source of life, not the blood. In my view, however, this can be interpreted without any conflict. Genesis 2:7 portrays the first time God gave the life to the first man, whom he made from the dust; therefore, the life was given from God through a breath he blew into the nostrils of the man. Nonetheless, the life God gave was designated by God himself to be in the blood of any living animal, as well as humankind, in the following Scriptures in the Pentateuch. These two aspects of life do not contradict each other.

4. Weinfeld, *Place of the Law*, 22–23. Miller asserts that it "represents a Priestly perspective that is echoed by other and somewhat different Priestly voices in the Noah story, where permission to eat flesh is given but not the eating of 'flesh with its life, that is, its blood' (Gen. 9:4)." Miller, *Religion of Ancient Israel*, 124. This congruent theme cannot be identified as coming from specific Priestly sources that are unique to the textual contexts of Genesis and Leviticus respectively; rather this consistent prohibition in Genesis 9 and Leviticus 17 – which is followed by the regulation in Deuteronomy 12 – is required because God has consistently appointed that life is in the blood, and also because it fits in the textual contexts of these three passages as teaching needed by the audience due to the permission of eating meat. Miller further points out that in the Israelite history, the people were expected to keep this regulation in their daily life. For example, it is recorded in 1 Samuel 14:31–34. Miller, *Religion of Ancient Israel*, 125, 134–35.

5. Miller also mentions this. Miller, 126; See Leviticus 17:13 and Deuteronomy 12:24; 15:23.

6. Snaith, "Sacrifices in Old Testament," 310. Snaith asserts, "It is not a meal which God shares with His faithful." De Vaux also mentions that offering blood and fat to God does not mean that God is fed by these offerings. It is because these belong to him alone. De Vaux, *Studies in Old Testament*, 42.

the sacrificial procedures prescribed in Leviticus. The word דָּם and its derivatives appear a total of 360 times in the OT, and 86 of these occurrences are in Leviticus.[7] Table 7 provides a summary of observations on the nature and functions of blood in the rituals in Leviticus.[8]

The primary function of blood in the rituals in Leviticus is to make atonement for the offerer, priests, congregation, officers, and sanctuary. Some procedures are performed by the priests to fulfill this purpose. After the animal was slaughtered within the tabernacle complex, actions undertaken to fulfill the purpose of atonement for an individual or specific group of people include: the priest shall bring the blood near and splash the blood all around on the altar, put it on the horns of the altar at the entrance or on the altar of fragrant incense, sprinkle the blood seven times in front of the veil in the sanctuary or in front of the mercy seat, and pour out the blood at the base of the altar of burnt offerings.[9] In Leviticus 16:18–19, the priest shall atone for the altar on the Day of Atonement by putting blood on the horns of the altar and sprinkling blood seven times in front of the altar. These procedures, with their purpose of atonement are found in Leviticus 1, 4–9, and 16 in the context of discussions of burnt offerings, sin offerings, and the guilt offering (Lev 5:6, 7).

I would like to especially highlight the role of blood in the sin offering and the burnt offering sacrificed to the Lord in Leviticus 8:14–21. It began with the washing rites – which symbolized the action of cleansing and consecrating in the OT – for Aaron and his sons (Lev 8:6).[10] Then Aaron put on his magnificent high priestly garments, which not only reflected God's holy presence and glory in the tent of meeting but also symbolized the royalty

7. Even-Shoshan, *New Concordance*, 266–68.

8. The summary of the nature and function of the blood in the rituals here does not include the following occurrences of דָּם, which appear in regulations but are not related to the rituals. In Leviticus 15:19 and 20:18, the word דָּם indicates the discharge of blood of a woman, while in Leviticus 20:11–13, 16 and 27, the word דָּם refers to the bloodguilt of committing a sin against the commandment of the Lord.

9. Heger mentions that we may regard "the absorption of the blood by the surrounding earth around it as a symbol of offering to the Deity." Heger, *Three Biblical Altar Laws*, 79, n.141. However, this concept or explanation is not included in biblical teaching, and it is just a way to dispose of the remaining blood after the ritual manipulation of the blood had been fulfilled.

10. In Exodus 19:10, YHWH also commanded the people to consecrate themselves by washing their garments.

Table 7. Summary of the Nature or Function of Blood in Leviticus

Nature/function of blood in the scriptural context	The action of blood ritual	Verses	The word that appears in the text	Notes
Make atonement for the offerer/sanctuary/priests or purify or consecrate the items to make atonement for it/them	The priests shall bring near the blood and throw (זָרַק) the blood all around on the altar.	1:5	אֶת־הַדָּם (1:5, two times)	Burnt offering (bull)
	The blood of the birds shall be drained out (מָצָה) on the side of the altar.	1:15	דָּמוֹ	Burnt offering (birds)
	The priest shall take (לָקַח) some blood and dip (טָבַל) his finger in the blood and sprinkle (נָזָה) part of the blood seven times before the Lord, in front of the veil of the sanctuary.	4:5–7	מִדַּם בַּדָּם מִן־הַדָּם	Sin offering (bull, for the anointed priest)
	The priest shall bring some blood and dip (טָבַל) his finger in the blood, sprinkle (נָזָה) seven times before the Lord in front of the veil of the sanctuary, put (נָתַן) some of the blood on the horns of the altar, and the rest of the blood he shall pour out (שָׁפַךְ) at the base of the altar of burnt offering.	4:16–18	מִדַּם מִן־הַדָּם וּמִן־הַדָּם כָּל־הַדָּם	Sin offering (bull, for congregation)
	The priest shall take (לָקַח) some blood and bring it to the tent of meeting, put (נָתַן) [it] on the horns of the altar of burnt offering and pour out (שָׁפַךְ) the rest of the blood at the base of the altar of burnt offering.	4:25	מִדַּם וְאֶת־דָּמוֹ	Sin offering (for officer, male goat)
	The priest shall take (לָקַח) some of its blood with his finger and put (נָתַן) [it] on the horns of the altar of burnt offering and pour out (שָׁפַךְ) all the rest of its blood at the base of the altar.	4:30	מִדָּמָהּ וְאֶת־כָּל־דָּמָהּ	Sin offering (for any individual, female goat)
	The priest shall take (לָקַח) some of its blood with his finger and put (נָתַן) [it] on the horns of the altar of burnt offering and pour out (שָׁפַךְ) all the rest of its blood at the base of the altar.	4:34	מִדַּם וְאֶת־כָּל־דָּמָהּ	Sin offering (for any individual, female lamb)

Nature/function of blood in the scriptural context	The action of blood ritual	Verses	The word that appears in the text	Notes
continued	The priest shall sprinkle (נָזָה) the blood of the sin offering on the side of the altar and the rest of the blood shall be drained out (מָצָה) at the base of the altar.	5:9	מִדַּם בַּדָּם	Sin offering (bird)
	Moses took (לָקַח) the blood and put (נָתַן) it on the horns of the altar around it (to purify it) and poured out (יָצַק) the blood at the base of the altar to consecrate (קָדַשׁ) it and make atonement (כָּפַר) for it	8:15	אֶת־הַדָּם וְאֶת־הַדָּם	Sin offering for the priests (bull; 8:1, 14, for the consecration of the priests)
	Moses killed [it] and threw (זָרַק) the blood all around on the altar.	8:19	אֶת־הַדָּם	Burnt offering (male lamb, for the consecration of the priests)
	Moses took (לָקַח) some of its blood and put (נָתַן) [it] on Aaron's earlobes, right thumbs, and right toes. He put (נָתַן) some of the blood on the earlobes, right thumbs, and right toes of the priests (to consecrate them, 8:30) and threw (זָרַק) the blood all around on the altar. He took (לָקַח) some of the blood and sprinkled (נָזָה) it on Aaron, his sons and their garments.	8:23–24, 30	מִדָּמוֹ מִן־הַדָּם אֶת־הַדָּם וּמִן־הַדָּם	The ram of ordination
	Aaron's sons brought (קָרַב) the blood to him and he dipped (טָבַל) his finger in the blood and put (נָתַן) it on the horns of the altar and poured out (יָצַק) the blood at the base of the altar.	9:9	אֶת־הַדָּם בַּדָּם וְאֶת־הַדָּם	Sin offering (bull, for the anointed priest themselves)
	Aaron killed the burnt offering and threw (זָרַק) the blood all around on the altar.	9:12	אֶת־הַדָּם	Burnt offering (male lamb for the anointed priests themselves)
	Any blood of all sin offering is brought (בּוֹא) into the tent of meeting to make atonement in the Holy Place.	6:23 [Eng 6:30]	מִדָּמָהּ	Sin offering

Nature/function of blood in the scriptural context	The action of blood ritual	Verses	The word that appears in the text	Notes
continued	The priests shall throw (זָרַק) the blood all around on the altar	3:2; 3:8, 13	אֶת־הַדָּם (3:2) אֶת־דָּמוֹ (3:8, 13)	Well-being offering (herd)
		9:18; 17:6	אֶת־הַדָּם	Well-being offering
		7:14, 33	אֶת־דַּם	Well-being offering for the priests themselves (ox, ram)
		7:2	וְאֶת־דָּמוֹ	The Guilt offering
	Day of Atonement: Aaron took (לָקַח) some blood of the bull and sprinkled (נָזָה) some of the blood both on the east side and in front of the mercy seat seven times to atone for the priests	16:14	מִדַּם מִן־הַדָּם	Day of Atonement: Burnt offering (bull)
	Day of Atonement: Aaron brought (בּוֹא) the blood of the goat and did (עָשָׂה) it as he did (עָשָׂה) with the blood of the bull. He sprinkled (נָזָה) it in front of the mercy seat	16:15	אֶת־דָּמוֹ אֶת־דָּמוֹ	Day of Atonement: Sin offering (goat)
	Day of Atonement: Aaron took (לָקַח) some blood of the bull and some of the goat to put (נָתַן) [it] on the horns of the altar and sprinkled (נָזָה) some blood on it seven times to consecrate it	16:18–19	מִדַּם וּמִדַּם מִן־הַדָּם	Day of Atonement: Sin offering (bull and goat)
	Day of Atonement: the summary of the usage of the blood. The blood was brought (בּוֹא) into the Holy Place to make atonement.	16:27	אֶת־דָּמָם	Day of Atonement: Sin offering (bull and goat)

Nature/function of blood in the scriptural context	The action of blood ritual	Verses	The word that appears in the text	Notes
Purification for the leper/ house	The priest dipped (טָבַל) them (several items) in the blood	14:6	בְּדַם	Purification ritual
	The priest took (לָקַח) from the blood and put (נָתַן) it on the earlobes, right thumbs, and right toes of the leper	14:14, 17, 25, 28	מִדַּם (14) דַּם (17) מִדַּם (25) דַּם (28)	Guilt offering (male lamb)
	The priest dipped (טָבַל) in the blood of the bird and sprinkled (נָזָה) [it] seven times on the house and with the blood it was cleansed (חָטָא)	14:51, 52	בְּדַם (51, 52)	Make atonement for the house
It belongs to the Lord	The blood of well-being offering	17:4 (two times)	דָּם	Well-being offering
	You shall not eat any fat or any blood	3:17; 7:26, 27	וְכָל־דָּם וְכָל־דָּם (7:26) כָּל־דָּם (7:27)	Well-being offering
	You shall not eat blood (10, 12, 14). The life is in the blood for atonement (11, 14).	17:10 (two times), 11 (two times), 12 (two times), 13, 14 (three times)	כָּל־דָּם (10) אֶת־הַדָּם (10) בַּדָּם (11) כִּי־הַדָּם (11) דָּם (12, two times) אֶת־דָּמוֹ (13) דָּמוֹ, דַּם, דָּמוֹ (14)	Well-being offering
It is most holy (6:20 [Eng 6:27])	When any of its blood is splashed on a garment, you shall wash that on which it was splashed in a holy place	6:20 [Eng 6:27]	מִדָּמָהּ	The sin offering
	Brought the blood within the inner part of the sanctuary	10:18	אֶת־דָּמָהּ	The sin offering
The people shall be holy because the Lord is holy (19:2)	Shall not eat with the blood	19:26	עַל־הַדָּם	Avoiding the custom of the Canaanites

of God, who ruled his kingdom on earth (Lev 8:7–9).[11] After anointing the tabernacle, all that was in it, the altar and all its vessels, Moses anointed Aaron with oil. The Scriptures clearly state that the purpose of this anointing was consecration. The act of anointing expressed the grace of YHWH's choosing; the oil also represented God's presence and strength that would be with Aaron as he was appointed to serve in the special role of high priest, and with the Israelites in the tabernacle.

To sum up, in Leviticus 8:1–13 Aaron and his sons were cleansed by water and were appointed as high priest and priests according to the words of the Lord. Moreover, in this section, Aaron, the high priest, and the tabernacle where the Lord dwelled with the Israelites were anointed by the oil – that is, both the personnel who drew near to the Lord and the place where the Lord was present among his people were designated by God himself. Through this designation, they obtained the status of consecration. Besides the rite of cleansing by water, one would observe that in this passage, for the personnel who served in the tabernacle, Aaron seemed to be the only representative to be appointed and acquire the status of consecration; however, if we read the interrelated text of Exodus 29:9, both Aaron and his sons were ordained to the perpetual status of priesthood. His sons thus joined him in the sacrificial rites described in the following passage from Leviticus 8, namely the sin offering and the burnt offering for Aaron and his sons, who laid their hands on the sacrificial animals.

According to Leviticus 1 and 4, the main purpose of these two sacrifices is to atone for the person who offers them. Moreover, the burnt offering is a pleasing aroma offered by the fire for YHWH – that is, it is a totally surrendered sacrifice, which pleases YHWH. The procedures for these two sacrifices include rituals of blood. In the case of the sin offering, the blood put on the horns of the altar could consecrate and make atonement for the altar, while for the burnt offering the blood was splashed all around on the altar. Splashing the blood all around on the altar was a way of putting the blood of the animal on the altar as part of the sacrifice of the whole animal.[12]

---

11. Hartley, *Leviticus*, 115. Hartley points out that "there was also a royal quality of these garments, indicating that the high priest ministered at the altar for a people who were God's kingdom on earth."

12. I thank Richard E. Averbeck for introducing the concept of splashing blood in the burnt offerings to this discussion. According to Milgrom, however, the blood here was not for

The last sacrifice described in this passage was the ram for ordination. In Leviticus 8:24, Moses took some of the blood and put it on the earlobes, right thumbs and right toes of the priests, and in Leviticus 8:30 he sprinkled oil and blood on the garments of the priests for the purpose of consecrating them. Leviticus 8:24 describes another blood rite, which involved pouring the blood all around on the altar. This procedure was consistent with the regulations for well-being offerings described in Leviticus 3:2, 8, and 13, because the blood belonged to YHWH.

We can summarize the nature or function of the blood rites involved in the three sacrifices in Leviticus 8 as follows: in terms of function, the blood carried the meaning of atonement, because the priests put their hands on the sacrificial animals of the sin and burnt offerings in order to identify themselves with the animals that died for them. According to Leviticus 1 and 3, laying hands on an animal to identify oneself with it brings the result of atonement for the offerers. The blood also carried the function of consecrating the altar, the priests, and their garments (Lev 8:15, 24 and 30). As for the nature of the blood, the requirement that it should be poured against the sides of the altar demonstrates that it belongs to YHWH, the Lord of all lives.

Second, as we discussed in the previous paragraph, another function of the blood is consecration or purification. This use of blood appears not only in Leviticus 8 but also in Leviticus 14 for the rites of purification for the leper and the house. Gane believes that, according to Leviticus 17:11, "blood represents life, and ritual application of animal blood to the Israelite altar enacted ransom of human life."[13] We may notice that in Israelite rituals, the blood was intentionally and meaningfully applied to persons, objects, or areas in order to atone or consecrate them. In the Mesopotamian or Ugaritic cults, however, there were no such rituals of blood.[14] In the Mesopotamian context, the rite of purification involved washing or rubbing with water, oil, or milk.

---

the purpose of burning up for the Lord. When he discussed the blood splashed against the walls of the altar in Leviticus 1:5, Milgrom concluded that the reason for not burning up the blood here in the burnt offering was that it was "not part of the offering but it is the life of the animal (17:10–14), which must be returned to God via the altar lest the slayer-offerer be considered a murderer (17:3–4)." Milgrom, *Leviticus 1–16*, 156. This is unlikly since the whole animal for the burnt offering is offered to God, including the life.

13. Gane, "Leviticus," 290.

14. Gane, 290; Also see Abusch, "Blood in Israel," 675–84; Olmo Lete, *Canaanite Religion*, 41.

We could not find any reference to the practice of purification by blood in Mesopotamian rites.[15] The only instance of a remotely similar practice was found among the Hittites, who, when they established a new temple for the goddess of the night, enacted bloody rituals to purify the new deity and the new temple. There were two different stages which involved the blood rites. At first, before the goddess was brought into the new temple, they performed an evocation rite at the old temple which included the smearing of the deity's statue with the blood of an offering. Fish were frequently employed in this cult.[16] Feder observes that "one may interpret the smearing of the deity's statue with blood as a means of attracting her from the underworld"[17] because such usage is consistent with belief in Hittite, Mesopotamian, and Greek sources; however, alternatively the blood rite is followed by the evocation sequences, Feder asserts that "the blood might better be viewed as an offering to greet the goddess upon her emergence from the underworld."[18]

Subsequently, on the following day there were other rites which reached a climax with the blood-smearing rite. The participants dug a ritual pit before the statue of the new deity and offered one sheep to her, slaughtering it in the pit as a reconciliation offering.[19] Then they bloodied the golden image of the deity, the wall, the cultic utensils, and all the implements of the new deity in order to purify and consecrate both the deity and the temple for the cult structure and apparatus for use.[20]

In summary, the blood rites in this ritual to the night goddess carry at least two different functions. On the one hand, Feder points out that "the animal chosen for the blood rite is idiosyncratic to the deity being worshipped."[21] A fish, for example, was involved in the night goddess's blood-smearing rite, and he concludes that this might indicate that the blood was an offering which could attract her from the underworld.[22] On the other hand, the blood

15. Vervenne, "'Blood is Life,'" 458.

16. Miller, *Studies in Origins, Development*, 284, n.435; Feder, *Blood Expiation*, 28.

17. Feder, 29.

18. Feder.

19. Feder, 32; "Establishing a New Temple for the Goddess of the Night," in Hallo, *Canonical Compositions*," 173–77.

20. Feder, 32.

21. Feder, 33.

22. Feder, 33.

smeared on the cultic objects including the statue of the deity herself was to consecrate them for ritual use. This function is similar to the blood which was smeared on the objects in the tabernacle to consecrate and purify them on the Day of Inauguration of the Priests (Lev 8–9) and on the Day of Atonement (Lev 16); however, the blood rites mentioned above in the rituals in Leviticus were offered to YHWH, who is the Most Holy One and above all creatures. He needs no purification from the sacrifices and the blood rituals in the Israelite rites could only purify the area, objects or people.[23]

Third, with regard to the nature of blood in the Levitical rituals, in Leviticus 3–5, 7–9, and 17, eating blood is prohibited because the blood belongs to YHWH. Vervenne points out that since only the cult of the dead and the netherworld stressed blood in the Greek sacrificial traditions, blood did not belong to the gods and therefore humans could eat it.[24] In contrast, the Israelite rituals of sacrifice are much more concerned about blood, which is reserved for YHWH and is a purifying agent.[25] Moreover, the prohibition of eating blood is connected with the prohibition of eating fat. For example, in Leviticus 7:22–27, it is stated that the blood and fat of a sacrificial animal belong to God, and therefore humans may not eat them.[26] We will discuss this in greater detail later in this book.

Lastly, Leviticus 6:18 [Eng. 6:25] states that the blood is the most holy in nature. It should therefore be treated according to this nature, which is described in Leviticus 6:20 [Eng. 6:27] ("when any of its blood is splashed on a garment, you shall wash that on which it was splashed in a holy place") and 10:18. The blood's most holy nature harmonizes well with its nature of belonging to YHWH. YHWH is the most holy God; thus anything which originates from him shall be most holy – the blood mentioned in the OT ritual system is no exception. Vervenne points out that Wellhausen and Smith have claimed, based on ancient evidence, that one common meaning which attributes a special power to blood in the blood rites is that "blood is divine and so is used in the ritual."[27] However, after McCarthy's thorough survey of ANE lit-

23. Gane, "Leviticus," 290.
24. Vervenne, "Blood Is Life,'" 459.
25. Vervenne, 460.
26. Vervenne, 457.
27. Vervenne, 458; Cf. Wellhausen, *Reste arabischen heidentums*.

erature, including Greek, Arab, Ugarit, Hittite, and Mesopotamian examples, he finally reached the conclusion that, outside the Hebrew Scriptures, blood is associated not with life but with unpleasantness, ghosts, death, darkness, and curse, and so on.[28] This concept is totally different from the OT view of the blood as divine.

The Prohibition of Eating Blood in the Pentateuch

There are at least three passages in the Pentateuch that mention the prohibition of eating blood: Genesis 9:3–6, Leviticus 17:10–16, and Deuteronomy 12:15–16, 20–25.[29] I would like to begin the following discussion by interpreting these three passages in their own literary contexts. From these understandings we may turn to a closer look at the meaning of blood in the Levitical rituals.

Genesis 9:3–6

Genesis 9:2 states that all the living creatures on the ground, in the air, or in the sea were given to Noah and his family. The following verse, Genesis 9:3, continues by proclaiming that all living creatures will be food for them, which introduces a tension in the form of the possibility of taking lives.[30] The restriction that follows in Genesis 9:4–6 must be taken together with this concession to kill. The Hebrew particle אַךְ appears at the beginning of both Genesis 9:4 and 9:5. The adverb אַךְ functions as "an emphatic and a restrictive particle."[31] In Genesis 9:4, this particle introduces the readers to the condition or restriction on the killing of animals in order to normalize the meat eating: אַךְ־בָּשָׂר בְּנַפְשׁוֹ דָמוֹ לֹא תֹאכֵלוּ׃. Westermann notes that there are some difficulties in understanding the meaning of this sentence.[32] בָּשָׂר here refers to the animals in the previous verse. The second word, בְּנַפְשׁוֹ, is "with its life."

---

28. McCarthy, "Further Notes," 205–10.

29. Cholewiński calls attention to the parallel between Leviticus and Deuteronomy, which includes Leviticus 17 and Deuteronomy 12. Walton and Matthews point out that "no comparable prohibition is known in the ancient world." Walton and Matthews, *IVP Bible Background Commentary*, 30.

30. Westermann, *Genesis 1–11*, 463.

31. Harman, "Particles," in VanGemeren, *NIDOTTE* 4:1031.

32. Westermann, *Genesis 1–11*, 464.

According to Gesenius, the prefix preposition בְּ expresses the idea of "*with* something."[33] Furthermore, Clines classifies this usage under the sub-category בְּ of essence, thus translating אַךְ־בָּשָׂר בְּנַפְשׁוֹ as "flesh (consisting of) its life," which is consistent with Gesenius's translation but more vivid in expression.[34]

Gesensius explains that the usage of the third word, דָמוֹ ("its blood"), belongs to permutation. The usage here is not complementary but rather "defines the preceding substantive . . . in order to prevent any possible misunderstanding."[35] The sentence should therefore be translated as: "Only the flesh with its life, (which is) its blood, you shall not eat."

The relationship of permutation between these two words, "life" and "blood," is mentioned in John Calvin's commentary on the book of Genesis. Calvin points out that, since there is no copulative conjunction between the words "life" and "blood," the word that appears later (blood) bears the exegetical usage to the previous word, life. Calvin therefore asserts that the blood is a token which represents life. Calvin explains this as follows: "flesh is in some sense devoured with its life, when it is eaten imbued with its own blood."[36]

Westermann agrees with Benno Jacob's view that the meaning of the prohibition here is built upon the idea of the pulsating of the blood, which is based on the rabbinic interpretation of later Judaism[37] and as one of the so-called "The Noachide Commandments." In different rabbinic traditions, "the Noachide Commandments" are varied. However, "the prohibition against eating flesh cut from a living animal" is included in the list of widest consensus.[38] Westermann further explains that "the life of every living being is identical with the pulsation of the blood."[39] Wenham notes that documents indicate that some Abyssinian tribes ate raw meat freshly cut from a living animal; however, the interpretation of the prohibition in Genesis 9:4 cannot

33. Gesenius, *Gesenius' Hebrew Grammar*, 380.

34. Clines, "בְּ," *Dictionary of Classical Hebrew*, 2:84.

35. Gesenius, *Gesenius' Hebrew Grammar*, 425. "Permutation" is a kind of apposition.

36. Calvin, *Genesis*, 293.

37. Jacob, *First Book*, 64.

38. Sarna, *Genesis*, 377. The translation of Genesis 9:4 in the *Hebrew-English Tanakh* reflects this interpretation: "You must not, however, eat flesh with its life-blood in it." Jewish Publication Society, *JPS Hebrew-English Tanakh*, 15. Walton specifies that "this view was expressed as early as the Talmud (*b. Sanb.* 59a)." Walton, "Genesis," 343, n.10.

39. Westermann, *Genesis 1–11*, 465.

rest solely on this background.[40] Wenham criticizes Westermann's interpretation as too narrow because it does not consider the commandment to drain the blood from the animals before they can be eaten (Lev 3:7; 7:25–26; 19:26; Deut 12:16–24).[41]

In Genesis 9:5–6, we see that the prohibition of eating animal blood in verse 4 is related to the discussion of homicide in verses 5–6.[42] Verse 5 begins with another adverb, אַךְ; however, it is not followed by a parallel prohibition as found in verse 4.[43] Instead, the verb דרשׁ appears three times in verse 5 in the first person imperfect.[44] The repetition and consistent usage of דרשׁ for emphasis conveys the idea that God insists on the need to reckon with his utmost authority as the Creator of all living creatures, including humans.[45] Moreover, in connection with verse 4, the word נֶפֶשׁ is used in three different senses in a type of word-play: בְּנַפְשׁוֹ in verse 4 means "together with its life;" in verse 5, לְנַפְשֹׁתֵיכֶם conveys the meaning of "belonging to your souls" – in other words, "of yourselves" – while אֶת־נֶפֶשׁ הָאָדָם expresses "the soul (actual life) of the man."[46] The word-play on נֶפֶשׁ also intensifies the meaning brought by דרשׁ– God's authorship and ownership of life. Lastly, Barré points out that the prepositional phrases connected to the verb דרשׁ in Genesis 9:5 are מִיַּד כָּל־חַיָּה, and מִיַּד אִישׁ אָחִיו, and they move from generic to more specific.[47] For example, the second phrase, "from the hand of the man," is developed to

40. Wenham, *Genesis 1–15*, 193. Walton points out that "in the ancient world where no refrigeration was available, sometimes an animal was kept alive as long as possible while it was used for meat." Walton, "Genesis," 343, n.10.

41. Wenham, *Genesis 1–15*, 193. See almost exactly the same paragraph in Vervenne, "Blood Is Life,'" 468. According to the publication date, this was first pointed out by Wenham; however, when Vervenne mentioned it in his article, he did not cite any source for this comment.

42. Vervenne, "Blood Is Life,'" 451.

43. Westermann also mentions this. Westermann, *Genesis 1–11*, 465.

44. Westermann, 466.

45. Cassuto, *Commentary*, 127. Barré discusses the poetic structure in Genesis 9:5. Barré, "Poetic Structure," 101–4.

46. Cassuto, 127.

47. Brown, Driver, and Briggs state that חַיָּה here specifically refers to the wild animals. Brown, Driver, and Briggs, *Brown-Driver-Briggs Hebrew*, 312. Barré, however, has a different opinion, mentioning that it may denote "clan," "community," or "group," which is the meaning of the second root of חַיָּה. Barré, "Poetic Structure," 103; Brown, Driver, and Briggs, 312–13.

a specific description in the third phrase, "from the hand of each man, his brother" to express "the responsibility of individual."[48]

The text of Genesis 9:6 focuses on the shedding of human blood. The first line of verse 6 is characterized by chiastic parallelism, in which the second part of the line repeats the words of the first part of the line in reverse order.[49] This line, with the participle of שׁפך at the beginning of the sentence, indicates a cause or condition; followed by the imperfect form of שׁפך at the end, it denotes the further consequence of the previous condition.[50] The first line thus expresses the idea that if anyone sheds man's blood, by man shall his blood be shed. Cassuto points out that this chiastic structure reflects "the principle of measure for measure,"[51] and Gunkel claims this word order also expresses that the murderer experiences precisely what he did to another.[52] The second line of verse 6 states the reason for the punishment listed in the first line – in the image of God he made man.[53] This penalty of death, with its reason, makes it clear that homicide is prohibited because it violates the principle of respecting God by eliminating a human – one created in the Divine image – from the world God made. Furthermore, if we relate the message of verse 6 with verses 4–5 in their immediate context of God's commandment following his blessing of Noah and his family after the flood (Gen 9:1–7), we can see a very strong textual connection with God's blessings and commandments following the creation of humans in Genesis 1:27–29 and the first account of murder in Genesis 4:8–24.[54] After the flood, humans are to respect God as the Creator of all the living creatures by not shedding the blood of other humans who are created in the Divine image and by not consuming blood,

48. Gesenius, *Gesenius' Hebrew Grammar*, 448. Gesenius mentions that in this phrase the second substantive is more likely in apposition to אִישׁ. Barré, "Poetic Structure," 102.

49. Turner, *Genesis*, 46. Turner also mentions about this chiastic structure and its relationship with Genesis 4. See also Reyburn and Fry, *Handbook on Genesis*, 205–6.

50. Gesenius, *Gesenius' Hebrew Grammar*, 361.

51. Cassuto, *Commentary*, 127.

52. Gunkel, *Genesis*, 149.

53. Cotter points out that this is "another reference back to the creation story of Genesis 1." That is "the divine image in which humanity has been created precludes the taking of human life." Cotter, *Genesis*, 60.

54. VanDrunen discusses the correlation between Genesis 1:26–28 and 9:1–7 in VanDrunen, "Natural Law," 137–39. On Genesis 4:8–24, see Wenham, *Genesis 1-15*, 192. Brodie also mentions this textual echoing in Brodie, *Genesis as Diaogue*, 180–81.

which God has designated as the symbol of life for both animals and humans.[55] These are not two separate prohibitions: they are closely related because these two restrictions will continually remind the Israelites that all life is sacred and belongs to God, the Author of life.[56] As Wenham says, "Respect for life, and beyond that, respect for the giver of life, means abstaining from blood."[57]

Deuteronomy 12:15–16, 20–25

Before we turn our attention to Leviticus 17, we will interpret another passage which provides instructions on how to deal with the blood in the meat consumed by the Israelites. As for the historical background, Deuteronomy 12 states that when the people enter Canaan, they will start a new way of life – settlement rather than nomadic life in the wilderness.[58] For this reason, YHWH reminds them through Moses of some important messages about worshiping him. The literary structure of Deuteronomy 12 is very clear.[59]

---

55. "God treats blood as symbolic of life, and thus forbids eating it in order to remind people that life is sacred." Assohoto and Ngewa, "Genesis," 24. Gammie also states that "there is clearly a didactic and ethical purpose behind the prohibition of blood." Gammie, *Holiness in Israel*, 11.

56. Gowan, *From Eden to Babel*, 103. Sprinkle also concludes that "the blood prohibition (Gen 9:3–6) taught the Israelite respect for animal life and for the Author of life whose permission was required to shed any blood, whether animal or human. This leads to a further moral implication: If taking mere animal life is not trivial, how much more serious is shedding human blood." Sprinkle, *Biblical Law*, 114; Also see the discussion in Walker, "Noah," 385–86; Cf. Sarna, *Genesis*, 61.

57. Wenham, *Genesis 1–15*, 193. Miguez Bonino also mentions this in Bonino, "Covenant of Life," 343–45. The prohibition of eating blood instills a respect for the sacredness of life. Waltke, *Genesis: A Commentary*, 144.

58. Deuteronomy 12:10, וִישַׁבְתֶּם־בֶּטַח ("and you dwell in safety").

59. Lundbom proposes a certain structural division of Deuteronomy 12. He provides a different parallel structure in his commentary. Lundbom, *Deuteronomy*, 420; Cf. Lundbom, "Inclusio and Other Framing," 307. The structure he identifies can be simplified as follows:

A These are the statutes and the ordinances (12:1)
  B Places of *their gods* to be destroyed (12:2–4)
    C On tithes and offerings (12:5–14)
    C' On the ritually clean and the unclean (12:15–28)
  B' Do not seek after *their gods* (12:29–31)
A' Every word that I am commanding you (13:1 [Eng 12:32])

Compared to the structure I propose, Lundbom does not differentiate the subunits in 12:15–28. McConville suggests a simple structure for this chapter, but does not distinguish between the paragraphs in Deuteronomy 12:15–28. McConville, *Deuteronomy*, 213. Woods proposes a structure based on the usage of pronominal suffixes. He observes that there are two main sections in Deuteronomy 12:1–32 and the first half (12:1–12) uses the second masculine plural, while the second half (12:13–32) mainly uses the second masculine singular with the only exception in verse 32 in which the second masculine plural is used. However, from this

A Introductory words: encouragement of obedience (v. 1)
  B Destroy their gods and worship only YHWH (vv. 2–4)
    C Worship YHWH at the central sanctuary via sacrifices (vv. 5–14)
      D The rules of eating nonsacrificial meat (vv. 15–16)
    C' Worship YHWH at the central sanctuary via sacrifices (vv. 17–19)
      D' The rules of eating nonsacrificial meat (vv. 20–25)
    C" Worship YHWH at the central sanctuary via sacrifices (vv. 26–28)
  B' Destroy their gods and worship only YHWH (vv. 29–31)
A' Conclusion: encouragement of obedience (13:1)

Aside from the introductory words (12:1) and the conclusion (13:1) – A and A' – both of which encourage obedience using the phrase, תִּשְׁמְרוּ לַעֲשׂוֹת,[60] the outer framework of this passage is Deuteronomy 12:2–4 and 12:29–31 (B and B' [v. 30, הִשָּׁמֶר לְךָ]), which emphasizes the first and second commandments in the Decalogue (Deut 5:7–10): the Israelites are to destroy all their gods and worship and seek only YHWH in the place they enter.[61] Under this guideline, Deuteronomy 12:5–28 focuses on how the Israelites are going to

point of view, in Woods's structure, two passages (12:13–14 and 12:26–28) could not be specified in terms of their contents. Woods, *Deuteronomy*, 185. Christensen proposes several possible parallel structures in his discussion. Christensen, *Deuteronomy 1:1–21:9*, 233–35. Block, Biddle, and Sherwood do not specify the parallel structure of this chapter. Block, *Deuteronomy*, 301–22; Biddle, *Deuteronomy*, 205–23; Sherwood, *Leviticus, Numbers, Deuteronomy*, 260.

60. Lundbom mentions this inclusio outer frame of this passage in both his article and his commentary. Moreover, he points out that הַחֻקִּים וְהַמִּשְׁפָּטִים in Deuteronomy 12:1 is balanced by כָּל־הַדָּבָר in Deuteronomy 13:1 [Eng 12:32] in this inclusio structure. Lundbom, "Inclusio and Other Framing," 306; Lundbom, *Deuteronomy*, 420. Hall makes similar comments, but does not mention the observations of Lundbom's article published in 1996 in his research. Hall, "Rhetorical Criticism, Chiasm," 98.

61. Lundbom identifies this inclusio as well, calling it "an inner frame" meant to "warn the audience to 'beware of *other gods*'" (italics in the original). However, he identifies the first part of this inclusio as vv. 2–3 instead of vv. 2–4, which I propose here. Lundbom, "Inclusio and Other Framing," 306. However, in his commentary, Lundbom includes v. 4 in the first part by identifying Deuteronomy 12:1–4 as a subunit of this passage. Lundbom, *Deuteronomy*, 413, 420. Hall also describes these two passages as a "secondary inclusion," but he does not mention Lundbom's observation in his article. Hall, "Rhetorical Criticism, Chiasm," 98.

worship YHWH in the Promised Land. There are two groups of parallel texts in verses 5–28.[62]

The first group, which consists of three paragraphs, contains verses 5–14, 17–19, and 26–28 (C [v. 13, הִשָּׁמֶר לְךָ], C' [v. 19, הִשָּׁמֶר לְךָ] and C" [v. 28, שְׁמֹר]). This group of texts focuses on how the Israelites should worship YHWH in the Promised Land in the future through sacrifices.[63] First, the phrase, בַּמָּקוֹם אֲשֶׁר־יִבְחַר יְהוָה/הַמָּקוֹם אֲשֶׁר־יִבְחַר יְהוָה (the place which YHWH shall choose), appears six times in Deuteronomy 12, and five out of six of these occurrences appear in this first group of passages, which emphasizes the sole obedience of the Israelites to YHWH and the uniqueness of the Israelites' worship to YHWH. Second, the word שמר appears in Deuteronomy 12:1, 13, 19, 28, 30, and 13:1, in which the message of worshiping God only according to his commandments has been stressed. We may conclude that the emphasis on this word, שמר, shows the importance of the message it bears.

The only occurrence of the phrase, בַּמָּקוֹם אֲשֶׁר־יִבְחַר יְהוָה/הַמָּקוֹם אֲשֶׁר־יִבְחַר יְהוָה (the place which YHWH shall choose), ouside this group is in verse 21, which denotes the importance of the second group of texts, verses 15–16 and 20–25 (D and D'). In response to the rules of offerings at the central sanctuary in the first group of texts, Moses instructs the people on eating nonsacrificial meat in their own future towns in Canaan. Verse 21 states that if the place YHWH shall choose is too far from them, they shall kill the animals and eat the meat in their own town as they desire. The conditional phrase, introduced by כִּי in verse 21, thus becomes a literary bridge between these two groups of texts through the repetition of the crucial term, בחר.

Thus, the theme of the second group of texts is how the Israelites should deal with the nonsacrificial meat they will consume in their own towns in Canaan. The Israelites, who were about to conclude their wandering journey in the wilderness and enter the Promised Land, received a commandment

62. Lundbom, "Inclusio and Other Framing," 296–315.

63. McConville and Hall have different views on the structure of Deuteronomy 12. McConville summarizes the macro-structure of Deuteronomy 12 as follows: 12:1–4 and 12:29–13:1 form the outer inclusio framework, while 12:5–12 and 13–28 form the inner parallel. McConville, *Law and Theology*, 59–63, 65–67. Hall concludes his observations on the structure of Deuteronomy 12 as follows: 12:1–4 and 12:29–13:1 form the outer inclusio framework, 12:5–7 and 12:8–12 are parallels, 12:13–14 and 12:26–28 are parallels as the key theme of this chapter, and 12:15–19 and 12:20–25 are parallels. Hall, "Rhetorical Criticism, Chiasm," 99–100.

regarding the eating of meat in their daily lives.[64] This instruction is more flexible than the similar regulation instructed in Leviticus 17 in terms of obtaining the meat for consuming in their daily life.[65] The text provides the reason of modifying the regulation stated in Leviticus 17: in the wilderness, it seems that people obtained meat for consumption mainly by offering well-being offerings at the tabernacle. During that historical stage, the Israelites lived surrounding the tabernacle, so they would not have trouble making well-being offerings at the tabernacle. In fact, when we compare these two paragraphs in the second group of texts, we see that Deuteronomy 12:20–22 develops from 12:15, while 12:16 is expanded into 12:23–25.

In Deuteronomy 12:20, it says, וְאָמַרְתָּ אֹכְלָה בָשָׂר ("And you will say 'Let me eat meat'"). Waltke and O'Connor points out that the אֹכְלָה is a cohortative, which expresses the desire of the speaker; however, since here the speaker could not effect the desire "without the consent of the one addressed, it connotes request."[66] Joüon points out that the precise meaning here is "I would like to eat some meat if it is allowed."[67] The rest of verse 20 confirms the permission for the Israelites to eat meat whenever they want to when they enter Canaan. Verse 21 implies that the regulation here in Deuteronomy is relevant to a new life stage that will arise in the near future when the Israelites enter the land of Canaan: the need to eat meat is now to be considered in a new light, as the previous regulation which only allows consumption of the meat of well-being offerings in Leviticus 17 might not be opportune. Milgrom points out that זבח, which is used to refer to "profane slaughter," is found only two times in Deuteronomy, both in this pericope (Deut 12:15, 21). "Elsewhere in biblical Hebrew and cognate languages it bears a sacral

64. Miller, *Religion of Ancient Israel*, 126. Miller mentions that "while there is an implicit indication that sacrificial slaughter at the altar is preferable, permission is given for slaughter of domestic animals for consumption in the towns."

65. "Later, when meat could be prepared for food without sacrifice, the blood still had to be treated in a special way (Deut. 12:23–24). There is no evidence that they thought the blood was sacred or contained some unique power (note that in Deuteronomy it is to be poured out 'like water'); the only reason ever given for this commandment about the blood is that it is the life of the animal. Only God can give life, and so every life that is taken involves responsibility to God for having done so." Gowan, *From Eden to Babel*, 103.

66. Waltke and O'Connor, *Introduction to Biblical Hebrew*, 573–74. See also Van der Merwe, Naudé, and Kroeze, *Biblical Hebrew Reference Grammar*, 152.

67. Joüon, *Grammar of Biblical Hebrew*, 375.

connotation."[68] Moreover, as the text states, וְזָבַחְתָּ . . . כַּאֲשֶׁר צִוִּיתִךָ, Milgrom concludes that this profane slaughter presumably follows the שחט method of killing prescribed in Leviticus for the sacrificial slaughter.[69] Lundbom defines זבח in Deuteronomy 12:15 and 21, as "simply 'slaughter,' not '(slaughter to) sacrifice,'"[70] and he regards the phrase כַּאֲשֶׁר צִוִּיתִךָ as indicating that "Moses realizes he is repeating what he said before."[71] Moreover, verse 22 states that this is similar to eating meat from hunted animals. Even though the animals must be listed in the clean animals, both the clean and the unclean could consume the meat, unlike the meat from the well-being offerings in Leviticus 7:19–21, which only the ritually clean were permitted to eat. However, Vogt argues that even though זבח in Deuteronomy 12:15 and 21 denotes the non-sacrificial slaughter, in the case of this nonsacrificial slaughter, "the Israelites are to imitate or mimic that which is done in sacrifice" because by the commanding of pouring the blood out in the practice of nonsacrificial slaughter, the connection between the sacrifice and nonsacrificial slaughter is built.[72] Therefore, Vogt concludes that "Deuteronomy 12 centralizes *sacrifice* to the central sanctuary, but *worship* is decentralized" (italics in the original).[73] In light of the structure of Deuteronomy 12 which I have proposed above, in Deuteronomy 12:5–28, there is an inclusio structure with worshiping the Lord at the place he chooses in the beginning and the end and the center as well. The two paragraphs on nonsacrificial slaughtering are inserted into the frame of sections on worship. This structure might take into consideration the concept of nonsacrificial slaughtering as an imitation of sacrifice, which is proposed by Vogt.

---

68. Milgrom, "Profane Slaughter," 1.

69. Milgrom, 1–3, 17. Low and Nicholls also point to the "the sacrificial animals Israel may slaughter 'in any of your towns' (v.15). The verb used here for 'slaughter,' which normally refers to a sacrifice, is puzzling." Low and Nicholls, *Book of Deuteronomy*, 140. Tigay suggests that, originally, domestic animals could only be slaughtered on altars, even if they were solely intended for food. Once Israel was settled in the land and had to reside away from the sanctuary, making this impractical, provisions for "profane slaughter" became necessary. The animal, however, still had to be slaughtered by the method used for sacrificial animals. The verb was thus a carry-over from the earlier custom. Tigay also agrees with the שחט method of killing. Tigay, *Deuteronomy*, 124–25.

70. Lundbom, *Deuteronomy*, 435.

71. Lundbom, 437.

72. Vogt, "Centralization and Decentralization," 131.

73. Vogt, 131; Cf. 137–38.

Verses 16 and 23–25 mention the prohibition of eating blood even in the context of this newly flexible regulation of eating nonsacrificial meat in one's own town. We will focus on the more elaborated passage, verses 23–25. The consumption of blood is prohibited three times in this passage, once in each verse: לְבִלְתִּי אֲכֹל הַדָּם in verse 23, לֹא תֹּאכְלֶנּוּ in verse 24, and לֹא תֹּאכְלֶנּוּ in verse 25. In verse 23, the reason for the prohibition immediatedly follows the prohibition itself: כִּי הַדָּם הוּא הַנָּפֶשׁ ("the blood, it [is] the life"). The blood, which represents the animal's life, must not be consumed but needs to be drained from the animal.[74] The second clause of this verse – וְלֹא־תֹאכַל הַנֶּפֶשׁ עִם־הַבָּשָׂר׃ – basically paraphrases the first half of the verse, even though halakhic exegesis saw it as an additional regulation to prohibit eating a limb immediately cut from a living animal.[75]

Verse 24 explains the method for dealing with the blood that may not be eaten: עַל־הָאָרֶץ תִּשְׁפְּכֶנּוּ כַּמָּיִם (the blood shall not be eaten; instead "it shall be poured on the ground as water.") On the one hand, as Gilders points out, the lack of explanation regarding the method of dealing with nonsacrificial blood prescribed in Deuteronomy 12:16 and Leviticus 17:14 may indicate that the blood is simply disposed because it is not to be accorded with the special treatment given to the blood of sacrifices in the cult.[76] Weinfeld argues that the reference to pouring out blood "as water" suggests that "blood has no more sacral value than water has."[77] Block futher comments that "this comparison relates to its liquid state rather than its religious significance."[78]

On the other hand, if we read the instructions on dealing with blood in the Pentateuch as symbolically related to respect for God, the Creator of all living creatures, we may see these instructions from a different point of view. In the case of sacrifices, the blood is returned to God by pouring it on the altar, sprinkling it in the sanctuary, or putting it on the horns of the altar – all of which show respect to God and carry ritual meanings and effects assigned by Him – while nonsacrificial blood must be either covered with dust (Lev

74. McConville, *Deuteronomy*, 226–27.

75. Tigay, *Deuteronomy*, 126.

76. Gilders, *Blood Ritual in Hebrew Bible*, 15. Von Rad also claims that "this pouring out of the blood is definitely denied the character of a sacrifice (it is to be like water)." Von Rad, *Deuteronomy*, 93.

77. Weinfeld, *Deuteronomy and Deuteronomic School*, 214.

78. Block, *Deuteronomy*, 318, n.6.

17:13) or poured on the ground as water.[79] In the former, which pertains to the blood of game animals, the shedding of blood must be covered up to show respect to the God of life.[80] In the latter case, Weinfeld claims that Deuteronomy permits profane slaughter, and has to dispense with this view by asserting that blood of profane slaughter has no more atoning value than water has.[81] This, too, shows respect for the Creator.[82]

Lastly, in verse 25 a promise from God is followed by the prohibition of eating blood: לְמַעַן יִיטַב לְךָ וּלְבָנֶיךָ אַחֲרֶיךָ – "in order that it may go well with you and your sons after you." This promise not only motivates the Israelites to follow the prohibition of eating blood, but also conveys that this regulation is integrated with other regulations in the Laws, especially those in Deuteronomy 12, emphasizing that God requires his people to respond obediently to his commandments. In summary, the key theme of Deuteronomy 12 is the worship of YHWH alone in Canaan (vv. 2–4, 29–31) by being obedient (v. 1 and 13:1) to his commandments concerning both sacrifices (vv. 5–14, 17–19, 26–28) and the consumption of nonsacrificial meat (15–16, 20–25). The literary structure of this passage suggests that respect for YHWH is the common principle underlying the rules in Deuteronomy 12.

79. "You shall pour it on the ground like water" (vv. 16, 24).

80. Weinfeld, *Deuteronomy and Deuteronomic School*, 214. Weinfeld mentions that "uncovered blood begs, as it were, for an avenger (Job 16:18 'O earth, cover not my blood . . .'; cf. Isa. 26:21; Ezek. 24:7–8)." However, the Scripture passages Weinfeld mentions to support this idea are all from the poetic genre. Therefore, his perspective regarding the avenger could not be confirmed here. However, in Weinfeld's discussion mentioned above, he does not discuss the related text in Genesis 4:10 which is recorded in the Cain-Abel narrative. Kidner asserts that Abel's blood crying out from the ground becomes a metaphor of avenger. Westermann even points out in his commentary that "it is this sentence that really gives the narrative its dramatic character. (B. Jacob: 'The speech is highly poetic and prophetic in its feeling')." Westermann, *Genesis 1–11*, 305. Thus, we may conclude that even though Genesis 4:10 is in the context of narrative, the description itself is metaphoric and poetic with expressions.

81. Weinfeld, *Deuteronomy and Deuteronomic School*, 214. See also Wright, *Deuteronomy*, 167. "This comparison relates to its liquid state rather than its religious significance." Block, *Deuteronomy*, 318, n.6. Moreover, Biddle points out that pouring blood on the ground like water could be seen to represent the blood returning to the ground, which might be the proximate source of it. However, he doesn't explain specifically why the ground is the proximate source of the blood. Biddle, *Deuteronomy*, 216. Harrison also mentions that the covering of blood with the earth in Leviticus 17:13 is to return the life "to the ground from which it had come." Harrison, *Leviticus*, 185.

82. Woods concludes that "it was not to be consumed, but poured out like water on the ground as belonging to God alone who gives life." Woods, *Deuteronomy*, 192. After a detailed discussion, Averbeck also agrees with Vogt's view that "handling of the blood by pouring it out on the ground" is "as a solemn act." Averbeck, "Cult in Deuteronomy," 31.

Leviticus 17:10–16

After examining the other two occurrences of the prohibition of eating blood in the Pentateuch outside the Sinai pericope, we now return to its occurrences in the Sinai covenant itself. The following sections will discuss the Sinai covenantal context, the structure, and the syntax and terminology of the prohibition of eating blood in Leviticus 17:10–16.

The Sinai Covenantal Context

We observe that only four passages in the Sinai pericope mention well-being offerings – Leviticus 3, 7:11–27, 17, and 22:17–25. Aside from 22:17–25, which discusses acceptable animals to be offered to YHWH, these occurrences also address the prohibition of eating blood. Leviticus 3 and 7:11–27 prohibit the consumption of both fat and blood. The reason for not eating fat is clearly stated in the texts (the fat belongs to YHWH and it should be burnt on the altar to him), but the reason for not eating blood is not clearly stated in these texts. However, the discussion of blood rituals required for the well-being offerings (Lev 3:2, 8, 13, and 7:14) suggests that the reason for the prohibition of eating blood in these literary contexts may be similar to the rules regarding fat: both are designated as belonging to YHWH.[83] Kiuchi asserts that "the burning of fat symbolizes the destruction of detestable things within a human's inner being."[84] So, the kidneys denote a human's inner being.[85] I do not agree with Kiuchi's explanation for burning the fat and kidneys in the well-being offering to Yahweh. On the one hand, the textual context clearly states that the fat could not be eaten because it belongs to Yahweh; on the other hand, in Kiuchi's argument, his explanation has been heavily based on the texts from the poetic genre, such as the books of Psalms and Job.[86] Leviticus 17 will be discussed below.

The prohibition of eating blood appears only once (in Lev 19:26) in the book of Leviticus outside discussions of well-being offerings. Here, this regulation accompanies other prohibitions related to Canaanite customs. In this context, we might speculate that eating blood was a pagan practice in Canaan.

83. Miller, *Religion of Ancient Israel*, 124. Miller mentions that this brief statement provides a clue for understanding the prohibition of eating fat and blood.

84. Kiuchi, *Leviticus*, 79.

85. Kiuchi, 79.

86. Kiuchi, 79.

Leviticus 19, then, contains the command not to eat blood (לֹא תֹאכְלוּ עַל־הַדָּם), due to its association with forbidden religious activities.

Based on observations of the occurrences of the well-being offering in Leviticus, we may conclude that in some cases it is a marking symbol that marks subunits in its literary context.[87] For example, in Leviticus 7:11–27 it comes at the end of both the discussions of priests' responsibilities during the sacrifices (Lev 6–7) and the whole discussion of sacrifices in Leviticus 1–7. As for Leviticus 17 and 22:17–25, chapter 2 of this book discusses the inclusio structure of these passages indicated by the same speech formula: דַּבֵּר אֶל־אַהֲרֹן וְאֶל־בָּנָיו וְאֶל כָּל־בְּנֵי יִשְׂרָאֵל (17:2; 22:18). This inclusio structure is also highlighted by the appearance of the regulations regarding the well-being offering in the respective texts.

The Structure of Leviticus 17

As for the structure of Leviticus 17, most scholars agree that it contains five instructions in it: vv. 3–7, 8–9, 10–12, 13–14, and 15–16. As Nihan points out, the chapter is a complex but unified composition.[88] The first four instructions are introduced by the same formula – אִישׁ אִישׁ (vv. 3, 8, 10 and 13);[89] only the fifth is introduced by וְכָל־נֶפֶשׁ (v. 15). The word נֶפֶשׁ is also a key word in this chapter, appearing nine times in verses 10–16.[90] It is this word, נֶפֶשׁ, which appears in verses 10, 11, 12, 14, and 15, that connects verses 15–16 to the previous two instructions in verses 10–14.[91]

Second, the כרת-threat also appears in the first three instructions (vv. 4, 9, and 10). While כרת does not appear in the main clause in the fourth instruction (v. 13), it appears in verse 14, and this כרת is basically a reinforcement in

---

87. Modéus, *Sacrifice and Symbol*, 382. Modéus points out that, on the level of structure, the well-being offering is a marking symbol.

88. Nihan, *Priestly Torah to Pentateuch*, 402–3. Nihan summarizes the most recent form- and source-critical reconstructions of Leviticus 17. He does not agree with them, but believes this chapter is a unified work. Nihan concludes that these critical reconstructions are unsupported by closer analysis of the structure of Leviticus 17. See also Schwartz, "Prohibition Concerning 'Eating,'" 34–66; Milgrom, *Leviticus 17–22*, 1447–51.

89. For discussion of the phrase אִישׁ אִישׁ, see Kiuchi, *Leviticus*, 314; Nihan, *Priestly Torah to Pentateuch*, 402; Schwartz, "Prohibition Concerning 'Eating,'" 38–39.

90. Even-Shoshan, *New Concordance*, 772–73, 775–76. It appears once in Leviticus 10, 12, and 15, and three times in Leviticus 17:11 and 14.

91. For why we find נֶפֶשׁ instead of אִישׁ אִישׁ in v. 15, see Schwartz, "Prohibition Concerning 'Eating,'" 41.

the motive clause of verse 13. The כרת in verse 14, therefore, is not directly connected to the instruction in verse 13.[92] Third, the key word דָּם appears thirteen times in this chapter, and ten out of the thirteen occurrences are located in Leviticus 17:10–14, and are closely related to the repeated word נֶפֶשׁ. These characteristics provide a basis for us to consider Leviticus 17 as a coherent literary unit in its context.[93]

Lastly, of the five instructions in Leviticus 17, the first two (vv. 3–7 and 8–9) are mainly concerned with the sacrificial practices of slaughtering the animals, especially in the well-being offerings, while the last two subunits (vv. 13–14 and 15–16) deal primarily with killing or eating nonsacrificial animals. Scholars disagree on how to interpret this arrangement. Milgrom identifies a chiastic pattern for these five instructions on a structural level, and Schwartz asserts that, on a thematic level, the prohibition of eating blood in verses 10–12 is the axiom of the other four instructions, and it is thus an absolute law.[94] Nihan, however, points out that it is difficult to agree with either Milgrom or Schwartz.[95] First, regarding a chiastic pattern in Leviticus 17 is concerned, neither the contents nor the terminology used in the texts demonstrate clear parallels between A (vv. 3–7) and A' (vv. 15–16) or between B (vv. 8–9) and B' (vv. 13–14).[96] Second, the theme of verses 3–9 is the proper location for worship and the only recipient of worship – YHWH – in Israelite sacrificial practice. It is not the prohibition of eating blood which could be the common theme for these five instructions.[97]

I regard Leviticus 17:10–12 in its literary context as an expansion of the blood prohibition which first appeared in Genesis 9:4. A review of the preceding passages may help clarify the importance of this text. The previous chapters in Leviticus (1–16) focus on setting up the sacrificial and priestly system after the building of the tabernacle; specifically, Leviticus 16 deals with the atonement of sins on the Day of Atonement. Leviticus 17:3–7 deals with

92. Nihan, *Priestly Torah to Pentateuch*, 404–5; Schwartz, 42.

93. Schwartz, 37–38. Schwartz also points out more common formulations of these five instructions in terms of the sentence structure and syntax of the verbal usages.

94. Milgrom, *Leviticus 17–22*, 1449; Schwartz, 42–43. Von Rad also considers Leviticus 17:10 as a further chief norm, forbidding any manner of eating of blood. Von Rad, *Studies in Deuteronomy*, 27.

95. Nihan, *Priestly Torah to Pentateuch*, 403, n.40, 424.

96. Nihan, 424, n.118.

97. Nihan, "Torah," 424.

the well-being offering, which is the only sacrifice in the OT system in which meat could be eaten by the common people. The prohibition of eating blood in Leviticus 17:10–12 thus makes a legitimate appearance in this context as a rationale and main principle for the Levitical ritual system.[98]

The Syntax and Terminology of Leviticus 17:10–16

Based on our previous discussion of the well-being offering, we will now focus on the exegesis of Leviticus 17:10–16, especially with regard to the prohibition of eating blood.

Leviticus 17:10–12

There are several exegetical points that must be considered in this text. First, it is noteworthy that the group of people to whom God addresses this prohibition differs from the recipients of the similar command in Genesis: verse 10 states that the prohibition of eating blood is specially announced to the community of the Israelites, including the sojourners among them. We also note that the prohibition refers to "whoever eats *any* blood" – verse 10 does not specify syntactically which kind of blood the people should avoid eating. However, based on its literary context, especially verses 3–9 and 13–14,[99] and the larger context of Leviticus 1–16, it is most likely that this prohibition should be understood within the Levitical ritual setting.

Second, the prohibition is followed by two sentences that convey the consequences of failure to comply with it. These two sentences, וְנָתַתִּי פָנַי בַּנֶּפֶשׁ הָאֹכֶלֶת אֶת־הַדָּם and וְהִכְרַתִּי אֹתָהּ מִקֶּרֶב עַמָּהּ:, in fact convey only one consequence for disobeying the prohibition: YHWH will set his face against the person, and the person will then be cut off among the people in logical sequence.[100]

98. Averbeck also points out that the sole reason for stating the blood prohibition in Leviticus 17 is because the well-being offering is the only kind of sacrifice of which common people could eat the meat. Averbeck, "כפר," in VanGemeren, *NIDOTTE* 2:695. Nihan also mentions similar ideas in Nihan, "Torah," 423.

99. Von Rad, *Studies in Deuteronomy*, 27. Von Rad contends that Leviticus 17:3–7 sets forth the chief regulation for killing animals in general, while Leviticus 17:8–9 deals with a specific sacrificial act, and that both of them make it necessary to go to the shrine. Moreover, Von Rad sees Leviticus 17:10 as a further chief norm forbidding any manner of eating of blood.

100. Kiuchi, *Leviticus*, 320. Kiuchi points out that in Leviticus 20, there are three occurrences (vv. 3, 5 and 6) where the phrase "set my face against [someone]" is followed by

Third, Leviticus 17:10–12 has a chiastic structure:[101]

A Whoever eats blood will be cut off from among his people (v. 10)
  B (כִּי) For it is the blood by means of the life that makes atonement (v. 11)
A (עַל־כֵּן) Therefore, no person among you may eat blood (v. 12)

This chiastic structure clearly conveys that the point of the prohibition is explained in verse 11.[102] Moreover, in verse 12 the phrase עַל־כֵּן "introduces the fundamental consequence of the preceding,"[103] and אָמַרְתִּי probably refers the rest of the words in this verse to the prohibition of eating blood in Leviticus 17:10.[104] We thus see a centric structure, with the law stated twice, both before and after the motive clause in the center. The purpose of this structure is to emphasize the rationale expressed by the motive clause rather than the law surrounding it.[105]

Fourth, let us turn our focus to verse 11 and try to understand what it conveys accurately. Schwartz suggests that there are three clauses in this verse, as shown in the following analysis.[106]

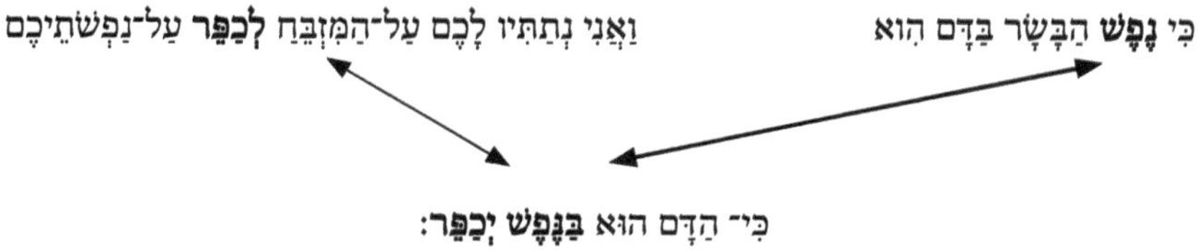

---

the cut off threat. Van der Merwe, Naudé, and Kroeze mention this function of the perfect aspect. Van der Merwe, Naudé, and Kroez, *Biblical Hebrew Reference Grammar*, 169.

101. Sklar also mentions this chiastic structure in Sklar, *Sin, Impurity, Sacrifice, Atonement*, 165.

102. Nihan, *Priestly Torah to Pentateuch*, 418. Nihan also observes that a motive clause introduced by כִּי in the beginning of v. 11 stands at the center of the structure.

103. Kiuchi, *Leviticus*, 322.

104. Nihan and Schwartz also regard this verse as a reference to Leviticus 17:11. Nihan, *Priestly Torah to Pentateuch*, 418; Schwartz, "Prohibition Concerning 'Eating,'" 46. However, Kiuchi sees this as a reference not only to Leviticus 17:10 but also to the relevant passages in Leviticus 3:17 and 7:26–27. Kiuchi, *Leviticus*, 323. For other scholars who support Kiuchi's view, see Schwartz, 46, n.1.

105. Schwartz, 45–46; Nihan, *Priestly Torah to Pentateuch*, 419.

106. Schwartz, 47.

Clause 3 (כִּי־הַדָּם הוּא בַּנֶּפֶשׁ יְכַפֵּר׃) in this structure provides a logical connection between clause 1 (כִּי נֶפֶשׁ הַבָּשָׂר בַּדָּם הִוא) and 2 (וַאֲנִי נְתַתִּיו לָכֶם עַל־הַמִּזְבֵּחַ לְכַפֵּר עַל־נַפְשֹׁתֵיכֶם).[107] Clause 2 is true because of clause 1. Clause 2 says that the blood is designated לְכַפֵּר; clause 3 combines the two and says that it is the blood that atones by means of life (כִּי־הַדָּם הוּא בַּנֶּפֶשׁ יְכַפֵּר).

In this verse, there are two clauses which bear a preposition, ב, in it. As for the first clause נֶפֶשׁ הַבָּשָׂר בַּדָּם הִוא, ב is a *beth essentiae*; it literally means "the life of the flesh is the blood."[108] ב could also be understood as *beth locative*, which would be translated as "the life of the flesh is in the blood."[109] This clause affirms that there is a close relationship between the animal's blood and the animal's life. However, the statement does not stop here, but continues in the second clause in verse 11, וַאֲנִי נְתַתִּיו לָכֶם עַל־הַמִּזְבֵּחַ לְכַפֵּר עַל־נַפְשֹׁתֵיכֶם. There is a conjunctive ו between these two clauses, which indicates that the following clause is also part of the rationale that the first clause is trying to convey. As Gilders correctly points out, "Consuming blood is not prohibited simply because it is identified with life. In this clause, YHWH indicates that he has done something with the life-identified blood."[110] YHWH claims that he has instituted the application of the blood to the altar for the Israelites, to atone them.[111]

There are several perspectives on the meaning of the ב in the third clause, כִּי־הַדָּם הוּא בַּנֶּפֶשׁ יְכַפֵּר. Averbeck points out that, among these perspectives,[112] the instrumental usage of this ב, which means "by" or "through," is the most possible interpretation "if one takes serious consideration of the parallel

---

107. Schwartz, 47. See also Feder, *Blood Expiation*, 203.

108. Milgrom, "Prolegomenon to Leviticus 17:11," 149. Milgrom points out that the ב in the phrase בַּדָּם is a *beth essentiae*. According to Joüon, "From a grammatical point of view the *Beth essentiae* is particularly important . . . ב indicating the predicate . . . (the ב adds practically nothing to the meaning)." Joüon, *Grammar of Biblical Hebrew*, 486.

109. Van der Merwe, Naudé, and Kroez, *Biblical Hebrew Reference Grammar*, 280; See also Rooker, *Leviticus*, 236.

110. Gilders, *Blood Ritual in Hebrew Bible*, 169.

111. Sprinkle, *Biblical Law*, 114. "The command not to eat the flesh with the blood not only reminded the Israelite of God's use of blood for atoning sacrifice but also inculcated respect for animal life." Regarding Leviticus 17:11 as clearly presenting an interpretation of blood manipulation, see Gilders, *Blood Ritual in Hebrew Bible*, 158–80.

112. Averbeck summarizes that there are three meanings proposed for the preposition ב. It is a ב of price, a ב of exchange, or an instrumental ב. See a brief discussion in Averbeck, "כפר," in VanGemeren, *NIDOTTE* 2:697. Also see detailed discussions of the perspectives of interpreting this proposition b in Hartley, *Leviticus*, 274–76, and Budd, *Leviticus*, 248–49.

between 'to make atonement (*l^{e}kappēr*) for your lives . . .' in Lev 17:11 with Exod 30:15–16."[113]

The focal point of the mention of blood, then, is not animal blood as it flows through the veins, which is identified with the animal's life, but the shedding of blood from the animal,[114] which indicated that life had ended and the atonement was done on the altar. Blood is the symbol of life assigned by YHWH for the purpose of atonement on the altar.[115] Schwartz thus explains that "the point is not that the blood is life." One might not completely agree with his claim, but another angle suggested by Schwartz can be used to understand this proclamation: "when blood is gone, there is no life."[116] The people's life could be atoned due to the blood shed by the sacrificial animal.[117]

---

113. Averbeck, "כפר," in VanGemeren, *NIDOTTE* 2:697–98. The following scholars hold similar perspectives on the interpretation of this ב in clause 3 in Leviticus 17:11. Schwartz point outs that the ב in בַּנֶּפֶשׁ יְכַפֵּר is a ב of agency. Schwartz, "Prohibition Concerning 'Eating,'" 47. Milgrom also emphasizes that the ב here is a *beth instrumenti* (instrument, "by means of life"), not a *beth essentiae* (essence, "is life") or a *beth pretii* (price, "for the cost of life"). Milgrom, *Leviticus 17–22*, 1448. Kiuchi, Sklar, Feder, Willis, and Hartley also consider the ב with the meaning of "by" or "through." Kiuchi, *Purification Offering*, 104–6; Kiuchi, *Leviticus*, 321–22; Sklar, *Sin, Impurity, Sacrifice, Atonement*, 168–74; Feder, *Blood Expiation*, 204; Willis, *Leviticus*, 154; Hartley, *Leviticus*, 274–77.

114. "To the Hebrews the blood of men, animals, and birds seemed to contain the very soul of the living creatures. In fact the blood was identical with the soul. . . . This also helps to explain why, amongst many ancient peoples, liver, which was regarded as a mass of coagulated blood, came to be synonymous with life. The liver often occurs in Semitic literatures as the seat of the emotions . . . in Lam. 2: 11, where Jerusalem, grieving over her destruction as a mother robbed of her children, exclaims, 'My liver is poured out on the ground,' meaning that her very life has been destroyed." Farbridge, *Studies in Biblical*, 228–29.

115. However, Ross sees the blood as not only the symbol of life, but life itself. "It is this higher use for shed blood that greatly enhanced the prohibition against eating blood. Since God had designed blood for atonement, it had to be brought to God. Eating it made common or profane something that God had intended for the sanctuary." Ross, *Holiness to the LORD*, 335–36. Schwartz disagrees with this view, contending that the prohibition of eating blood in Leviticus 17 is restricted to the sacrificial animals rather than all the animals. See Schwartz, "Prohibition Concerning 'Eating,'" 60–61.

116. Schwartz, 49. Vervenne explains that "to the so-called primitive mind, the blood seems to be the visible 'soul' or principle of life; the loss of blood is the discernible threat of death. As already said, however, blood is not only a life-giving substance but also a symbol of death." Vervenne, "Blood Is Life,'" 453.

117. Wenham, *Genesis 1–15*, 193. "God's provision of animal life to sustain human life is paradoxical. To preserve man's respect for life, he is forbidden to eat 'flesh with its life, i.e. blood.'" Milgrom, *Leviticus 1–16*, 154–55. Milgrom adds that the food laws, in accord with the ethical purpose of inculcating reverence for animal life, limited the slaughtering of animals: only for food, only certain species, and only certain procedures. However, this view has been criticized by some of Milgrom's own students, especially Firmage and Wright. See Firmage, "Biblical Dietary Laws," 195 n.24; Wright, "Observations on Ethical Foundations," 193–98.

Leviticus 17:13–14

According to Leviticus 17:11 and 14, כִּי נֶפֶשׁ הַבָּשָׂר בַּדָּם הִוא וַאֲנִי נְתַתִּיו לָכֶם עַל־הַמִּזְבֵּחַ לְכַפֵּר עַל־נַפְשֹׁתֵיכֶם כִּי־הַדָּם הוּא בַּנֶּפֶשׁ יְכַפֵּר: and כִּי־נֶפֶשׁ כָּל־בָּשָׂר דָּמוֹ בְנַפְשׁוֹ הוּא וָאֹמַר לִבְנֵי יִשְׂרָאֵל דַּם כָּל־בָּשָׂר לֹא תֹאכֵלוּ כִּי נֶפֶשׁ כָּל־בָּשָׂר דָּמוֹ הִוא כָּל־אֹכְלָיו יִכָּרֵת:, the text uses a similar structure three times to explain the relationship between blood and life: כִּי נֶפֶשׁ הַבָּשָׂר בַּדָּם הִוא (v. 11), כִּי־נֶפֶשׁ כָּל־בָּשָׂר דָּמוֹ בְנַפְשׁוֹ הוּא (v. 14), and כִּי נֶפֶשׁ כָּל־בָּשָׂר דָּמוֹ הִוא (v. 14) This identification of blood with life is unique in the ANE world.[118] Sprinkle explains that "the blood symbolic of the life, had to be poured back to God even for nonatoning slaughter to symbolize that only by divine permission could even animal life be taken."[119] The draining of blood presumably reflected the belief that the blood contained the life force of the animal.[120] The blood must therefore be "covered" or expiated by bringing it to the altar.[121] As for the blood to be covered by dirt in Leviticus 17:14, the context does not provide an explanation of how the identification of life and blood relates to the requirement that blood be covered by dirt after being poured out. Schwartz points out that it is easy enough to conclude that the pouring out and covering are intended to dispose of the blood, which may not be eaten.[122]

118. "The Hebrew treatment of the oath sacrifice points up the symbolism of blood peculiar to OT texts . . . it gives blood a very different meaning – life and not death. . . . Its conclusion: careful regard for the evidence indicates that the Hebrew attitude toward blood is unique." McCarthy, "Further Notes," 210.

119. Sprinkle refers to this purpose as the "ethical lesson." Sprinkle, *Biblical Law*, 113–14.

120. "In ancient times blood was considered a life force (Deut 12:23). The prohibition does not require that no blood at all be consumed, but only that the blood must be drained. The draining of the blood before eating the meat was a way of returning the life force of the animal to the God who gave it life. This offers recognition that they have taken the life with permission and are partaking of God's bounty as his guests." Walton and Matthews, *IVP Bible Background Commentary*, 30. However, Walton points out that "ritual draining of blood is not attested in ancient Near Eastern literature." Walton, "Genesis," 53; Cf. Gorman, *Ideology of Ritual*, 181–89; Vervenne, "Blood Is Life,'" 451–70.

121. Hallo, "Origins of Sacrificial Cult," 5.

122. Schwartz, "Prohibition Concerning 'Eating,'" 61–62. See also Noth, *Leviticus*, 132. A different perspective, which I do not agree with, interprets the disposal of the blood of nonsacrificial animals as a special kind of instruction from YHWH. I regard any kind of disposal of blood, whether the blood of nonsacrificial animals or the blood of the sacrificial animals that is not used for the ritual purposes, as the simple action of disposal without any ritual meaning. For example, Gilders explains that these instructions establish disposal of blood from nonsacrificial animals as a ritualized activity prescribed by YHWH, since the method of disposing it is specifically defined and is different from any normal or casual disposal of other waste products. Gilders, *Blood Ritual in Hebrew Bible*, 23–24. Furthermore, Gilders points out that while he does not agree with Schwatz's narrow understanding of "ritual" activity and

Leviticus 17:15–16

The regulation here, which is a continuation of the previous sections (17:10–12 and 13–14), obviously has a contextual and literary connection with the prohibition of eating blood. Milgrom argues that, since Leviticus 17:15–16 is located in the context of the threefold prohibition of eating blood in verses 11, 12, and 14, its point is that an animal that died naturally or violently must presumably be drained of its blood before it is eaten.[123] This argument is not logical, however. For example, if an animal died from sickness without the presence of its owner, its blood might not be drained from its body when it was found dead. Such a requirement could only be met in the case of animals torn by beasts, where the blood of the animal would be drained because of the wound. One of the possible reasons that eating clean animals found dead makes a person unclean is that the blood of this kind of animal has not been properly drained before the meat is consumed.[124] Moreover, since the blood in the dead animals has dried and there is no reason to drain the blood before preparing the food, its flesh has no "life" in it.[125] The meat from it is therefore not banned, just regarded as unclean.[126]

We may observe in the text that this regulation does not strictly prohibit eating animals found dead, since Leviticus 11:39–40 discusses the procedure for cleansing from this unclean situation. In fact, this procedure is identical to the one required for cleansing after touching or moving a dead animal body.[127] It is possible, then, that a person who eats an animal found dead is pronounced ceremonially unclean due to their contact with death rather than possible remnants of blood in the animal's body.[128]

---

argument that the pouring out and covering are not ritual activities at all, he agrees with Schwartz that it "is right to question the explanations of the treatment of blood that identify it as a means of returning the blood to God or fulfilling some other cultic purpose." Gilders, *Blood Ritual in Hebrew Bible*, 200, n.51. For Schwartz's view on this topic, see Schwartz, "Prohibition Concerning 'Eating,'" 61 n.3.

123. Milgrom, *Leviticus 17–22*, 1487. Baker also holds to a similar stand of explanation. He concludes, "their blood was drained and buried, in conformity with the last law, even though this was not specifically mentioned." Baker, "Leviticus," 127.

124. Also see in Hartley, *Leviticus*, 277; Rooker, *Leviticus*, 238.

125. Willis, *Leviticus*, 155.

126. Kleinig, *Leviticus*, 366.

127. Rooker also mentions this. Rooker, *Leviticus*, 238.

128. Gerstenberger, *Leviticus*, 239.

What is the connection between these two verses related to cleansing after eating dead animals and the prohibition of eating blood in Leviticus 17:10–14? Sprinkle suggests that the prohibition of eating blood associates YHWH with life and wholeness rather than death and disorder. Therefore, he asserts, eating or touching carcasses rendered a person unclean because they obviously have to do with death; however, "purification rituals symbolize movement from death toward life and accordingly involved blood, the color red, and living water, all of which are symbols of life (Lev 17:11; 14:5, 50; Num 19:2, 17, etc.)."[129]

Theological Implications

On the level of literary context, the prohibition of eating blood in the Pentateuch magnifies the concept of fear of YHWH who is the Creator, the only God, the solemn and holy One. After the flood, in Genesis 9:3–6, YHWH gives the command that while human beings are allowed to eat meat from animals, they must not eat the meat with its blood, its life. This first prohibition of eating blood is located in a context of covenant between YHWH and Noah, who represents the human being later in history. The preceding passage (Gen 9:1–2) discusses YHWH's blessings and commandments, which echo those recorded after creation in Genesis 1–2. Moreover, the following section (Gen 9:5–6) continues with the theme of blood, developing it into an ethical statement that reflects the blood-for-blood principle, which relates the consequences of homicide to the fact that God made the people in his own image (Gen 9:6).[130] We suggest, therefore, that this very first passage regarding the prohibition of eating blood occurs against a distinct contextual background focused on the fear of YHWH as the Creator of life. It is he who associates the life with blood, and obedience to this prohibition reflects the holiness of YHWH – especially his ethical holiness.

Second, Leviticus 17:10–16 offers a new perspective on the designation of blood as life – it is used for the atonement on the altar. This not only

129. Sprinkle, *Biblical Law*, 114–15.

130. "Not only do humans kill animals for substance, some humans resort to killing other humans, at times for profit. Still, God prohibits the shedding of human life, because humans are created in the image of God, the *imago Dei*. Whosoever sheds the blood of humans shall have his or her own blood spilled by humans, blood for blood." De La Torre, *Genesis*, 122.

identifies the blood with life, but also specifically points out that the purpose of the blood given to the Israelites is to atone for them on the altar. This is expressed in a cultic textual context. As we have seen, Leviticus 17:10–12 clearly states that the purpose of identifying blood with life is to provide atonement through the sacrifices prescribed in Leviticus 1–16. Moreover, the locus of Leviticus 17:10–12 is the Mosaic covenant on Mount Sinai, and the text is located not only after the instructions for the sacrifices and the inauguration of the priests, but also after the first sin of death conducted by the priests (Lev 10), the first observation of the Day of Atonement (Lev 16), and the regulation of cleanness and uncleanness between them. This association of the blood with the clear purpose of atonement in Leviticus 17:10–12 is obviously related to the holiness of YHWH and the adoration of him by his covenantal people, the Israelites. It thus takes the concept of fear of YHWH – the Creator, the only God, the solemn and holy One – a step further, into the aspect of ritual holiness. In Leviticus 17:10–12, YHWH identifies the blood with life, and prohibits the Israelites and the people in their community from eating it, in order to assign the shedding of blood as the symbol of atonement, especially in the context of covenantal relationship between YHWH and the Israelites. In contrast, we see in Leviticus 17:13–16 that blood not used for atonement on the altar – the blood of game animals – loses its symbolic association with atonement and it is poured out on the ground and covered by dirt to prevent ingestion. This represents a return to the basic principle behind the prohibition of eating blood stated in Genesis 9:3–6, in which obeying the regulation demonstrates fear of YHWH as the Creator and the holy One and expresses ethical holiness.

Third, in Leviticus 19:26a we find another occurrence of the prohibition of eating blood, this time located among the warnings delivered to the Israelites when they enter the land of Canaan. Even though there is no clear purpose for this prohibition stated in the text, by its context we may infer that its purpose is ethical holiness. The Israelites belong to YHWH, so they must reflect his image – including his holiness – in their daily behaviors. The Israelites are expected to be different and distinct among the nations because of their covenantal relationship with YHWH.

Finally, in Deuteronomy 12:15–16 and 20–25 we see the prohibition of eating blood in a literary context that emphasizes the giving of worship to YHWH alone. These verses announce no specific purpose for the prohibition, but their literary context is a discussion of the expectation that the Israelites display ethical holiness in their future lives in Canaan. Again, the blood of nonsacrificial animals does not carry the symbolic meaning of atonement, and can be disposed of by pouring it out like water.

To sum up, this prohibition consistently occurs in the context of covenant. Among these seven occurrences in the Pentateuch, only Leviticus 17:10–12 clearly states that the purpose of not eating blood is its designation for atonement on the altar, and this passage is situated in the conclusion of the sacrificial system instructed by YHWH. These features make it clear that the blood is assigned to be a symbol to life, and that only the blood shed on the altar is reserved for the use of atonement.[131] Blood shed by animals hunted for game, like blood remaining in the body of animals subject to natural deaths, totally forfeits any association with atonement.

131. "The prohibition of consumption of blood expressly indicates its symbolic value in representing life and in being given for atonement (see Lev 17:11; also Lev 3:17; 7:26–27; 19:26; etc.). The fact that animals may be eaten means that animal blood may be shed, though not consumed." Kuruvilla, *Genesis*, 125. See also Hamilton, *Book of Genesis*, 314.

CHAPTER 5

Conclusion

The aim of the study is to define the role of Leviticus 17 in the macrostructure of Leviticus, so that we may treat the exegetical debates regarding altar centralization and the prohibition against the consumption of blood in relation to each other, and also in relation to the role of Leviticus 17 in the book of Leviticus and with regard to the holistic framework of the Mosaic covenant at Sinai (Exod 19–Num 10). As we approach the end of this journey, I would like to offer the following observations, focusing particularly on the correlation among the chapters of this book:

In chapter 1, I reviewed several crucial topics related to a thorough exegetical consideration of Leviticus 17. First, I examined the debate on the Priestly Document and Holiness Code. Not only is this debate related to the macrostructure of Leviticus as a book, it also develops into the issue of dating. This discussion was followed by a consideration of the macrostructure of Leviticus in light of the Sinai covenant as a whole, which led to the conclusion that the primary issue in the structure of Leviticus is the role or location of Leviticus 17 in the book as a whole. In the scholarly debate on the structure of Leviticus, the most prominent inconsistency is the placement of Leviticus 17: some group it with the succeeding chapters, Leviticus 18–26; some exclude it from Leviticus 18–26; some regard it as a transitional chapter between Leviticus 1–16 and 18–26; some isolate Leviticus 16–17 as a literary subunit that forms a bridge between Leviticus 1–15 and 18–26. This diversity of opinion prompted us to discuss the role of Leviticus 17 in detail in chapter 2.

The literature review portion of this study covered a number of issues. As described in the problem statement, following the investigation of the structure of Leviticus, the approach to the meaning of rituals is of foremost importance. I concluded that the rituals in the OT are prescribed within a context of relationship-building between Yahweh and the Israelites, and that they convey the meanings assigned by the author in their textual contexts. While similar rituals exist in different cultural or textual contexts, the symbolic meanings attached to the rituals may be varied. Therefore, the specific meaning of a ritual in an OT text should be identified in its literary context. Finally, the literature review addressed scholarly arguments regarding altar centralization and the prohibition of eating blood in Leviticus 17. These two exegetical issues have been basically treated from a theological perspective, while the textual contexts of Leviticus and the Sinai covenant as a whole have been neglected.

In chapter 2, I moved on to a comprehensive survey of different approaches to the structure of Leviticus that have been proposed by scholars throughout the history of Levitical studies. In the Pentateuch, laws and narratives are woven together. The narratives provided the historical contexts for Yahweh's revelation and his laws, and testified to the relationship between Yahweh and the Israelites. In the Sinai pericope – Exodus 19 to Numbers 10:10 – the inclusio framework of Leviticus 1:1 and Numbers 1:1 emphasizes the tent of meeting through the use of the specific formula וַיְדַבֵּר יְהוָה אֵלָיו מֵאֹהֶל מוֹעֵד and וַיְדַבֵּר יְהוָה אֶל־מֹשֶׁה בְּמִדְבַּר סִינַי בְּאֹהֶל מוֹעֵד, which appear only in these two verses. This structural element denotes the importance of Leviticus within the Sinai pericope. Moreover, since the OT presents us with ritual texts rather than live ritual actions, literary devices such as the narrative framework and rhetorical emphases are more important than the social context which we might try to rebuild.

In terms of the structure of Leviticus per se, we identified the close relationship between the first part of Leviticus (chapters 1–16) and Leviticus 17 by identifying the thematic similarity of chapters 16 and 17. The theme of animal sacrifices appears in both chapters. Furthermore, even though it is the well-being offering which appears in Leviticus 17 rather than the sacrifices of atonement discussed in the previous chapter, the theme of atonement is not absent in Leviticus 17. It recurs in the second half of chapter 17 as the reason of the prohibition of eating blood is revealed. Furthermore, we noticed that the beginning of Leviticus 17 does not include a specific formula to introduce a new paragraph, such as we find elsewhere in the Sinai pericope (Exod 19:3;

Lev 1:1; and Num 1:1). Instead, the close connection between chapters 16 and 17 supports the continuity between Leviticus 1–16 and 17.

At the same time, however, we also observed the connection between Leviticus 17 and 18–27. These two parts are joined through the appearance of the exodus theme, the repetitive motive clause and keyword (קדשׁ), the commandment to keep the Sabbath, the use of personal pronouns, and the repetition of the כרת punishment. In addition, the chiastic structure of the speech formulas demonstrates the unity of Leviticus 17–22 in particular, and highlights the emphasis placed the structure and message of this passage. Based on all these factors, I proposed the following structure: Leviticus 1–7, 8–16, 17–22, 23–27.

Once we concluded, based on observation of the speech introductory formula and the contents of the regulations in these chapters, that Leviticus 17 belongs to a subunit with the following chapters (Lev 17–22), we could clearly see the parallel structures of the nonritual sections in the Sinai pericope (Exod 20:22–Exod 24; Lev 17–27; and Deut 12–26), as Averbeck points out.[1] On the other hand, it is helpful to discuss the altar centralization and blood atonement in Leviticus 17 in relation to the other so-called altar laws, found in the beginning of its parallel sections in Exodus and Deuteronomy. This approach helps the readers understand the two exegetical issues in Leviticus 17 within the whole structure of the Sinai covenant, which extends from Exodus 20 to Deuteronomy 30.

In chapter 3, we focused our discussion on the first exegetical issue in Leviticus 17: the regulation of well-being offerings. First, we reexamined the occurrences of זֶבַח שְׁלָמִים in the OT, excluding those appearing in poetic and wisdom literature. This led us to the following conclusions regarding the meaning of this type of offering. The well-being offering accents the status of well-being in the offerer's relationships with Yahweh and with other humans. It denotes not only the covenantal relationship with Yahweh but also the reconfirmation of the covenant. Moreover, well-being offerings expressed people's willingness to seek Yahweh's guidance in their lives, bearing the concept of collective dedication to Yahweh when kings offered them to dedicate the temple to Yahweh.

1. Averbeck, "Cult in Deuteronomy," 258–59

Second, I reviewed what we know about well-being offerings elsewhere in the ANE context, especially in the Ugaritic ritual documents. This discussion revealed several similarities between well-being offerings in Israel and Ugarit. In both cases, the people would eat and drink from the offerings after the ceremony; both involved blood sacrifices; both denoted a certain level of harmony between the offerers and the deities; both involved offerers of either gender; and both are recorded to have been offered by kings. A number of differences could also be observed. The purpose of sacrificial banquets in Ugarit was to provide food to satisfy the deities in order to receive blessings from them; in the OT, Yahweh is never described as eating the offerings. Moreover, there was a distinctive boundary between the offerers and the offering recipient (Yahweh) among the Israelites, while in Ugarit the lists of sacrifices for the gods seem to indicate that the gods enjoyed a high social status in Ugaritic society. As for the animals used in the well-being offerings, both OT and Ugaritic documents describe blood sacrifices, but the donkey is included in the lists of sacrifices only in Ugaritic documents.

Finally, in chapter 3 I addressed the scholarly debate around altar centralization, and arrived at the conclusion that in the Pentateuch's three major passages of so-called "altar laws" (Exod 20:24–26; Lev 17:1–7; and Deut 12:2–5), we can see a development from the most lenient laws, to the strictest, and finally to a moderate position. We concluded that the best strategy for interpreting this textual phenomenon is not to rearrange the chronological sequence of these passages based on the concepts they express, but to examine their textual contexts – the surrounding narratives – in order to understand the transition hermeneutically, sociologically, and chronologically. This approach shows us that the altar laws discussed in different textual passages vary in response to the different needs arising in the different historical periods in which each specific law was announced.

Chapter 4 covered the prohibition of eating blood. The Pentateuch contains three passages that discuss this regulation. Genesis 9:3–6 appears against a distinct contextual background focused on the fear of Yahweh as the Creator of life. It is he who associates the life with blood, and obedience to this prohibition reflects Yahweh's holiness, especially his ethical holiness. In Leviticus 17:10–12, Yahweh identifies the blood with life and prohibits the Israelites and others in their community from eating it. This establishes the shedding of blood as the symbol of atonement, especially in the context of the covenantal relationship between YHWH and the Israelites. Finally, Deuteronomy 12:15–16 and 20–25 announce no specific purpose for the prohibition, but their literary context is a discussion of the expectation that the Israelites display ethical holiness in their future lives in Canaan. Across these three passages, we can see that this prohibition consistently occurs in the context of covenant. Moreover, Leviticus 17:10–12 clearly states that the purpose of not eating blood is its designation for atonement on the altar, and this passage is situated in the conclusion of the sacrificial system instructed by YHWH. These features make it clear that the blood is assigned to be a symbol to life, and that only the blood shed on the altar was reserved for the use of atonement.

I would now like to sum up several contributions of this research. First, this book has examined the interpretation of ritual texts. Yahweh assigned symbolic meanings when he annouced the ritual regulations to the Israelites, and one can usually discern the meanings in the OT ritual texts. Second, recognizing the importance of the relationship between narratives and laws, we have examined the relationship between the speech formula, audiences, and contents of the ritual regulations in Leviticus. Subsequently, we discovered the very close sturcture in Leviticus 17–22 as a subunit in the book of Leviticus. This observation, along with the macro-pattern in the Sinai pericope proposed by Richard E. Averbeck with regard to the literary unit of Leviticus 17–27,[2] provides a better understanding not only of Leviticus but of the Sinai pericope as a whole. Third, this research applies an understanding of the literary structure of Leviticus to the interpretive issues of altar centralization and the blood atonement in Leviticus 17. We not only interpreted these two issues in their own literary context in Leviticus, but also extended the discussion to related passages in the corpus of Pentateuch. This gives us a more comprehensive understanding of the development of these two issues in their literary contexts, both diachronically and synchronically.

Let us now turn to the final part of this research: the application of the understanding of the blood atonement principle in Leviticus 17 to a particular context. In Chinese culture, there is a common dietary habit of eating cooked blood pudding. Here at the end of this conclusion, I would like to devote a

2. Averbeck, "The Cult in Deuteronomy," 256–58.

section to discussing how the theological implications of this study could be applied to daily life in Chinese culture.

The Practice of Eating Blood in Chinese Culture and the Prohibition of Eating Blood

In Chinese culture, some concepts of dietetic therapy or food therapy are passed down through the generations. Even though people acquire these concepts unwittingly as they grow up in their cultural setting, in this section we would like not only to summarize some concepts obtained from oral tradition, but also to present some documentation of the teachings of dietetic therapy in the traditional Chinese medicine. This section will focus on the practice of eating blood in Chinese culture.

The Practice of Eating Blood in Chinese Oral Tradition

A major contributor to practice of eating blood in Chinese culture is the concept of "like nourishes like" (以形補形), which is very common in Chinese society.[3] Applied to Chinese daily diets, the concept of "like nourishes like" expresses the idea that "if one eats an organ of an animal, then it will be good for the corresponding organ in one's body."[4] For example, "eating brain nourishes your brain" (吃腦補腦), "eating liver nourishes your liver" (吃肝補肝), and so on – thus, "eating blood nourishes your blood" (吃血補血). Moreover, according to Chinese tradition, some foods benefit specific organs in the body because of their similar shape or appearance. For example, since a walnut has a similar appearance to the brain, there is a traditional belief that "eating walnuts benefits your brain" (吃核桃補腦). Similarly, "eating beans benefits your kidneys" (吃豆補腎), while "eating apricot kernel benefits your heart" (吃杏仁補心).[5]

3. For a detailed discussion of different practices of eating blood in Chinese culture, see Li, "Culture of Blood." This article is in Chinese.

4. Sheik, "Like Nourishes Like." See also Shen-Nong Limited, "Like Nourishes Like." "The Chinese commonly use animal organs in their recipes to fortify the corresponding organs in humans' bodies, because these organs carry out similar functions in animals, and therefore; they can be used to enhance weakened organs. E.g. chicken feet are eaten for nourishing the legs, pig brain is said to benefit the brain." Both articles cited here are in Chinese.

5. *People.Cn*, "Walnuts Benefit Brain." This article is in Chinese.

These concepts have been passed down from generation to generation for thousands of years in Chinese culture, and despite a historical lack of specific and objective proof for the effectiveness of these health principles, Chinese people still believe them and unconsciously practice them in their everyday diet. In the twenty-first century, however, it has been discovered that there are some scientific foundations to the concept of "like nourishes like" (以形補形). For example, some hormones and enzymes extracted from animal hearts are used clinically to treat patients who suffer from heart disease or other illnesses. Animal livers contain vitamin A, the mineral iron, and RNA, which benefit those who suffer from jaundice, anemic disorders, or hepatitis and liver cirrhosis.[6] As for the brain, a 2014 report indicated that there is a specific part of a sequence of peptide in pig's brain which might be beneficial to the treatment of Alzheimer disease. Extracting this particular element from the pig's brain is a challenge, however, and the necessary technology is still under development.[7] Moreover, recent research has asserted "that dietary supplementation with walnuts may have a beneficial effect in reducing the risk, delaying the onset, or slowing the progression of, or preventing AD [Alzheimer's disease]."[8]

Another tradition which might reinforce the prevalence of the practice of eating blood in Chinese culture is that Chinese people regard red, purple, or black colored foods as nourishing to the body – especially benefitting "blood reproduction" (補血). Foods such as red beans, red dates, red wine, purple grapes, purple rice, black rice, black chicken, and pig's blood pudding, among others, are regarded as beneficial to human blood. The preference for the color red in Chinese culture is also relevant to this discussion. Chinese people favor the color red not only in ideology but also in the practices of daily lives. In

6. "For example, Cytochrome C, Corhormone and Coenzyme A could be extracted from the animal heart and these are applied to the clinical treatments for some heart diseases and other diseases. As for liver, it contains many nutrients, for instance, Vitamin A could treat jaundice, iron could treat anemia and its RNA could treat hepatitis and cirrhosis. The specific biological cells extracted from kidney could be used to treat chronic nephritis." Xiaoyan, "In Terms of Like." (This article appears in Chinese. Translation provided by the author of this book.) For the medical usage of cells extracted from kidney, see also *Yuhengfengbio.Com*, "Human Renal Glomerular." This article is available in both English and Chinese.

7. Lin and Li, "Specific Peptide Sequences." This article is in Chinese.

8. Balu Muthaiyah et al., "Dietary Supplementation of Walnuts," 1197–1405. See also Kunkle, "Walnuts Appear to Delay."; Lyu, "Cause of Alzheimer's Disease." This article is in Chinese.

Chinese tradition, red symbolizes a life connection, the powerful material of fire, the sun that sustains life,[9] and the element which drives evil away and brings prosperity to the people.[10] Therefore, in Chinese culture people not only prefer the color red for food, believing that it will benefit the body, but also prefer to use red in decorations to denote a celebratory atmosphere for Chinese New Year, weddings, and any other important festival or place.[11]

The Teaching of Eating Blood in Ancient Chinese Literature

What does ancient Chinese literature teach regarding the concept of "like nourishes like" (以形補形)? How can we understand this from the perspective of dietetic therapy in traditional Chinese medicine? We may consider the following discussion regarding the documents.

The earliest traceable document to discuss the benefit of eating blood is entitled *Invaluable Prescriptions for Ready Reference*, written by Simiao Sun (孫思邈, AD 581–682) during the Tang Dynasty. Sun believed that correct diet can not only take care of health but also cure diseases.[12] Sun wrote that eating an animal's lung could cure coughing, eating animal's heart could be helpful in dealing with forgetfulness, and eating pig's blood could stop bleeding and strokes.[13]

Second, according to the category of animal (獸部) in *Compendium of Materia Medica* (本草綱目, Ben Cao Gang Mu), written by Shizhen Li (李時珍) during the Ming Dynasty (明朝), pig's brain could treat dizziness, pig's bone

9. There is an ancient Chinese idiom, "the arrival of the sun gives birth to all the creatures (日至而萬物生)" which is recorded in *The Handbook of Astronomy by Huainazi* (淮南子天文訓). There is a positive attitude toward the color red rather than the color white, which symbolizes death, bloodless and evil, in Chinese culture. Yang, "Preliminary Study." This article is in Chinese.

10. Li, "Impression Chinese Red." This article is in Chinese.

11. Regarding the preference for red and yellow in Chinese culture, see "Analysis of Difference." This article appears in Chinese with an English abstract.

12. In Chinese, it is called "千金要方, Qian Jin Yao Fang" or "千金翼方, Qian Jin Yi Fang." Regarding the development of Sun's concept of diet and health, please refer to Lin, "Study of Sun Si-Miao's." Also see Wang, "Investigation of Suan Sy-Meau's." (These two dissertations are in Chinese.) Sun's medical theory has a wide influence on the Chinese and Japanese traditional medicine in following centuries; therefore, people call him "the king of medicine" (藥王).

13. Sun, *Collection*, 394–95. "Lung: moderate, nourishing lung and stopping coughing; . . . heart: preventing forgetfulness; . . . pig's blood: moderate, astringent, non-toxic, benefit for those who bleed constantly . . . and for those who have stroke or are wounded." For discussion of other benefits of eating the blood of different animals, see Sun, *Invaluable Prescriptions*, 7:41–45. These two texts are in Chinese.

marrow could benefit bone marrow, eating blood could benefit our blood, and so on.[14]

The Attitude of Chinese Christians toward the Practice of Eating Blood in Chinese Culture

How should the Pentateuch passages prohibiting the eating of blood be applied for Chinese Christians today? It was easy for the Israelites to know clearly what they should do in response to the food laws and the prohibition of eating blood given by YHWH in the days of the OT, but what is the principle we should follow as Christians today? In Sprinkle's discussion on "Understanding Laws of Clean and Unclean," he analyzes the rationale behind the Levitical purity laws in detail. Among seven articles he lists, the most plausible rationales for the purity laws are separation from the Gentiles and the contrast between the holiness of God and the contamination of humans.[15] These principles give us something to think about when we ponder the rationale for the prohibition of eating blood within its literary context.

As we have summarized in the second point of the previous section "Theological Implications" above, the cultic reason for the prohibition of eating blood – revealed only in Leviticus 17:10–12 – is related to the atonement of sin. God has assigned the blood as the symbol of life, and once it is shed in the sacrifices it is for atonement. This ritual function of shed blood has a strong connection with the holiness of God versus the contaminations of humanity: only through the atonement fulfilled by the shed blood of animals could sinful humans approach the holy God.

14. "According to the category of animal in *Compendium of Materia Medica* written by Shizhen Li in Ming Dynasty, as for any of the animals in the genus Sus alone, it is recorded as the following: the pig marrow can nourish your marrow and benefit those who are weak and tired; the pig heart can reduce perspiration and the coughing up of blood caused by a weak heart or acute heart pain; the pig liver can nourish your liver, improve your eyesight and cure abdominal edema caused by liver failure; the pig spleen can strengthen a weak stomach and spleen; the pig kidney can improve the functions carried out by your kidney and benefit your bladder, etc. Moreover, in *Compendium of Materia Medica*, it is stated that eating the stomach of an animal cures your stomach, eating the heart of an animal benefits your heart, eating the blood of an animal cleanses your blood, eating the bone of an animal benefits your bone, eating the marrow of an animal nourishes your marrow and eating the skin of an animal treats your skin. From this point of view, we can see that Chinese Traditional Medicine values the theory of 'Like nourishes like.'" "Foundation of Like." This article is in Chinese; the author of this book provided the above translation.

15. Sprinkle, *Biblical Law*, 116–19.

Moreover, we have seen that all the passages that prohibit eating blood in the Pentateuch occur in the context of a relationship between God and humans/Israelites that is initiated by God himself. After humanity's fall in the garden of Eden, God determines to restore his relationship with humanity by his own initiative, through actions such as making a covenant with human beings. In God-human relationship, then, we must not minimize the absolute holiness of God or the total depravity of human beings; however, the nature of atonement in this relationship is crucial, since it is only through the atonement provided for in the covenant that human beings can access the holy God. In the OT, blood is an important symbol of life and atonement, but the NT reveals that, since Christ shed his blood on the cross, salvation comes upon those who believe in him. Through the blood of Christ, our sins have been atoned, and we may come to worship the holy God without any fear. The symbolic identification of shed blood with life and atonement was fully fulfilled in the death of Christ on the cross. Furthermore, in Leviticus 19:26 we see another rationale behind the prohibition of eating blood: the OT separation of the Israelites from the Gentiles, was meant to ensure that the Israelites would worship the only God and remain unaffected by the pagan worship in Canaan.

Evangelical Christians today do not follow the purity laws in the OT since they are abolished in the NT (Mark 7:19; Acts 10:15; 11:9; Rom 14:14) and today are seen to metaphorically symbolize moral purity and impurity.[16] Likewise, as taught in Hebrews 9:11–28, the reality of the blood atonement in the OT sacrificial system is fulfilled in the covenant made by Christ's blood. Therefore, the death of Christ on the cross has ultimately fulfilled the symbolic meaning of the blood shed in the Israelites' sacrifices. The tension arose in the NT church when Gentiles entered the congregation. John Calvin comments on this as follows:

> Yet we must remember, that this restriction was part of the old law. Wherefore, what Tertullian relates, that in his time it was unlawful among Christians to taste the blood of cattle, savours of superstition. For the apostles, in commanding the Gentiles to observe this rite, for a short time, did not intend to inject a

16. Sprinkle, 117–23.

> scruple into their consciences, but only to prevent the liberty which was otherwise sacred, from proving an occasion of offence to the ignorant and the weak.[17]

One of the main purposes of the decision in Acts 15 was to maintain the harmony between Jewish Christians and Gentile Christians when the Gentiles joined the Jewish Christian community. As Ross rightly points out in his conclusion about the prohibition of eating blood, "Paul ruled that if what people ate was associated with the pagan temple and therefore part of the worship of demons, or if it was open to misunderstanding and offensive to others, then it should not be eaten. Otherwise, it was permissible to eat (1 Cor 10:20– 27). It was not wrong; but it might not be wise or beneficial."[18]

17. Calvin, *Genesis*, 293–94.

18. Ross, *Holiness to the LORD*, 336–37.

APPENDIX 1

Observations on the Speeches of YHWH in the Sinai Pericope (Exodus 19–Numbers 10:10)

Exodus 19–40

Verse	Speech Giver	Verb Used (Receiver)	Speech Receiver	Speech Audience	Verb Used (Audience)	Length of Speech
19:3	יְהוָה	וַיִּקְרָא אֵל	מֹשֶׁה (אֵלָיו)	לְבֵית יַעֲקֹב לִבְנֵי יִשְׂרָאֵל	תֹאמַר וְתַגֵּיד	19:3–6 19:7–25 Narrative
20:1	אֱלֹהִים	וַיְדַבֵּר	--	--	--	20:1–17 (Ten Commandments) 20:18–21 Narrative
20:22	יְהוָה	וַיֹּאמֶר	מֹשֶׁה	אֶל־בְּנֵי יִשְׂרָאֵל	תֹאמַר	20:22–26 (Altar law) 20:24 Well-being offering
21:1	--	--	--	--	--	וְאֵלֶּה הַמִּשְׁפָּטִים אֲשֶׁר תָּשִׂים לִפְנֵיהֶם Chapters 21–23
						Chapter 24 Narrative 24:5 Well-being offering
25:1–2	יְהוָה	וַיְדַבֵּר	אֶל־מֹשֶׁה	אֶל־בְּנֵי יִשְׂרָאֵל	דַּבֵּר	25:1–30:10 29:28 Well-being offering
30:11	יְהוָה	וַיְדַבֵּר	אֶל־מֹשֶׁה	--	--	30:11–16
30:17	יְהוָה	וַיְדַבֵּר	אֶל־מֹשֶׁה	--	--	30:17–21
30:22	יְהוָה	וַיְדַבֵּר	אֶל־מֹשֶׁה	--	--	30:22–33
30:34	יְהוָה	וַיְדַבֵּר	אֶל־מֹשֶׁה	--	--	30:34–38
31:1	יְהוָה	וַיְדַבֵּר	אֶל־מֹשֶׁה	--	--	31:1–11
31:12–13	יְהוָה	וַיֹּאמֶר	אֶל־מֹשֶׁה	אֶל־בְּנֵי יִשְׂרָאֵל	דַּבֵּר	(31:12–17 Observe the Sabbaths) 31:18–32:35 Narrative
33:1	יְהוָה	וַיְדַבֵּר	אֶל־מֹשֶׁה	--	--	33:1–3 33:4 Narrative
33:5	יְהוָה	וַיְדַבֵּר	אֶל־מֹשֶׁה	--	--	33:5–39:43 (35:1–3 Observe the Sabbaths)
40:1	יְהוָה	וַיְדַבֵּר	אֶל־מֹשֶׁה	--	--	40:1–15 40:16–38 Narrative

Leviticus

Verse	Speech Giver	Verb Used (Receiver)	Speech Receiver	Speech Audience	Verb Used (Audience)	Length of Speech
1:1	[יְהוָה]	וַיִּקְרָא אֶל מֵאֹהֶל (מוֹעֵד)				
1:2	יְהוָה	וַיְדַבֵּר	מֹשֶׁה	בְּנֵי יִשְׂרָאֵל	דַּבֵּר אֶל	Chapters 1–3 Chapter 3 Regulation of Well-being offerings (3:17 Prohibition of eating fat and blood)
4:1	יְהוָה	וַיְדַבֵּר	מֹשֶׁה	בְּנֵי יִשְׂרָאֵל	דַּבֵּר אֶל	Chapter 4–5:13
5:14	יְהוָה	וַיְדַבֵּר	מֹשֶׁה (as a judge?)	--	--	5:14–19 5:15 בְּעֶרְכְּךָ 5:18 בְּעֶרְכְּךָ
5:20	יְהוָה	וַיְדַבֵּר	מֹשֶׁה (as a judge?)	--	--	5:20–26 [Eng. 6:1–7] 5:25 בְּעֶרְכְּךָ
6:1–2 [Eng. 6:8–9]	יְהוָה	וַיְדַבֵּר	מֹשֶׁה	אֶת־אַהֲרֹן וְאֶת־בָּנָיו	צַו	6:1–11 [Eng. 6:8–18] Burnt, Cereal Offerings
6:12 [Eng. 6:19]	יְהוָה	וַיְדַבֵּר	מֹשֶׁה	--	--	6:12–16 [Eng. 6:19–23] Day of Anointing – Cereal Offerings
6:17–18 [Eng. 6:24–25]	יְהוָה	וַיְדַבֵּר	מֹשֶׁה	אֶל־אַהֲרֹן וְאֶל־בָּנָיו	דַּבֵּר	6:17–7:21 [Eng. 6:24–7:21] Sin, Guilt, Well-being Offerings 7:11–21 Regulation of Well-being offerings

Verse	Speech Giver	Verb Used (Receiver)	Speech Receiver	Speech Audience	Verb Used (Audience)	Length of Speech
7:22–23	יְהוָה	וַיְדַבֵּר	מֹשֶׁה	בְּנֵי יִשְׂרָאֵל	דַּבֵּר אֶל	7:22–27 (Prohibition of eating fat and blood)
7:28–29	יְהוָה	וַיְדַבֵּר	מֹשֶׁה	בְּנֵי יִשְׂרָאֵל	דַּבֵּר אֶל	7:28–38 The portion of Aaron and his sons 7:38 Conclusion – Mount Sinai
8:1	יְהוָה	וַיְדַבֵּר	מֹשֶׁה	--	--	8:1–3 8:4–10:7 Narrative
10:8	יְהוָה	וַיְדַבֵּר	אַהֲרֹן Yahweh first spoke to Aaron after the anointing ceremony and after his two sons died.	--	--	10:8–11 10:12–20 Narrative
11:1–2	יְהוָה	וַיְדַבֵּר	אֶל־מֹשֶׁה וְאֶל־אַהֲרֹן	אֶל־בְּנֵי יִשְׂרָאֵל	דַּבְּרוּ	Chapter 11 11:46–47 Conclusion
12:1–2	יְהוָה	וַיְדַבֵּר	מֹשֶׁה	אֶל־בְּנֵי יִשְׂרָאֵל	דַּבֵּר	Chapter 12 (Purification after giving birth)
13:1	יְהוָה	וַיְדַבֵּר	אֶל־מֹשֶׁה וְאֶל־אַהֲרֹן	--	--	Chapter 13 (Priestly regulation of dealing with the skin disease)

Verse	Speech Giver	Verb Used (Receiver)	Speech Receiver	Speech Audience	Verb Used (Audience)	Length of Speech
14:1	יְהוָה	וַיְדַבֵּר	מֹשֶׁה	--	--	14:1–31 (Purification from the skin disease) 14:32 – statement
14:33	יְהוָה	וַיְדַבֵּר	אֶל־מֹשֶׁה וְאֶל־אַהֲרֹן	--	--	14:34–53 (Purification of the houses with the "skin disease" in Canaan) 14:54–57 – statement
15:1–2	יְהוָה	וַיְדַבֵּר	אֶל־מֹשֶׁה וְאֶל־אַהֲרֹן	אֶל־בְּנֵי יִשְׂרָאֵל	דַּבֵּר	15:1–31 15:32–33 – statement
16:1–2	יְהוָה יְהוָה	וַיְדַבֵּר וַיֹּאמֶר	אֶל־מֹשֶׁה (Narrative) אֶל־מֹשֶׁה (Speech)	אֶל־אַהֲרֹן	דַּבֵּר	Chapter 16 (16:31 Sabbath)
17:1–2	יְהוָה	וַיְדַבֵּר	אֶל־מֹשֶׁה	אֶל־אַהֲרֹן וְאֶל־בָּנָיו וְאֶל כָּל־בְּנֵי יִשְׂרָאֵל	דַּבֵּר	Chapter 17 17:3–9 Regulation of Well-being offerings (17:10–16 Prohibition of eating fat and blood)
18:1–2	יְהוָה	וַיְדַבֵּר	אֶל־מֹשֶׁה	אֶל־בְּנֵי יִשְׂרָאֵל	דַּבֵּר	Chapter 18
19:1–2	יְהוָה	וַיְדַבֵּר	אֶל־מֹשֶׁה	אֶל־כָּל־עֲדַת בְּנֵי־יִשְׂרָאֵל	דַּבֵּר	Chapter 19 (19:3, 30 Sabbath)
20:1–2	יְהוָה	וַיְדַבֵּר	אֶל־מֹשֶׁה	וְאֶל־בְּנֵי יִשְׂרָאֵל (1st word in v.2)	תֹּאמַר (2nd word in v.2)	Chapter 20

Verse	Speech Giver	Verb Used (Receiver)	Speech Receiver	Speech Audience	Verb Used (Audience)	Length of Speech
21:1	יְהוָה	וַיֹּאמֶר	אֶל־מֹשֶׁה	אֶל־הַכֹּהֲנִים בְּנֵי אַהֲרֹן (1st word in sentence) אֱלֵהֶם (3rd word)	וְאָמַרְתָּ (2nd word)	21:1–15
21:16–17	יְהוָה	וַיְדַבֵּר	אֶל־מֹשֶׁה	אֶל־אַהֲרֹן	דַּבֵּר	21:16–23 21:24–Narrative statement וַיְדַבֵּר מֹשֶׁה אֶל־אַהֲרֹן וְאֶל־בָּנָיו וְאֶל־כָּל־בְּנֵי יִשְׂרָאֵל
22:1–3	יְהוָה	וַיְדַבֵּר	אֶל־מֹשֶׁה	אֶל־אַהֲרֹן וְאֶל־בָּנָיו אֱלֵהֶם	דַּבֵּר אֱמֹר	22:1–16
22:17–18	יְהוָה	וַיְדַבֵּר	אֶל־מֹשֶׁה	אֶל־אַהֲרֹן וְאֶל־בָּנָיו וְאֶל כָּל־בְּנֵי יִשְׂרָאֵל	דַּבֵּר	22:17–25 Regulation of Well-being offerings
22:26	יְהוָה	וַיְדַבֵּר	אֶל־מֹשֶׁה			22:26–33
23:1–2	יְהוָה	וַיְדַבֵּר	אֶל־מֹשֶׁה	אֶל־בְּנֵי יִשְׂרָאֵל	דַּבֵּר	23:1–8 23:2–3 Sabbath 23:4–8 Passover
23:9–10	יְהוָה	וַיְדַבֵּר	אֶל־מֹשֶׁה	אֶל־בְּנֵי יִשְׂרָאֵל	דַּבֵּר	23:9–22 Pentecost
23:23–24	יְהוָה	וַיְדַבֵּר	אֶל־מֹשֶׁה	אֶל־בְּנֵי יִשְׂרָאֵל	דַּבֵּר	23:23–25 New Year

Verse	Speech Giver	Verb Used (Receiver)	Speech Receiver	Speech Audience	Verb Used (Audience)	Length of Speech
23:26	יְהוָה	וַיְדַבֵּר	אֶל־מֹשֶׁה			23:26–32 Day of Atonement
23:33–34	יְהוָה	וַיְדַבֵּר	אֶל־מֹשֶׁה	אֶל־בְּנֵי יִשְׂרָאֵל	דַּבֵּר	23:33–43 Tabernacle 23:44 statement
24:1–2	יְהוָה	וַיְדַבֵּר	אֶל־מֹשֶׁה	אֶת־בְּנֵי יִשְׂרָאֵל	צַו	24:1–9 Light and Bread 24:10–12 Narrative (frame)
24:13	יְהוָה	וַיְדַבֵּר	אֶל־מֹשֶׁה			24:13–22 Regulation 24:10–12, 23 Narrative (frame)
25:1	יְהוָה	וַיְדַבֵּר	אֶל־מֹשֶׁה בְּהַר סִינַי	אֶל־בְּנֵי יִשְׂרָאֵל	דַּבֵּר	25:1–26:45 26:46 concluding statement בְּהַר סִינַי בְּיַד־מֹשֶׁה
27:1–2	יְהוָה	וַיְדַבֵּר	אֶל־מֹשֶׁה	אֶל־בְּנֵי יִשְׂרָאֵל	דַּבֵּר	27:1–33 27:34 concluding statement בְּהַר סִינָי

Numbers 1:1–10:10

Verse	Speech Giver	Verb Used (Receiver)	Speech Receiver	Speech Audience	Verb Used (Audience)	Length of Speech
1:1	יְהוָה	וַיְדַבֵּר (בְּמִדְבַּר סִינַי בְּאֹהֶל מוֹעֵד)	אֶל־מֹשֶׁה	--	--	1:1–1:53 1:54 statement
2:1	יְהוָה	וַיְדַבֵּר	אֶל־מֹשֶׁה וְאֶל־אַהֲרֹן	--	--	

APPENDIX 2

The Translation of *KTU* 1.40 (RS 1.002)[1]

Text and word analysis	**Translation**
Observe Section ? (I or II) 1. [. . .]⌜*w*⌝ *n*⌜*py*⌝[. . .] *n*⌜*py*⌝ – n.m. atonement, expurgation (Olmo Lete, 638), Akk. nappu; however, Pardee suggests "well-being."[2]	Observe Section ? (I or II) . . . ⌜and⌝ well-being . . .
2. [. . .] *npy* . *ʾu*[*grt*. . .]	. . . well-being for U[garit. . .]
3. [. . .]*y* . *ʾu l p* . [. . .] *ʾu* – "whether . . . or"[3] *l* – "according to" *p* – "the mouth, statement," פֶּה, (HALOT, 914)	. . . whether (be it) according to the statement . . .

1. This Ugaritic text is taken from Pardee, *Ritual and Cult*, 79–80.

2. Pardee, 80.

3. Pardee, 111. In n.113, Pardee mentions that "another key expression is *ʾu l p*, here taken as representing three words: the conjunction *ʾu*, 'whether . . . or,' the preposition *l*, 'to, according to,' and *p*, 'mouth, statement of.'"

Text and word analysis	**Translation**
4. [. . .]⌜*ǵ*⌝*br* . *ʾu*⌜*l*⌝[*p*. . .] ⌜*ǵ*⌝*br* – (Olmo Lete, 317), it occurs only in cultic context, identification unclear. "Ḫapiru"[4] *ʾu* – "whether . . . or"[5] *l* – "according to" *p* – "the mouth, statement," פֶּה, (HALOT, 914)	. . . ⌜Ḫ⌝apiru, whether (be it) ⌜according to⌝ [the statement . . .]
5. [. . .]⌜--⌝[. . .]	. . . . . .
. . . .	. . . .
Section II 6. [*ṯʿ ntʿ*]⌜*y*⌝ *ṯʿ* – (I) n. m., offering (from *ṯʿy*), (Olmo Lete, 892) // זֶבַח *ntʿ*]⌜*y*⌝ – G, yqtl, 1cp, ṮʿY, (Olmo Lete, 894), that we offer, Pardee suggests that this is a N, yqtl, 3ms.	Section II . . . the offering that we offer (parallel: line 24, suggested by Olmo Lete) Pardee[6] – [the *ṯʿ*-sacrifice, it is offer]ed
7. [*d*]*r* . *b*⌜*n*⌝ ⌜*ʾi*⌝[*l*] *d*]*r* – n.m. circle, דּוֹר (HALOT, 217), is it possible the second meaning, "generation" is used here? ⌜*ʾi*⌝[*l*] – god, spelling in *ilu*, אֵל (HALOT, 48–50)	. . . the circle of the sons of god
8. [ ]	. . . . . .
Section III 9. [ ] ⌜.⌝ *w npy* *npy* – n.m. atonement, expurgation (Olmo Lete, 638), Akk. nappu; however, Pardee suggests "well-being."	Section III . . . and well-being
10. [ ]*y* . *ʾugr*⌜*t*⌝ It follows line 2.	. . . well-being for Ugari⌜t⌝
11. [*qṭ*]*y* *qṭ*]*y* – cf. line 36, Qaṭ]ien, (gentilic, Olmo Lete, 721)	. . . Qaṭ]ien
12. [ ]⌜-⌝	. . . . . .
13. [ ]	. . . . . .

4. De Moor and Sanders suggest accepting "Gordon's proposal to regard this word as a variant spelling of the name of the Ḫapiru (normally *ʿprm* in Ugaritic)." De Moor and Sanders, "Ugaritic Expiation Ritual," 293.

5. Pardee, *Ritual and Cult*, 111, n.113.

6. Pardee, 81.

Text and word analysis	**Translation**
14. [ ]	. . . . . .
15. [*ndb*]*ḥ* *ndb*]*ḥ* – G, yqtl, 1cp (Olmo Lete, 261), DBḤ, to sacrifice, זָבַח (HALOT, 261) However Pardee suggests N, yqtl, 3ms.[7]	. . . we sacrifice Pardee – . . . is sacrificed
16. [ ]⸢*yt* ⸣[*šʾi*] ⸢*yt* ⸣ – foreman, person in charge?? (Olmo Lete, 989) *šʾi* – in broken context, sheep, ram, שֶׂה (HALOT, 1310)	. . . ⸢foreman⸣ [a ram . . .]
17. [*mpḫ*]⸢*r*⸣*t* . [*bn* . *ʾil* *ṯkmn w šn*]*m hn š* *mpḫ*]⸢*r*⸣*t* – assembly, gathering, cf. line 25 *ʾil* – god, spelling in *ilu*, אֵל (HALOT, 48–50) *ṯkmn w šn*]*m* – DN, (Olmo Lete, 903), Ṯukamuna-wa-Šuna]ma[8] *hn* – here (Olmo Lete, 342), הִנֵּה (HALOT, 251) *š* – n.m., ram, sheep, שֶׂה (HALOT, 1310)	. . . the assembly of [the sons of god, *Ṯukamuna-wa-Šuna]ma*: Here is the ram.
Section IV 18. [. *w n*]*py* . *g*⸢*r*⸣ [. *ḥmyt* . *ʾugrt* . *w np*]*y* *npy* – n.m. atonement, expurgation (Olmo Lete, 638), Akk. nappu; however, Pardee suggests "well-being." *g*⸢*r*⸣ – guest, foreigner, גֵּר (HALOT, 201) *ḥmyt* – pl. of *ḥmt*, walls, חוֹמָה (HALOT, 298)	Section IV . . . and well-being of the foreigner (line 35–36) [(within)[9] the walls of Ugarit, and well-being of
19. [ ]⸢-⸣ . *w n*⸢*p*⸣[*y*]⸢-⸣ . *ʾu tḫṭ* ⸢*ʾi*⸣[*n* . *ʾu l p* . *qṭy*] *ʾu* – whether, אוֹ (HALOT, 20) *tḫṭ* ⸢*ʾi*⸣[*n* – G, yqtl, 2f.pl.[10] , ḪṬʾ, to sin, חטא (HALOT, 305) *ʾu* – "whether . . . or"[11] *l* – "according to" *p* – "the mouth, statement," פֶּה, (HALOT, 914) *qṭy* – cf. line 36, Qaṭien, (gentilic, Olmo Lete, 721)	. . . and well-being of]; whether you have sinned, whether (be it) according to the statement of the Qaṭien.]

7. Pardee, 81.
8. Pardee, 81.
9. Pardee, 81.
10. Sivan, *Grammar of Ugaritic Language*, 111.
11. Pardee, *Ritual and Cult*, 81, 111, n.113.

Text and word analysis	**Translation**
20. *ʾu l p . ddmy . ʾu l* ⸢*p*⸣ [*. ḫry . ʾu*] ⸢*l*⸣ *p . ḫty . ʾu l p* [*. ʾalty . ʾu l p .*] *ǵbr* *ʾu* – "whether. . .or"[12] *l* – "according to"	Whether (be it) according to the statement (/custom, Olmo Lete, 385) of Didima. Whether (be it) according to ⸢the statement of⸣ [Hurrian. Whether (be it)] ⸢according to⸣ the statement of Hittite.
p – "the mouth, statement," פֶּה (HALOT, 914) *ddmy* – gentilic, m., TN (place name), *Didima* (Olmo Lete, 266) *ḫry* – gentilic, m., "Hurrian," III חֹרִי o (HALOT, 353) *ḫty* – gentilic, m., "Hittite," חִתִּי (HALOT, 363) *ʾalṯy* – (Olmo Lete, 68) gentilic, m., Cypriots[13] or ʾAlashian[14] *ǵbr* – (Olmo Lete, 317), it occurs only in cultic context, identification unclear "Ḫapiru;" however, Wyatt suggests "Subarean"[15]	Whether (be it) according to the statement of [ʾAlashian. Whether (be it) according to the statement of] Ḫapiru.
21. *ʾu l p . ḫbtkn . ʾu l* ⸢*p*⸣ *. md*[*llk*]*n . ʾu l p . q*[*rzbl*] *ʾu* – "whether . . . or"[16] *l* – "according to" *p* – "the mouth, statement," פֶּה (HALOT, 914) *ḫbtkn* – 2 f. pl., suffix, from *ḫbt*, Akk. *ḫabātu*, "those who pillage you," (Olmo Lete, 385) your pillagers *md*[*llk*]*n* – D, ptc. Active, 2 f. pl., DLL, to oppress (Olmo Lete, 270), דלל (HALOT, 223) your oppressors *q*[*rzbl*] – a place by Astour: modern Karzbil[17]	Whether (be it) according to the statement of your pillagers. Whether (be it) according to ⸢the statement of⸣ your oppressors. Whether (be it) according to the statement of Q[RZBL].

12. Pardee, 81, 111, n.113.

13. Wyatt, *Religious Texts from Ugarit*, 344.

14. Pardee, *Ritual and Cult*, 81.

15. Wyatt, *Religious Texts from Ugarit*, 344.

16. Pardee, *Ritual and Cult*, 81, 111, n.113.

17. Wyatt, *Religious Texts from Ugarit*, 344. Also see Olmo Lete and Sanmartin, *Dictionary of Ugaritic Language*, 2:715.

Text and word analysis	**Translation**
22. *ʾu tḫṭʾin . b ʾapkn . ʾu b ⸢q⸣ṣrt . npš [kn . ʾu b qṭt]* *ʾu* – whether,אוֹ (HALOT, 20) *tḫṭʾin* –G, yqtl, 2f.pl., *ḪṬ*ʾ, to sin, חטא (HALOT, 305) *b ʾapkn* – in/by+ n.m. with 2f.pl. suffix, by your anger, אַף; (HALOT, 76) *b ⸢q⸣ṣrt* – in/by + (Olmo Lete, 717) n. f. s. constr., shortness of, Akk. *kiṣru* *npš [kn* – n. f. s. 2 f. pl. suffix, your soul, נֶפֶשׁ (HALOT, 711) *b qṭt]* – in/by+n. f., repugnance(s)	Whether you sin in your anger, in the shortness of your soul, [in repugnance(s)] . . . (connects to the first word of next line)
23. *tqṭṭn ʾu tḫṭʾin . l bḥ⸢m⸣ w l ṯʿ . db[ḥn . ndb]⸢ḥ⸣* *tqṭṭn* – L, 2 f. pl., QṬ, to fell repugnance (HALOT, 1083) *ʾu* – whether, אוֹ (HALOT, 20) *tḫṭʾin* –G, yqtl, 2f.pl., *ḪṬ*ʾ, to sin, חטא (HALOT, 305) *l bḥ⸢m⸣* – *l* , in connection with (Olmo Lete, 262). Pardee suggests that *bḥ⸢m⸣* should be read as <*d*>*bḥ⸢m⸣*,[18] n. m. pl., sacrifices, זֶבַח (HALOT, 262). *ṯʿ* – n. m., offering(s) *db[ḥn* – n. m., sacrifice *ndb]⸢ḥ⸣* – G, yqtl, 1c. pl., DBḤ, to sacrifice, זָבַח (HALOT, 261). Pardee suggests that this is a N, yqtl, 3ms.	you have felt. Whether you sin in connection with the sacrifices or in connection with the offering. The sacrifice that we sacrifice, Pardee[19] – the sacrifice, it is offered
24. *hw . ṯʿ . nṯʿy . hw . nkt . n⸢k⸣t*[20] *. ytšʾi[. l ʾab . bn ʾil]* *hw* – demostr. pn., this (Olmo Lete, 348), הוּא (HALOT, 240) *nṯʿy* – G, yqtl, 1cp, ṮʿY, (Olmo Lete, 894), that we offer, Pardee suggests that this is a N, yqtl, 3ms. *nkt* – n. m. s., victim *n⸢k⸣t* – G, qtl, 1c. pl./N, qtl, 3m.s., NKT, to immolate, Arab. *nakata* *ytšʾi* – Gt, 3 m. s., jussive (Olmo Lete, 649),[21] NŠʾ, to rise, נשׂא (HALOT, 724)	This is the offering we offer. This is the victim we immolate. May it rise [to the father of the sons of god.]

18. Pardee, *Ritual and Cult*, 110, n.107.

19. Pardee, *Ritual and Cult*, 82.

20. "NKT denotes basic 'slaughtering' and corresponds to the use of the West-Semitic verb *qatālu* and the Akkadian verb *dâku*, both meaning 'to kill' and both used in the Mari donkey-sacrifice texts." Pardee, *Ritual and Cult*, 112, n.115.

21. Also see Pardee, *Les textes rituels*, 108.

Text and word analysis	**Translation**
25. *ytš'i . l dr . bn . 'il . l . ⸢m⸣pḫrt . bn ⸢'i⸣[l . l ṯkmn . w š]nm hn š* *dr* – n.m. circle, דּוֹר (HALOT, 217), is it possible the second meaning, "generation" here? *'il* – god, spelling in *ilu*, אֵל (HALOT, 48–50) *⸢m⸣pḫrt* – assembly, gathering, cf. line 25 ṯkmn w šn]m – DN, (Olmo Lete, 903), Ṯukamuna-wa-Šuna]ma[22] *hn* – here (Olmo Lete, 342), הֵנָּה (HALOT, 251) *š* – n.m., ram, sheep, שֶׂה (HALOT, 1310)	May it rise to the circle of the sons of god, to the assembly of the sons of god, to *Ṯukamuna-wa-Šu]nama*. Here is the ram.
Section V 26. *w . šqrb . 'r . mšr mšr* [.] *⸢b⸣n . 'ugrt . ⸢w⸣ [npy] 'ugr* *šqrb* – Š, imperative, QRB, to offer[23] /to bring near,[24] קרב (HALOT, 1132) *'r* – donkey, עַיִר (HALOT, 822) *mšr* – justification,מִישׁוֹר (HALOT, 578) *npy* – n.m. atonement, expurgation (Olmo Lete, 638), Akk. nappu; however, Pardee suggests "well-being."[25]	Section V And offer/bring near a donkey of justification, of justification, sons of Ugarit! ⸢And⸣ [well-being] for Ugarit.
27. *w npy . ym'an . w npy . 'rmt ⸢. w⸣ npy .* ⸢-⸣[ ] *npy* – n.m. atonement, expurgation (Olmo Lete, 638), Akk. nappu; however, Pardee suggests "well-being."[26] *ym'an* – place name (Olmo Lete, 966) *'rmt* – place name (Olmo Lete, 183)	And well-being of YM'AN, and well-being of 'RMT, ⸢and⸣ well being of [ ],

22. Pardee, *Ritual and Cult*, 81.
23. Olmo Lete and Sanmartin, *Dictionary of Ugaritic Language*, 709.
24. Pardee, *Ritual and Cult*, 82.
25. Pardee, 80.
26. Pardee, 80.

Text and word analysis	**Translation**
28. *w npy . nqmd . ʿu šn . ypkm . ʾu l p . q[ṯy . ʾu l p . ddm]y* *nqmd* – personal name of several kings of Ugarit (Olmo Lete, 640), *Niqmaddu*[27] *ʾu* – “whether. . .or”[28] *šn* – marred.[29] *ypkm* – 2 m. pl. suffix, your beauty/dignity (Olmo Lete, 972), יְפִי (HALOT, 424) *q[ṯy* – cf. line 36, Qaṭien, (gentilic, Olmo Lete, 721) *ddm]y* – gentilic, m., TN (place name), *Didima* (Olmo Lete, 266)	and well-being of Niqmaddu. Whether your beauty/dignity (is) marred, whether (be it) according to the statement of the Qa[ṭien, whether (be it) according to the statement of the *Didim]a*,
29. *ʾu l p . ḫry . ʾu l p . ḫ⸢t⸣y . ʾu l p . ʾalty . ʾu ⸢l⸣ [p ǵbr .] ⸢ʾu⸣ l p* *ḫry* – gentilic, m., “Hurrian,” III חֹרִי o (HALOT, 353) *ḫ⸢t⸣y* – gentilic, m., “Hittite,” חִתִּי (HALOT, 363) *ʾalṯy* – (Olmo Lete, 68) gentilic, m., Cypriots[30] or ʾAlashian[31] *ǵbr* – (Olmo Lete, 317), it occurs only in cultic context, identification unclear “Ḫapiru;” however, Wyatt suggests “Subarean”[32]	Whether (be it) according to the statement of Hurrian. Whether (be it) according to the statement of Hittite. Whether (be it) according to the statement of ʾAlashian. Whether (be it) ⸢according to⸣ [the statement of Ḫapiru.] ⸢Whether (be it)⸣ according to the statement of

27. Pardee, 82; Olmo Lete, *Canaanite Religion*, 640.

28. Pardee, *Ritual and Cult*, 111, n.113.

29. Wyatt, *Religious Texts from Ugarit*, 345, n.19; Cf. De Moor and Sanders, “Ugaritic Expiation Ritual,” 286.While the origin and meaning of this word are uncertain, “the whole expression *u šn ypkm/kn* must have approximately the same meaning as the parallel *ʾu ṯḫṭ ʾu/ ṯḫṭ ʾin*.” De Moor and Sanders, “Ugaritic Expiation Ritual,” 292.

30. Wyatt, *Religious Texts from Ugarit*, 344.

31. Pardee, *Ritual and Cult*, 81.

32. Wyatt, *Religious Texts from Ugarit*, 344.

Text and word analysis	Translation
30. *ḫbtkm . ʾu l p . m*⌜*d*⌝*[l]lkm . ʾu l p . qrzbl . ʾu* ⌜*šn*⌝ [.] *ypkm* *ḫbtkm* – 2 m. pl., suffix, from *ḫbt*, Akk. *ḫabātu*, "those who pillage you," (Olmo Lete, 385) your pillagers *m*⌜*d*⌝*[l]lkm* – D, ptc. Active, 2 m. pl., DLL, to oppress (Olmo Lete, 270), דלל (HALOT, 223) your oppressors *qrzbl* – a place by Astour: modern Karzbil[33] *ʾu* – "whether . . . or"[34] *šn* – marred.[35] *ypkm* – 2 m. pl. suffix, your beauty/dignity (Olmo Lete, 972), יְפִי (HALOT, 424)	your pillagers. Whether (be it) according to the statement of your oppressors. Whether (be it) according to the statement of QRZBL. Whether your beauty/dignity (is) ⌜marred⌝,
31. *ʾu b ʾapkm . ʾu b q[ṣ]*⌜*r*⌝*t . npškm . ʾu b qṭt . tqṭṭ* *ʾu* – whether, אוֹ (HALOT, 20) *b ʾapkm* – in/by+ n.m. with 2 m. pl. suffix, by your anger, אַף; (HALOT, 76) *b q[ṣ]*⌜*r*⌝*t* – in/by + Olmo Lete, 717) n. f. s. constr., shortness of, Akk. *kiṣru* *npškm* – n. f. s. 2 m. pl. suffix, your soul, נֶפֶשׁ (HALOT, 711) *b qṭt* – in/by+n. f., repugnance(s) *tqṭṭ* – L, 2 m. pl., QṬ, to feel repugnance, (HALOT, 1083)	whether in your anger, or in the shortness of your soul, or in repugnance(s) you have felt.

33. Wyatt, 344. See also Olmo Lete, *Canaanite Religion*, 715.

34. Pardee, *Ritual and Cult*, 111, n.113.

35. Wyatt, *Religious Texts from Ugarit*, 345, n.19; De Moor and Sanders, "Ugaritic Expiation Ritual," 286, 292.

Text and word analysis	**Translation**
32. *ʾu šn . ypkm . l d*[*b*]*ḥm . w l . ṯʿ . dbḥn . ndbḥ . hw . ṯʿ n ṯʿy* *ʾu* – "whether. . .or"[36] *šn* – marred.[37] *ypkm* – 2 m. pl. suffix, your beauty/dignity (Olmo Lete, 972), יְפִי (HALOT, 424) *l d*[*b*]*ḥm* – *l*, in connection with (Olmo Lete, 262). n. m. pl., sacrifices, זֶבַח (HALOT, 262). *ṯʿ* – n. m., offering(s) *dbḥn* – n. m., sacrifice *ndbḥ* – G, yqtl, 1c. pl., DBḤ, to sacrifice, זָבַח (HALOT, 261). Pardee suggests that this is a N, yqtl, 3ms. *hw* – demostr. pn., this (Olmo Lete, 348), הוּא (HALOT, 240) *nṯʿy* – G, yqtl, 1cp, ṮʿY, (Olmo Lete, 894), that we offer, Pardee suggests that this is a N, yqtl, 3ms.	Whether your beauty/dignity is marred in connection with the sacrifices or in connection with the offering. The sacrifice that we sacrifice. This is the offering we offer.
33. *hw . nkt . nkt .* ⸢*y*⸣[*t*]*šʾi . l ʾab . bn . ʾil . ytšʾi . l dr* *nkt* – n. m. s., victim *nkt* – G, qtl, 1c. pl./N, qtl, 3m.s., NKT, to immolate, Arab. *nakata* ⸢*y*⸣[*t*]*šʾi* – Gt, 3 m. s., jussive (Olmo Lete, 649),[38] NŠʾ, to rise, נשׂא (HALOT, 724) *dr* – n.m. circle, דּוֹר (HALOT, 217), is it possible the second meaning, "generation" is used here?	This is the victim we immolate. May it rise to the father of the sons of god. May it rise to the circle of
34. *bn ʾil . l ṯkmn* [*. w*] *šnm . hn . ʿr* *ṯkmn* [*. w*] *šnm* – DN, (Olmo Lete, 903), Ṯukamuna-wa-Šuna]ma[39] *hn* – here (Olmo Lete, 342), הֵנָּה (HALOT, 251) *ʿr* – donkey, עַיִר (HALOT, 822)	the sons of god, to *Ṯukamuna-[wa]-Šunama*. Here is the donkey.

36. Pardee, *Ritual and Cult*, 111, n.113.

37. Wyatt, *Religious Texts from Ugarit*, 345, n.19; De Moor and Sanders, "Ugaritic Expiation Ritual," 286, 292.

38. Also see Pardee, *Les textes rituels*, 128.

39. Pardee, *Ritual and Cult*, 81.

Text and word analysis	**Translation**
Section VI 35. *w . tb . l mspr . m[š]⌜r⌝ mšr . bt . ʾugrt . w npy* ⌜.⌝ *gr* *t̠b* – G, imperative, m. s., T̠B, to go back, return, שׁוּב (HALOT, 1427) *l mspr* – recitation, story, narrative, מִסְפָּר (HALOT, 607) *mšr* – justification, מִישׁוֹר (HALOT, 578) *npy* – n.m. atonement, expurgation (Olmo Lete, 638), Akk. nappu; however, Pardee suggests "well-being."[40] *gr* – guest, foreigner, גֵּר (HALOT, 201)	Section VI Now go back to the narrative/ recitation of justification: Justification of the daughter of Ugarit. And well-being of foreigner
36. *ḥmyt . ʾugrt . w [np]y* ⌜. *ʾa*⌝*tt . ʾu šn . ypkn . ʾu l p* ⌜.⌝ *qṭy* *ḥmyt* – pl. of *ḥmt*, walls, חוֹמָה (HALOT, 298) *ʾa*⌝*t̠t* – n. f. s./pl. woman/women, אִשָּׁה (HALOT, 93) *ʾu* – "whether . . . or"[41] *šn* – marred.[42] *ypkn* – 2 f. pl. suffix, your beauty/dignity (Olmo Lete, 972), יֳפִי (HALOT, 424) *qṭy* – cf. line 36, Qaṭien, (gentilic, Olmo Lete, 721)	(within) the walls of Ugarit, and well-being of women/woman. Whether your beauty/dignity (is) marred, whether (be it) according to the statement of the Qaṭien,
37. *ʾu l p . ddmy . ʾu l [p . ḫ]ry . ʾu l p . ḫty . ʾu l p . ʾalty* *ddmy* – gentilic, m., TN(place name), *Didima* (Olmo Lete, 266) *ḫry* – gentilic, m., "Hurrian," III חֹרִי o (HALOT, 353) *ḫty* – gentilic, m., "Hittite," חִתִּי (HALOT, 363) *ʾalt̠y* – (Olmo Lete, 68) gentilic, m., Cypriots[43] or ʾAlashian[44]	whether (be it) according to the statement of the *Didima*. Whether (be it) according to the statement of Hurrian. Whether (be it) according to the statement of Hittite. Whether (be it) according to the statement of ʾAlashian.

40. Pardee, 80.

41. Pardee, 111, n.113.

42. Wyatt, *Religious Texts from Ugarit*, 345, n.19; De Moor and Sanders, "Ugaritic Expiation Ritual," 286, 292.

43. Wyatt, *Religious Texts from Ugarit*, 344.

44. Pardee, *Ritual and Cult*, 81.

Text and word analysis	**Translation**
38. *ʾu l p* [.] *ǵbr* . *ʾu l p* . ⸢*ḫ*⸣[*bt*]⸢*kn* . *ʾu l*⸣ *p* . *mdllkn* . *ʾu l p* ⸢.⸣ *qrz*⸢*bl*⸣ *ǵbr* – (Olmo Lete, 317), it occurs only in cultic context, identification unclear "Ḫapiru;" however, Wyatt suggests "Subarean"[1] ⸢ *ḫ*⸣[*bt*]⸢*kn* – 2 f. pl., suffix, from *ḫbt*, Akk. *ḫabātu*, "those who pillage you," (Olmo Lete, 385) your pillagers *mdllkn* – D, ptc. Active, 2 m. pl., DLL, to oppress (Olmo Lete, 270), דלל (HALOT, 223) your oppressors *qrz*⸢*bl*⸣ – a place by Astour: modern Karzbil[2] (Olmo Lete, 715)	Whether (be it) according to the statement of your pillagers. Whether (be it) according to the statement of your oppressors. Whether (be it) according to the statement of QRZ[BL].
39. *l šn ypkn* . *b ʾap*⸢*k*⸣[*n* . *ʾu b q*]⸢*ṣ*⸣*rt* . *npškn* ⸢.⸣ *ʾu b q*⸢*ṭt*⸣ *l* – Pardee suggests it should be read as "*ʾu*"[3] – "whether . . . or" *šn* – marred.[4] *ypkn* – 2 f. pl. suffix, your beauty/dignity (Olmo Lete, 972), יְפִי (HALOT, 424) *b ʾap*⸢*k*⸣[*n* – in/by+ n.m. with 2 f. pl. suffix, by your anger, אַף; (HALOT, 76) *b q*]⸢*ṣ*⸣*rt* – in/by + (Olmo Lete, 717) n. f. s. constr., shortness of, Akk. *kiṣru* *npškn* – n. f. s. 2 f. pl. suffix, your soul, נֶפֶשׁ (HALOT, 711) *b qṭt* – in/by+n. f., repugnance(s)	Whether your beauty/dignity (is) marred in your anger, or in the shortness of your soul, or in repugnance(s)

1. Wyatt, *Religious Texts from Ugarit*, 344.
2. Wyatt, 344. Also see Olmo Lete, *Canaanite Religion*, 715.
3. Pardee, *Ritual and Cult*, 111, n.110.
4. Wyatt, *Religious Texts from Ugarit*, 345, n.19; De Moor and Sanders, "Ugaritic Expiation Ritual," 286, 292.

Text and word analysis	**Translation**
40. *tqṯṯn . ʾu šn y*⸢*p*⸣[*kn . l dbḥm .*] *w l ṯʿ dbHn* *tqṯṯn* – L, 2 f. pl., Qˆ, to fell repugnance, (HALOT, 1083) *ʾu* – "whether . . . or"[1] *šn* – marred.[2] *y*⸢*p*⸣[*kn* – 2 f. pl. suffix, your beauty/dignity (Olmo Lete, 972), יְפִי (HALOT, 424) *l dbḥm* – *l*, in connection with (Olmo Lete, 262). n. m. pl., sacrifices, זֶבַח (HALOT, 262). *ṯʿ* – n. m., offering(s) *dbḥn* – n. m., sacrifice	you have felt. Whether your beauty/dignity is marred in connection with the sacrifices or in connection with the offering. The sacrifice
41. *ndbḥ . hw . ṯʿ n*[*ṯʿy . hw . nkt . n*]⸢*k*⸣*t .* ⸢*yt*⸣[*š*]⸢ *ʾi .*⸣ *l ʾab bn ʾil* *ndbḥ* – G, yqtl, 1c. pl., DBḤ, to sacrifice, זָבַח (HALOT, 261). Pardee suggests that this is a N, yqtl, 3ms. *hw* – demostr. pn., this (Olmo Lete, 348), הוּא (HALOT, 240) *ṯʿ* – n. m., offering(s) *n*[*ṯʿy* – G, yqtl, 1cp, ṮʿY, (Olmo Lete, 894), that we offer, Pardee suggests that this is a N, yqtl, 3ms. *nkt* – n. m. s., victim *n*]⸢*k*⸣*t* – G, qtl, 1c. pl./N, qtl, 3m.s., NKT, to immolate, Arab. *nakata* ⸢*yt*⸣[*š*]⸢ *ʾi* – Gt, 3 m. s., jussive (Olmo Lete, 649),[3] NŠʾ, to rise, נשׂא (HALOT, 724)	that we sacrifice. This is the offering we offer. This is the victim we immolate. May it rise to the father of the sons of god.
Reverse 42. *ytšʾi . l* ⸢*d*⸣[*r . bn ʾil . l*] *mpḫrt . bn ʾil* *ytšʾi* – Gt, 3 m. s., jussive (Olmo Lete, 649),[4] NŠʾ, to rise, נשׂא (HALOT, 724) ⸢*d*⸣[*r* – n.m. circle, דּוֹר (HALOT, 217), is it possible the second meaning, "generation" is used here? *ʾil* – god, spelling in *ilu*, אֵל (HALOT, 48–50) *mpḫrt* – assembly, gathering.	Reverse May it rise to the circle of the sons of god, to] the assembly of the sons of god,

1. Pardee, *Ritual and Cult*, 111, n.113.

2. Wyatt, *Religious Texts from Ugarit*, 345, n.19; De Moor and Sanders, "Ugaritic Expiation Ritual," 286, 292.

3. Also see Pardee, *Les textes rituels*, 128.

4. Pardee, *Les textes rituels*, 128.

Text and word analysis	Translation
43. *l ṯkm*⸢*n*⸣[. *w šnm* .] *hn* ⸢ *ʿr*⸣ *ṯkm*⸢*n*⸣[. *w šnm*] – DN, (Olmo Lete, 903), Ṯukamuna-[wa-Šunama][1] *hn* – here (Olmo Lete, 342), הֵנָּה (HALOT, 251) *ʿr* – donkey, עַיִר (HALOT, 822)	to *Ṯukamu*⸢*na*⸣*-[wa-Šunama.]* Here is ⸢the donkey.⸣

1. Pardee, *Ritual and Cult*, 81.

APPENDIX 3

The Structure of *KTU* 1.40 (RS 1.002)

Section IV

18. . . . and well-being of the foreigner (within) the walls of Ugarit,
    and well-being of
19. . . . and well-being of];
    whether you have sinned,
    whether (be it) according to the statement/custom of the Qaṭien.
20. Whether (be it) according to the statement of Didima.
    Whether (be it) according to the statement of Hurrian.
    Whether (be it) according to the statement of Hittite.
    Whether (be it) according to the statement of ʾAlashian.
    Whether (be it) according to the statement of Ḫapiru.
21. Whether (be it) according to the statement of your pillagers.
    Whether (be it) according to the statement of your oppressors.
    Whether (be it) according to the statement of Q[RZBL].
22. Whether you sin in your anger,
    in the shortness of your soul,
    in repugnance(s)
23. you have felt.
    Whether you sin in connection with the sacrifices
    or in connection with the offering.
    The sacrifice that we sacrifice,
24. This is the offering we offer.
    This is the victim we immolate.
    May it rise to the father of the sons of god.
25. May it rise to the circle of the sons of god,
    to the assembly of the sons of god,
    to *Ṯukamuna-wa-Šunama*.
    Here is the ram.

Section V

26. And offer/bring near a donkey of justification,
of justification, sons of Ugarit!
And well-being for Ugarit.

27. And well-being of YM'AN,
and well-being of 'RMT,
and well being of [ ],

28. and well-being of Niqmaddu.
Whether your beauty/dignity (is) marred,
whether (be it) according to the statement of the Qaṭien,
whether (be it) according to the statement of the *Didima*,

29. Whether (be it) according to the statement of Hurrian.
Whether (be it) according to the statement of Hittite.
Whether (be it) according to the statement of 'Alashian.
Whether (be it) according to the statement of Ḫapiru.
Whether (be it)according to the statement of

30. your pillagers.
Whether (be it) according to the statement of your oppressors.
Whether (be it) according to the statement of QRZBL.
Whether your beauty/dignity (is) marred,

31. whether in your anger,
or in the shortness of your soul,
or in repugnance(s) you have felt.

32. Whether your beauty/dignity is marred
in connection with the sacrifices
or in connection with the offering.
The sacrifice that we sacrifice.
This is the offering we offer.

33. This is the victim we immolate.
May it rise to the father of the sons of god.
May it rise to the circle of

34. the sons of god,
to *Ṯukamuna-wa-Šunama.*
Here is the donkey.

Section VI

35. Now go back to the narrative/recitation of justification:
Justification of the daughter of Ugarit. And well-being of foreigner

36. (within) the walls of Ugarit,
and well-being of women/woman.

Whether your beauty/dignity (is) marred,
whether (be it) according to the statement of the Qaṭien,
37. whether (be it) according to the statement of the *Didima*,
Whether (be it) according to the statement of Hurrian.
Whether (be it) according to the statement of Hittite.
Whether (be it) according to the statement of ʾAlashian.
38. Whether (be it) according to the statement of Ḫapiru.
Whether (be it) according to the statement of your pillagers.
Whether (be it) according to the statement of your oppressors.
Whether (be it) according to the statement of QRZBL.
39. Whether your beauty/dignity (is) marred in your anger,
or in the shortness of your soul,
or in repugnance(s)
40. you have felt. Whether your beauty/dignity is marred in connection with the sacrifices
or in connection with the offering.
The sacrifice
41. that we sacrifice.
This is the offering we offer.
This is the victim we immolate.
May it rise to the father of the sons of god.
Reverse
42. May it rise to the circle of the sons of god,
to the assembly of the sons of god,
43. to *Ṯukamuna-wa-Šunama*.
Here is the donkey.

APPENDIX 4

The Translation of *KTU* 1.109 (RS 24.253)

Obverse 1. *b ʾarbʿt . ʿšr*[*t*] *b ʾarbʿt* – on + four, אַרְבַּע (HALOT, 83) *ʿšr*[*t*] – ten, עֲשֶׂרֶת (HALOT, 895)	Obverse On the fourteenth [the day of the month],[1]
2. *yrtḥṣ . mlk .* ⌜*b*⌝[*rr*] *yrtḥṣ* –Gt, yqtl, 3m.s., to wash himself, רחץ (HALOT, 1220) *mlk* – n.m. king, מֶלֶךְ ⌜*b*⌝[*rr*] – pure, purified, clean, בַּר II, בָּרוּר (HALOT, 153, 155), Akk. *Barru*	the king will wash himself clean.
3. *b ym . mlʾat* *b ym* – on the day of, יוֹם *mlʾat* – n. f. s./pl., fullness/full moon, מְלֵאָה (HALOT, 585)	On the day of fullness/full moon
4. *tqln . ʾalpm* *tqln* – G, 2 m. du., to fall, QL, Akk. *qiālu, qâlu* *ʾalpm* – m. du., two cattle, אֶלֶף (HALOT, 59)	two cattle fall
5. *yrḫ . ʿšrt . l bʿ*[*l . ṣpn*] *yrḫ* – the Moon god (Olmo Lete, 979), *Yariḫu*[2] *ʿšrt* – a banquet offering (Olmo Lete, 190) *l bʿ*[*l* – for + Baal *ṣpn*] – north (Olmo Lete, 788), צָפוֹן (HALOT, 1046)	(for) the Moon god/ *Yariḫu*, a banquet offering for Ba[al in the north.]
6. *dqtm . w ynt . qr*[*t*] *dqtm* – n. f. du., two ewes/sheep (Olmo Lete, 279) *w ynt* – and + n. f. constrc., a dove of, יוֹנָה (HALOT, 402) *qr*[*t*] – n. f., city, קֶרֶת (HALOT, 1149)	Two ewes and a dove of city/a domestic dove[3]

1. Pardee, *Ritual and Cult*, 30.
2. Pardee, *Ritual and Cult*, 30.
3. Olmo Lete, *Canaanite Religion*, 972.

7. *w mtntm* . ⸢*w*⸣ *š l rm*⸢*š*⸣ *mtntm* – n. f. du., two loin (Olmo Lete, 601)/two kidneys[4] *š* – n.m., ram, sheep, שֶׂה (HALOT, 1310) *l rm*⸢*š*⸣ – for + unknown deity, RM⸢Š⸣	and two kidneys ⸢and⸣ a ram for RM⸢Š⸣.
8. *w kbd* . *w š* . *l šlm* ⸢*k*⸣*bd* *kbd* – a liver, כָּבֵד (HALOT, 456) *šlm* – the god of dusk (Olmo Lete, 820)/ Šalimu, שָׁלֵם (HALOT, 1538)	A liver and a ram for Šalimu, a liver of
9. *ʾalp* . *w š l bʿl cpn* *ʾalp* – m. s., cattle, אֶלֶף (HALOT, 59)	a cattle and a ram for Baal in the north.
10. *dqt l ṣpn* . *šrp* . *w šlmm* *dqt* – n. f. s., an ewe/a sheep (Olmo Lete, 279) *ṣpn* – 2) DN, mountain god/Ṣapunu[5] (Olmo Lete, 788),צָפוֹן (HALOT,1046) *šrp* – a burnt offering *šlmm* – s. with encl. *m*,[6] a peace offering, שֶׁלֶם (HALOT, 1536)	An ewe for Ṣapunu as a burnt offering. And as a peace offering:
11. *kmm* . *w b bt* . *bʿl*. *ʾugrt* *kmm* – ditto/the same	Ditto. And in the temple/house of Baal of Ugarit,
12. *kkdm* . *w npš* . *ʾilʾib* *kkdm* – kbdm,[7] two livers. *npš* – n. f., (piece of) offal (Olmo Lete, 637–38),[8] (HALOT, 711) *ʾilʾib* – father El/ father god/ *ʾiluʾibi*, אֱלִיאָב (cf. HALOT, 55)	two livers and a piece of offal: for *ʾIluʾibi*
13. *gdlt* . *ʾil š* . *bʿl š* . *ʿnt* *gdlt* – n. f. a cow *ʿnt* – name of the goddess, Baal's "sister," ʿAnatu	a cow, for El a ram, for Baal a ram, for ʿAnatu
14. *ṣpn* . *ʾalp* . *w š* . *pdry š* *pdry* – DN, daughter of Baal, Pidray	in the north[9] a cattle and a ram, for Pidray a ram
15. *šrp* . *w šlmm ʾilʾib š* *šrp* – a burnt offering *šlmm* – s. with encl. *m*,[10] a peace offering, שֶׁלֶם (HALOT, 1536) *ʾilʾib* – father El/ father god/ *ʾiluʾibi*, אֱלִיאָב (cf. HALOT, 55)	as a burnt offering. And as a peace offering for *ʾiluʾibi* a ram,

4. Pardee, *Ritual and Cult at Ugarit*, 30.

5. Pardee, 31

6. Pardee, 31.

7. Olmo Lete suggests this is a scribal error. Olmo Lete, "Rituales sacrificiales," 183, n.6; Cf. Olmo Lete and Sanmartin, *Dictionary of Ugaritic Language*, 1:425. Pardee suggests it is an unknown word KKD. Pardee, *Ritual and Cult*, 31.

8. Pardee suggests this word means "neck." Pardee, *Les textes rituels*, 603.

9. Pardee translates this as "ʿAnatu of Ṣapunu." Pardee, *Ritual and Cult*, 31.

10. Olmo Lete, *Dictionary of Ugaritic Language*, 819.

16. *b ʿl ʾugrt š . b ʿl ḫlb š* *ḫlb* – place name, *Ḫalab* "Aleppo"	for Baal of Ugarit a ram, for Baal of Aleppo a ram,
17. *yr– š . ʿnt ṣpn . ʾalp* *yrḫ* – the Moon god (Olmo Lete, 979), *Yariḫu*[1]	for *Yariḫu* a ram, for ʿAnatu in the north a cattle
18. *w š . pdry š . ddmš . š* *ddmš* – DN, Hurro-Anat, Dadmiš	and a ram, for Pidray a ram, for Dadmiš a ram
19. *w b ʾurbt . ʾil ʾib š* *ʾurbt* – a cult installation, "opening,"[2] אֲרֻבָּה (HALOT, 83)	And in the opening for *ʾilu ʾibi* a ram,
Lower Edge 20. *b ʿl. ʾalp w š*	Lower Edge for Baal a cattle and a ram,
Reverse 21. *dgn . š . ʾil t ʿḏr* *dgn* – DN, Dagan, דָּגוֹן (cf. HALOT, 213) *ʾil t ʿḏr* – the helper gods of	Reverse for Dagan a ram, for the helper gods of
22. *b ʿl š . ʿnt š . ršp š* *ršp* – god of pestilence/plague, Rašap,רֶשֶׁף (HALOT, 1297)	Baal a ram, for ʿAnatu a ram, for Rašap a ram,
23. *šlmm.*	as a peace offering.
24. *w šnpt . ʾil š* *šnpt* – an unspecified type of general offering	And as a ŠNPT offering:[3] or El a ram.
25. *l ʿnt ḥlš . tn šm* *ḥlš* – ḤLŠ, cf. חלש (HALOT, 324) *ṯn* – two, שְׁנַיִם (HALOT, 1605)	For ʿAnatu-ḤLŠ two rams,
26. *l gtrm . ǵṣb šm ʾal* *gṯrm* – DN, Gaṯarūma *ǵṣb* – fold of bull's body, ǴṢB *šm ʾal* – left, שְׂמֹאל (HALOT, 1332)	for Gaṯarūma the left ǴṢB of
27. *d ʾalpm . w ʾalp* ⌜*w*⌝ *š* *d* – which	which (is) two cattle and a cattle and a ram
28. *šrp . w šlmm kmm* *šrp* – a burnt offering *šlmm* – s. with encl. *m*,[4] a peace offering, שָׁלֵם (HALOT, 1536) *kmm* – Ditto/the same	as a burnt offering. And a peace offering: Ditto.
29. *l b ʿl . ṣpn b ʿr ʿr* *b ʿl . ṣpn* – Baal in the north *b ʿr ʿr* – with the tamarisk, עַרְעָר (HALOT, 887)	For Baal in the north with the tamarisk

1. Pardee, *Ritual and Cult*, 30.
2. Pardee, 31.
3. Pardee, 31. Pardee translates this as "presentation offering."
4. Olmo Lete, *Dictionary of Ugaritic Language*, 819.

30. *pʿamt ṯlṯm . š l qẓrt* *pʿamt* – times, פַּעַם (HALOT, 952) *ṯlṯm* – thirty, שְׁלֹשׁוּם (HALOT, 1545) *qẓrt* – n. f. "brazier, incense-burner" (OLMO LETE, 722)/ *Qẓrt*[1]	thirty times; a ram for the *Qẓrt*/incense-burner of
31. *ṯlḥn . bʿlt . bhtm* *ṯlḥn* – table, שֻׁלְחָן (HALOT, 1519) *bʿlt* – lady, בַּעֲלָה (HALOT, 145) *bhtm* – pl. palace, בַּיִת (HALOT, 124)	the table of Lady of the Palace
32. *ʿlm⸢ .⸣ ʿlm . gdlt . l bʿl* *ʿlm*–II, adv., next, in addition (Olmo Lete, 157) *ʿlm*–III, offspring (Olmo Lete, 157), עֲוִיל (HALOT, 797) *gdlt* – n. f. a cow	Next: a offspring of a cow for Baal Pardee – On the day after next: a cow for . . .[2]
33. *ṣpn . ḫlb ⸢. w kb⸣d .⸢ d⸣[q]⸢t⸣* *ḫlb* – place name, *Ḫalab* "Aleppo" *dqt* – n. f. s., a ewe/sheep (Olmo Lete, 279)	in the north Aleppo,[3] and a liver (of?) an ewe
34. *l ṣpn⸢ .--(-)⸣ [.] ⸢b⸣ʿl . ʾu⸢g⸣[rt. . .]* *ṣpn* – 2) DN, mountain god/Ṣapunu[4] (Olmo Lete, 788), צָפוֹן (HALOT,1046)	for Ṣapunu. . . . . .⸢Ba⸣al of U⸢ga⸣[rit. . .]
35. *ʾilʾib . g⸢dlt .⸣ bʿ⸢l⸣[. . .]*	for *ʾiluʾibi* a cow, for Ba⸢al⸣. . .
36. *ʾugr⸢t⸣ [-?] [ʿ]⸢nt ṣ⸣pn [. . .]*	Ugari⸢t⸣. . .ʿAnatu in the north (refer to line 17). . .
37. ⸢ ⸣*šl*⸢-⸣[. . .]	ŠL. . .[5]

1. Pardee, *Ritual and Cult*, 31. See also Clemens, *Sources for Ugaritic Ritual*, 893, n.1278.

2. Pardee, *Ritual and Cult*, 31.

3. In line 16, Pardee translates *ḫlb* as "Aleppo"; however, here he doesn't translate it. Pardee, *Ritual and Cult*, 31.

4. Pardee, 31.

5. Pardee, 100, n.9. Pardee notes that this may read "as a peace [offering], but the presence of a wedge, which appears to be "ʿ" before this formula is unexplained."

APPENDIX 5

The Structure of *KTU* 1.109 (RS 24.253)

Obverse

1. On the fourteen [the day of the month],
2. the king will wash himself clean.
3. On the day of fullness/full moon
4. two cattle fall
5. (for) the Moon god/ *Yariḫu*,
a banquet offering for Baal in the north:
6. two ewes and a dove of city/ a domestic dove;
7. and two kidneys and a ram for RM⸢Š⸣.
8. A liver and a ram for Šalimu,
a liver of
9. a cattle and a ram for Baal in the north.
10. An ewe for Ṣapunu
as a burnt offering.
And as a peace offering:
11. ditto.
And in the temple/house of Baal of Ugarit,
12. two livers and a piece of offal:
for *ʾIluʾibʾi*
13. a cow,
for El a ram,
for Baal a ram,
for ʿAnatu
14. in the north a cattle and a ram,
for Pidray a ram
15. as a burnt offering.
And as a peace offering
for *ʾiluʾibʾi* a ram,
16. for Baal of Ugarit a ram,

for Baal of Aleppo a ram,
17. for *Yariḫu* a ram,
for ʿAnatu in the north a cattle
18. and a ram,
for Pidray a ram,
for Dadmiš a ram
19. And in the opening
for *ʾiluʾibʾi* a ram,
Lower Edge
20. for Baal a cattle and a ram,
Reverse
21. for Dagan a ram,
for the helper gods of
22. Baal a ram,
for ʿAnatu a ram,
for Rašap a ram,
23. as a peace offering.

---

24. And as a ŠNPT offering:[1]
for El a ram.
25. For ʿAnatu–ḪLŠ two rams,
26. for Gaṯarūma the left ǴṢB of
27. which (is) two cattle and a cattle and a ram
28. as a burnt offering.
And a peace offering: ditto.
29. For Baal in the north with the tamarisk
30. thirty times;
a ram
for the *Qẓrt*/incense-burner of
31. the table of Lady of the Palace
32. Next: a offspring of a cow
for Baal
33. in the north Aleppo,
and a liver (of?) an ewe
34. for Ṣapunu. . . . . .Baal of Ugarit. . .
35. for *ʾiluʾibʾi* a cow,
for Baal. . .
36. Ugarit. . .ʿAnatu in the north. . .
37. ŠL. . .

1. Pardee translates this as "presentation offering." Pardee, 31.

Bibliography

Abramson, Henry M. *Maimonides on Teshuvah: The Ways of Repentance*. 5th ed. Brooklyn: Touro College, 2017. Retrieved from https://touroscholar.touro.edu/lcas_books/1/?utm_source=touroscholar.touro.edu%2Flcas_books%2F1&utm_medium=PDF&utm_campaign=PDFCoverPages

Abusch, T. "Blood in Israel and Mesopotamia." In *Emanuel: Studies in Hebrew Bible, Septuagint, and Dead Sea Scrolls in Honor of Emanuel Tov*, edited by Shalom M. Paul, 675–84. Supplements to Vetus Testamentum 94. Boston: Brill, 2003.

Alt, Albrecht. "The Origins of Israelite Law." In *Essays on Old Testament History and Religion*, 79–132. Translated by R. A. Wilson. Oxford: Basil Blackwell, 1966.

Assohoto, Barnabe, and Samuel Ngewa. "Genesis." In *Africa Bible Commentary*, edited by Tokunboh Adeyemo, 9–84. Grand Rapids: Zondervan, 2006.

Auld, Graeme. "Leviticus: After Exodus and Before Numbers." In *The Book of Leviticus: Composition and Reception*, edited by Rolf Rendtorff and Robert A. Kugler, 41–54. Leiden: Brill, 2003.

———. "Leviticus at the Heart of the Pentateuch." In *Reading Leviticus: A Conversation with Mary Douglas*, edited by John F. A. Sawyer, 40–51. Sheffield: Sheffield Academic, 1996.

Averbeck, Richard E. "Ancient Near Eastern Mythography as It Relates to Historiography in the Hebrew Bible: Genesis 3 and the Cosmic Battle." In *The Future of Biblical Archaeology: Reassessing Methodologies and Assumptions: The Proceedings of a Symposium, August 12–14, 2001 at Trinity International University*, edited by James Karl Hoffmeier and Alan Millard, 328–56. Grand Rapids: Eerdmans, 2004.

———. "The Cult in Deuteronomy and Its Relationship to the Book of the Covenant and the Holiness Code." In *Sepher Torath Mosheh: Studies in the Composition and Interpretation of Deuteronomy*, edited by Daniel I. Block and Richard L. Schultz, 232–59. Peabody: Hendrickson, 2017.

———. "The Form Critical, Literary, and Ritual Unity of Exodus 19:3–24:11." Paper presented to the Biblical Law Group at the annual meeting of Society of Biblical Literature. Philadelphia, 20 November 1995.
———. "Law." In *Cracking Old Testament Codes: A Guide to Interpreting the Literary Genres of the Old Testament*, edited by D. Brent Sandy and Ronald L. Giese, Jr., 113–38. Nashville: Broadman & Holman, 1995.
———. "Sacrifices and Offerings." In *Dictionary of the Old Testament: Pentateuch*, edited by T. Desmond Alexander and David W. Baker, 706–33. Downers Grove: InterVarsity, 2003.
———. "Sumer, the Bible, and Comparative Method: Historiography and Temple Building." In *Mesopotamia and the Bible: Comparative Explorations*, edited by Mark W. Chavalas and K. Lawson Younger, Jr., 88–125. Grand Rapids: Baker Academic, 2002.
Baker, David W. "Leviticus." In *Leviticus, Numbers, Deuteronomy*. Cornerstone Biblical Commentary 2, 1–214. Carol Stream: Tyndale House, 2008.
Bar-Efrat, Shimon. *Narrative Art in the Bible*. Sheffield: Sheffield Academic, 1989. Reprint. New York: T&T Clark International, 2004.
Barr, James. "The Synchronic, the Diachronic and the Historical: A Triangular Relationship?" In *Synchronic or Diachronic? A Debate on Method in Old Testament Exegesis*, edited by Johannes C. De Moor, 1–14. New York: Brill, 1995.
Barré, Lloyd M. "The Poetic Structure of Genesis 9:5." *Zeitschrift fur die alttestamentliche Wissenschaft* 96, no. 1 (1984): 101–4.
Bell, Catherine. *Ritual: Perspectives and Dimensions*. New York: Oxford University Press, 1997.
———. *Ritual Theory, Ritual Practice*. New York: Oxford University Press, 1992.
Bergen, Wesley J. *Reading Ritual: Leviticus in Postmodern Culture*. New York: T&T Clark International, 2005.
Berlin, Adele. *Poetics and Interpretation of Biblical Narrative*. Sheffield: Almond, 1983.
Bibb, Bryan D. *Ritual Words and Narrative Worlds in the Book of Leviticus*. New York: T&T Clark, 2009.
Biddle, Mark E. *Deuteronomy*. Smyth and Helwys Bible Commentary. Macon: Smyth & Helwys, 2003.
Birch, Bruce C., Walter Brueggemann, Terence E. Fretheim, and David L. Petersen. *A Theological Introduction to the Old Testament*. Nashville: Abingdon, 1999.
Blenkinsopp, Joseph. *The Pentateuch: An Introduction to the First Five Books of the Bible*. Anchor Bible Reference Library. New York: Doubleday, 1992.
Block, Daniel I. *Deuteronomy*. NIV Application Commentary. Grand Rapids: Zondervan, 2012.

Bloom, Harold. "'Before Moses Was, I Am': The Original and Belated Testaments." In *Notebooks in Cultural Analysis: An Annual Review*, edited by Norman F. Cantor and Nathalia King, 3–14. Durham: Duke University Press, 1984.

Blum, Erhard. *Studien zur komposition des Pentateuch*. New York: Walter de Gruyter, 1990.

Boyce, Richard N. *Leviticus and Numbers*. Louisville: Westminster John Knox, 2008.

Bratcher, Dennis R. "Torah as Holiness: Old Testament 'Law' as Response to Divine Grace." A paper presented at the annual meeting of the Wesleyan Theological Society. Dayton, Ohio, 5 November 1994. Accessed 28 February 2016. http://www.crivoice.org/torahholiness.html.

Brett, Mark G. "The Future of Old Testament Theology." In *Congress Volume: Oslo 1998*, edited by A. Lemaire and M. Sæbø, 465–88. Leiden: Brill, 2000.

Brodie, Thomas L. *Genesis as Dialogue: A Literary, Historical and Theological Commentary*. Oxford: Oxford University Press, 2001.

Brown, Francis, S. R. Driver, and Charles A. Briggs. *The Brown-Driver-Briggs Hebrew and English Lexicon*. Peabody: Hendrickson, 1996.

Brown, Michael L. "*Kippēr* and Atonement in the Book of Isaiah." In *Ki Baruch Hu: Ancient Near Eastern, Biblical, and Judaic Studies in Honor of Baruch A. Levine*, edited by Robert Chazan, William W. Hallo, and Lawrence H. Schiffman, 189–202. Winona Lake: Eisenbrauns, 1999.

Brueggemann, Walter. *An Introduction to the Old Testament: The Canon and Christian Imagination*. Louisville: Westminster John Knox, 2003.

Budd, Philip J. *Leviticus*. New Century Bible Commentary. Grand Rapids: Eerdmans, 1996.

Calvin, John. *Genesis*. Translated by John King. Edinburgh: Banner of Truth Trust, 1984.

Campbell, Antony F., and Mark A. O'Brien. *Rethinking the Pentateuch: Prolegomena to the Theology of Ancient Israel*. Louisville: Westminster John Knox, 2005.

Carmichael, Calum M. *Illuminating Leviticus: A Study of Its Laws and Institutions in the Light of Biblical Narratives*. Baltimore: Johns Hopkins University Press, 2006.

———. *Law and Narrative in the Bible: The Evidence of the Deuteronomic Laws and the Decalogue*. London: Cornell University Press, 1985.

———. *The Laws of Deuteronomy*. Ithaca: Cornell University Press, 1974.

———. *The Spirit of the Laws*. Athens: University of Georgia Press, 1996.

Cassuto, U. *A Commentary on the Book of Genesis: Part II from Noah to Abraham*. Translated by Israel Abrahams. Jerusalem: Magnes Press, Hebrew University, 1992.

Cazelles, Henri. "Le Pentateuque comme Torah." In *Les règles de l'interprétation*, edited by Michel Tardieu, 35–68. Paris: Cerf, 1987.

Chirichigno, G. C. "The Narrative Structure of Exod 19–24." *Biblica* 68 (1987): 457–79.

Cholewinski, Alfred. *Heiligkeitsgesetz und Deuteronomium: Eine vergleichende Studie*. Rome: Biblical Institute Press, 1976.

Christensen, Duane L. *Deuteronomy 1:1–21:9*. Rev. ed. Word Biblical Commentary 6A. Nashville: Thomas Nelson, 2001.

Clemens, David M. *Sources for Ugaritic Ritual and Sacrifice: Ugaritic and Ugarit Akkadian Texts*. Münster: Ugarit-Verlag, 2001.

Clements, Ronald E. "The Deuteronomic Law of Centralisation and the Catastrophe of 587 B.C.E." In *After the Exile: Essays in Honour of Rex Mason*, edited by John Barton and David J. Reimer, 5–25. Macon: Mercer University Press, 1996.

Clines, David J. A., ed. *The Dictionary of Classical Hebrew*. 8 vols. Sheffield: Sheffield Academic, 1995.

Cogan, Mordechai. *1 Kings*. Anchor Bible. New York: Doubleday, 2000.

Cotter, David W. *Genesis*. Berit Olam: Studies in Hebrew Narrative and Poetry. Collegeville: Liturgical Press, 2003.

Cox, Howard H. *The Pentateuch: History or Story?* New York: University Press of America, 2005.

Crüsemann, Frank. "Der Exodus als Heiligung: Zur rechtgeschichtlichen Bedeutung des Heiligkeitsgesetzes." In *Die Hebräische Bibel und ihre zweifache Nachgeschichte: Festschrift für Rolf Rendtorff zum 65. Geburtstag*, edited by Erhard Blum, Christian Macholz, and Ekkehard W. Stegemann, 117–29. Neukirchen-Vluyn: Neukirchener Verl, 1990.

Daly, Robert J. *Sacrifice Unveiled: The True Meaning of Christian Sacrifice*. New York: T&T Clark, 2009.

Damrosch, David. *The Narrative Covenant: Transformations of Genre in the Growth of Biblical Literature*. Ithaca: Cornell University, 1987.

Davies, Philip R., and John Rogerson. *The Old Testament World*. 2nd ed. Louisville: Westminster John Knox, 2005.

De La Torre, Miguel A. *Genesis*. Belief: A Theological Commentary on the Bible. Louisville: Westminster John Knox, 2011.

De Moor, Johannes C., and Paul Sanders. "An Ugaritic Expiation Ritual and Its Old Testament Parallels." *Ugarit Forschungen* 23 (1991): 283–300.

De Vaux, Roland. *Ancient Israel: Its Life and Institutions*. London: Darton, Longman & Todd, 1973.

———. *Les sacrifices de L'Ancien Testament*. Paris: Gabalda, 1964.

———. *Studies in Old Testament Sacrifice*. Cardiff: University of Wales Press, 1964.

Dever, William G. *What Did the Biblical Writers Know and When Did They Know It?: What Archaeology Can Tell Us about the Reality of Ancient Israel*. Grand Rapids: Eerdmans, 2001.

Dietrich, Manfried, Oswald Loretz, and Joaquín Sanmartín, ed. *Die keilalphabetischen Texte aus Ugarit (KTU)*. Münster: Ugarit-Verlag, 2013. 3rd enl. Ed. of *KTU: The Cuneiform Alphabetic Texts from Ugarit, Ras Ibn Hani, and Other Places*. Edited by Manfried Dietrich, Oswald Loretz, and Joaquín Sanmartín. Münster: Ugarit-Verlag, 1995.

Dillmann, A. *Die Bücher Numeri, Deuteronomium und Josu* Kurzgefasstes exegetisches Handbuch zum Alten Testament. Leipzig: S. Hirzel, 1886.

Doorly, William J. *The Laws of Yahweh: A Handbook of Biblical Law*. New York: Paulist, 2002.

Dorsey, David A. *The Literary Structure of the Old Testament: A Commentary on Genesis–Malachi*. Grand Rapids: Baker, 1999.

Doty, William G. *Mythography: The Study of Myths and Rituals*. 2nd ed. Tuscaloosa: University of Alabama Press, 2000.

Douglas, Mary. "The Forbidden Animals in Leviticus." *Journal for the Study of the Old Testament* 59 (1993): 3–23.

———. *Leviticus as Literature*. New York: Oxford University Press, 2000.

———. "Poetic Structure in Leviticus." In *Pomegranates and Golden Bells: Studies in Biblical, Jewish, and Near Eastern Ritual, Law, and Literature in Honor of Jacob Milgrom*, edited by David P. Wright, David Noel Freedman, and Avi Hurvitz, 239–56. Winona Lake: Eisenbrauns, 1995.

———. *Purity and Danger: An Analysis of the Concepts of Pollution and Taboo*. London: Routledge, 1991.

Dozeman, Thomas B. *God on the Mountain*. Atlanta: Scholars Press, 1989.

Driver, S. R. *A Critical and Exegetical Commentary on Deuteronomy*. 3rd ed. Edinburgh: T&T Clark, 1996.

———. *An Introduction to the Literature of the Old Testament*. Cleveland: World, 1967.

Durkheim, Émile. *The Elementary Forms of the Religious Life*. New York: Macmillan, 1954.

Eissfeldt, Otto. *The Old Testament: An Introduction, including the Apocrypha and Pseudepigrapha, and also the Works of Similar Type from Qumran: The History of the Formation of the Old Testament*. New York: Harper & Row, 1965.

Elliger, Karl. *Leviticus*. Tübingen: J. C. B. Mohr, 1966.

Enns, Peter. *Exodus*. NIV Application Commentary. Grand Rapids: Zondervan, 2000.

Even-Shoshan, Abraham. *A New Concordance of the Old Testament: Using the Hebrew and Aramaic Text*. 2nd ed. Jerusalem: Sivan Press, 1989.

Falk, Ze'ev W. *Hebrew Law in Biblical Times: An Introduction*. 2nd ed. Winona Lake: Eisenbrauns, 2001.

Farbridge, Maurice H. *Studies in Biblical and Semitic Symbolism*. Library of Biblical Studies. New York: KTAV, 1970.

Feder, Yitzhaq. *Blood Expiation in Hittite and Biblical Ritual: Origins, Context, and Meaning*. Society of Biblical Literature Writings from the Ancient World Supplement Series. Atlanta: Society of Biblical Literature, 2011.

Feucht, Christian. *Untersuchungen zum Heigkeitsgesetz*. Theologische Arbeiten 20. Berlin: Evangelische Verlagsanstalt, 1964.

Firmage, E. "The Biblical Dietary Laws and the Concept of Holiness." In *Studies in the Pentateuch*, edited by J. A. Emerton, 177–208. Supplements to Vetus Testamentum 41. New York: Brill, 1990.

Firth, Raymond. *Symbols: Public and Private*. Symbol, Myth, and Ritual Series. Ithaca: Cornell University Press, 1973.

Fohrer, G. *Introduction to the Old Testament*. Nashville: Abingdon, 1968.

Fretheim, Terence E. *The Pentateuch*. Nashville: Abingdon, 1996.

Gammie, John G. *Holiness in Israel*. Minneapolis: Fortress, 1989.

Gane, Roy E. *Cult and Character: Purification Offerings, Day of Atonement, and Theodicy*. Winona Lake: Eisenbrauns, 2005.

———. "Leviticus." In *Genesis, Exodus, Leviticus, Numbers, Deuteronomy*. Vol. 1 of Zondervan Illustrated Bible Backgrounds Commentary, 284–337. Grand Rapids: Zondervan, 2009.

———. *Leviticus, Numbers*. NIV Application Commentary. Grand Rapids: Zondervan, 2004.

Gemser, B. "The Importance of the Motive Clause in Old Testament Law." In *Congress Volume: Copenhagen*, 50–66. Leiden: Brill, 1953.

Genette, Gérard. *Figures III*. Paris: Seuil, 1972.

———. *Narrative Discourse: An Essay in Method*. Translated by Jane E. Lewin. Ithaca: Cornell University Press, 1980.

Gerstenberger, Erhard S. *Leviticus: A Commentary*. Louisville: Westminster John Knox, 1996.

Gesenius, Wilhelm. *Gesenius' Hebrew Grammar*. Edited by E. Kautzsch. Translated by A. E. Cowley. Mineola: Dover, 2006.

Gignilliat, Mark S. *A Brief History of Old Testament Criticism: From Benedict Spinoza to Brevard Childs*. Grand Rapids: Zondervan, 2012.

Gilders, William K. *Blood Ritual in the Hebrew Bible: Meaning and Power*. Baltimore: John Hopkins University Press, 2004.

Gluckman, Max. "Ritual." In *Magic, Witchcraft, and Religion: An Anthropological Study of the Supernatural*, edited by Arthur C. Lehmann and James E. Myers, 40–44. Mountain View: Mayfield, 1997.

Goldingay, John. *Israel's Faith*. Vol. 2 of *Old Testament Theology*. Downers Grove: IVP Academic, 2006.

———. *Israel's Life*. Vol. 3 of *Old Testament Theology*. Downers Grove: IVP Academic, 2009.

Gorman, Frank H. *Divine Presence and Community: A Commentary on the Book of Leviticus*. Grand Rapids: Eerdmans, 1997.

———. *The Ideology of Ritual: Space, Time and Status in the Priestly Theology*. Sheffield: Sheffield Academic, 1990.

Gowan, Donald E. *From Eden to Babel: A Commentary on the Book of Genesis 1–11*. International Theological Commentary. Grand Rapids: Eerdmans, 1988.

Grabbe, Lester L. *Leviticus*. Old Testament Guides. Sheffield: Sheffield Academic, 1993.

Graetz, Heinrich. *The Structure of Jewish History and Other Essays*. Translated by Ismar Schorsch. New York: Jewish Theological Seminary of America, 1975.

Graf, Karl Heinrich. *Die geschichtlichen bücher des Alten Testaments: Zwei historisch-kritische untersuchungen*. Leipzig: Weigel, 1866.

Grimes, Ronald L. *Ritual Criticism: Case Studies in Its Practice, Essays on Its Theory*. Columbia: University of South Carolina Press, 1990.

Gunkel, Hermann. *Genesis*. Translated by Mark E. Biddle. Macon: Mercer University Press, 1997.

Gutzwiller, Kathryn. "Comments on Rolf Rendtorff." In *Reading Leviticus: A Conversation with Mary Douglas*, edited by John F. A. Sawyer, 36–39. Sheffield: Sheffield Academic, 1996.

Hall, Gary. "Rhetorical Criticism, Chiasm, and Theme in Deuteronomy." *Stone-Campbell Journal* 1 (1998): 85–100.

Hallo, William W. "Compare and Contrast: The Contextual Approach to Biblical Literature." In *Scripture in Context III: The Bible in the Light of Cuneiform Literature*, edited by William W. Hallo, Bruce William Jones, and Gerald L. Mattingly, 1–30. Lewiston: Edwin Mellen, 1990.

———. "The Origins of the Sacrificial Cult: New Evidence from Mesopotamia and Israel." In *Ancient Israelite Religion: Essays in Honor of Frank Moore Cross*, edited by Patrick D. Miller, Jr., Paul D. Hanson, and S. Dean McBride, 3–13. Philadelphia: Fortress, 1987.

Hallo, William W., ed. *Canonical Compositions from the Biblical World*. Vol. 1 of *The Context of Scripture*. Leiden: Brill, 1997.

Hamilton, Victor P. *The Book of Genesis Chapters 1–17*. New International Commentary on the Old Testament. Grand Rapids: Eerdmans, 1990.

Haran, M. "Holiness Code." In *Encyclopaedia Judaica*, 820–25. Jerusalem: Encyclopaedia Judaica, 1971.

Haran, Menahem. *Temples and Temple Service in Ancient Israel: An Inquiry into the Character of Cult Phenomena and the Historical Setting of the Priest School.* Oxford: Clarendon, 1978.

Harrison, R. K. *Leviticus: An Introduction and Commentary*. Tyndale Old Testament Commentaries. Downers Grove: InterVarsity, 1980. Reprint, 2008.

Hartley, John E. *Leviticus*. Word Biblical Commentary 4. Dallas: Word, 1992.

Heger, Paul. *The Three Biblical Altar Laws: Developments in the Sacrificial Cult in Practice and Theology – Political and Economic Background*. Beihefte zur Zeitschrift für die alttestamentliche Wissenschaft. New York: Walter de Gruyter, 1999.

Hess, Richard S. *Israelite Religions: An Archaeological and Biblical Survey*. Grand Rapids: Baker Academic, 2007.

Hildenbrand, Michael Dean. *Structure and Theology in the Holiness Code*. North Richland Hills: Bibal, 2004.

Hill, Andrew E. *1 and 2 Chronicles*. The NIV Application Commentary. Grand Rapids: Zondervan, 2003.

Hillers, Delbert R. *Covenant: The History of a Biblical Idea*. Baltimore: Johns Hopkins Press, 1969.

Hoffmeier, James K. *Ancient Israel in Sinai: The Evidence for the Authenticity of the Wilderness Tradition*. New York: Oxford University Press, 2005.

Hoppe, L. J. "Jerusalem in the Deuteronomistic History." In *Das Deuteronomium. Entstehung, gestalt und botschaft – Deuteronomy: Origin, Form and Message*, edited by Norbert Lohfink and S. Amsler, 107–10. Bibliotheca Ephemeridum Theologicarum Lovaniensium. Leuven: Leuven University Press, 1985.

House, Paul R. *Old Testament Theology*. Downers Grove: InterVarsity, 1998.

"Human Renal Glomerular Endothelial Cells." *Yuhengfengbio.com*. Accessed 24 September 2015. http://www.yuhengfengbio.com/display03.asp?id=277.

Jacob, Benno. *The First Book of the Bible: Genesis*. Translated by Ernest I. Jacob and Walter Jacob. New York: KTAV, 1974.

Janzen, David. *The Social Meanings of Sacrifice in the Hebrew Bible: A Study of Four Writings*. Beihefte zur zeitschrift für die alttestamentliche wissenschaft. New York: Walter de Gruyter, 2004.

Jenson, Philip P. "The Levitical Sacrificial System." In *Sacrifice in the Bible*, edited by Roger T. Beckwith and Martin J. Selman, 25–40. Grand Rapids: Baker, 1995.

Jewish Publication Society, ed. *JPS Hebrew-English Tanakh*. Philadelphia: Jewish Publication Society, 1999.

Johnstone, W. "Reactivating the Chronicles Analogy in Pentateuchal Studies." *Zeitschrift für die alttestamentliche wissenschaft* 99, no. 1 (1987): 16–37.

Joosten, J. *People and Land in the Holiness Code*. Supplements to Vetus Testamentum 67. New York: Brill, 1996.

Joüon, Paul. *A Grammar of Biblical Hebrew*. Translated by T. Muraoka. 2 vols. Subsidia Biblica. Rome: Editrice Pontificio Istituto Biblico, 2005.

Jüngling, Hans-Winfried. "Das Buch Levitikus in der Forschung seit Karl Elligers Kommentar aus dem Jahr 1966." In *Levitikus als Buch*, edited by Heinz-Josef Fabry and Hans-Winfried Jüngling, 1–45. Berlin: Philo, 1999.

Kayser, August. *Das vorexilische Buch der Urgeschichte Israels und seine Erweiterungen: Ein Beitrag zur Pentateuch-kritik*. Strassburg: C. F. Schmidt's Universitäts-Buchhandlung, 1874. ATLA fiche 1987–1271.

Kertzer, David, I. *Ritual, Politics, and Power*. New Haven: Yale University Press, 1988.

Kilian, Rudolf. *Literarkritische und formgeschichtliche Untersuchung des Heiligkeitsgesetzes*. Bonner biblische Beiträge 19. Bonn: P. Hanstein, 1963.

Kitchen, Kenneth A., and Paul J. N. Lawrence. *Overall Historical Survey*. Vol. 3 of *Treaty, Law and Covenant in the Ancient Near East*. Wiesbaden: Harrassowitz, 2012.

Kiuchi, Nobuyoshi. *Leviticus*. Apollos Old Testament Commentary. Downers Grove: InterVarsity, 2007.

———. *Purification Offering in the Priestly Literature: Its Meaning and Function*. Journal for the Study of the Old Testament Supplement Series 56. Sheffield: JSOT Press, 1987.

———. "Spirituality in Offering a Peace Offering." *Tyndale Bulletin* 50, no. 1 (1999): 23–31.

Kleinig, John W. *Leviticus*. Concordia Commentary. Saint Louis: Concordia, 2003.

Klingbeil, Gerald A. *Bridging the Gap: Ritual and Ritual Texts in the Bible*. Bulletin of Biblical Research Supplements 1. Winona Lake: Eisenbrauns, 2007.

Klostermann, August. *Der Pentateuch: Beitrage zu seinem verstandnis und seiner Entstehungsgeschichte*. Leipzig: A. Deichert (Georg Böhme), 1893.

Kluckhohn, Clyde. "Myths and Rituals: A General Theory." *Harvard Theological Review* 35, no. 1 (1942): 45–79.

Knierim, Rolf P. "The Composition of the Pentateuch." In *Society of Biblical Literature 1985 Seminar Papers*, edited by Kent Harold Richards, 393–415. Atlanta: Scholars Press, 1985.

Knohl, Israel. *The Sanctuary of Silence: The Priestly Torah and the Holiness Code*. Minneapolis: Fortress, 1995.

Knoppers, Gary N. *1 Chronicles 10–29*. Anchor Yale Bible Reference Library. New Haven: Yale University Press, 2004.

Koehler, Ludwig, Walter Baumgartner, and J. J. Stamm. *The Hebrew and Aramaic Lexicon of the Old Testament (HALOT)*. Translated and edited under the supervision of M. E. J. Richardson. 4 vols. Leiden: Brill, 1994–99.

Kornfeld, Walter. *Die neue Echter Bibel: Kommentar zum Alten Testament mit der Einheitsübersetzung*. Würzburg: Echter, 1983.

Kunkle, Fredrick. "Walnuts Appear to Delay Onset of Alzheimer's Disease, New Study Finds." *The Washington Post*. 21 October 2014. Accessed 9 July 2015. https://www.washingtonpost.com/national/health-science/walnuts-appear-to-delay-onset-of-alzheimers-disease-new-study-finds/2014/10/20/d357bc7e-58a6-11e4-b812-38518ae74c67_story.html.

Kuruvilla, Abraham. *Genesis: A Theological Commentary for Preachers*. Eugene: Resource, 2014.

Labuschagne, Casper J. "The Pattern of the Divine Speech Formulas in the Pentateuch: The Key to Its Literary Structure." *Vetus Testamentum* 32, no. 3 (1982): 268–96.

Leach, Edmund R. "Ritual." In *International Encyclopedia of the Social Sciences*, edited by David L. Sills and Robert K. Merton, 520–26. New York: Crowell Collier & Macmillan, 1968.

Lemche, Niels Peter. "On the Use of 'System Theory,' 'Macro Theories' and 'Evolutionistic Thinking' in Modern OT Research and Biblical Archaeology." *Scandinavian Journal of the Old Testament* 2 (1990): 73–88.

Levine, Baruch A. *In the Presence of the LORD: A Study of Cult and Some Cultic Terms in Ancient Israel*. Leiden: Brill, 1974.

———. "Leviticus: Its Literary History and Location in Biblical Literature." In *The Book of Leviticus: Composition and Reception*, edited by Rolf Rendtorff and Robert A. Kugler, 11–23. Leiden: Brill, 2003.

———. *Leviticus: The Traditional Hebrew Text with the New JPS Translation*. JPS Torah Commentary. Philadelphia: Jewish Publication Society, 1989.

———. "*Lpny* YHWH – Phenomenology of the Open-Air-Altar in Biblical Israel." In *Biblical Archaeology Today, 1990: Proceedings of the Second International Congress on Biblical Archaeology*, 196–205. Jerusalem: Israel Exploration Society/Keterpress, 1993.

Levinson, Bernard M. *Deuteronomy and the Hermeneutics of Legal Innovation*. New York: Oxford University Press 1997.

———. "The Right Chorale: From the Poetics to the Hermeneutics of the Hebrew Bible." In *'Not in Heaven': Coherence and Complexity in Biblical Narrative*, edited by Jason P. Rosenblatt and Joseph C. Sitterson, Jr., 129–53. Bloomington: Indiana University Press, 1991.

Levy, David M. *The Tabernacle: Shadows of the Messiah – Its Sacrifices, Services, and Priesthood*. Grand Rapids: Kregel, 2003.

Li, Ershan. "Impression Chinese Red." *Chinese Herritage*. February 2007. Accessed 9 July 2015. http://doc.qkzz.net/article/93b0673e-c8e4-4d1d-8378-af86206d2962.htm. [in Chinese]

李爾山。〈印象中國紅〉。《中華遺產》, 2007年2月。2015年7月9日存取。Accessed 9 July 2015. http://doc.qkzz.net/article/93b0673e-c8e4-4d1d-8378-af86206d2962.htm.

Li, Zhixiang. "The Culture of Blood." *Blog.Ifeng.com*. 28 January 2010. Accessed 9 July 2015. http://blog.ifeng.com/article/4171732.html. [in Chinese]
李之祥。〈血文化〉。《尋找中國人的信仰》，2010年1月28日張貼。2015年7月9日存取。Accessed 9 July 2015. http://blog.ifeng.com/article/4171732.html.

Lin, Tianfen. "A Study of Sun Si-Miao's Medical Health Preserving Theory." Master's thesis, Aletheia University, 2007. [in Chinese] 林天芬。〈孫思邈醫藥養生之研究〉。碩士論文，真理大學，2007。

Lin, Zhiming, and Qihua Li. "The Specific Peptide Sequences of Pig's Brain Can Treat Alzheimer's Disease." *Taiwan Association for Traditional and Complementary Medicine*. 13 June 2014. Accessed 9 July 2015. http://www.tatcm.org.tw/%E8%B1%AC%E8%85%A6%E7%89%B9%E5%AE%9A%E8%83%9C%E8%82%BD%E5%BA%8F%E5%88%97-%E5%8F%AF%E6%B2%BB%E7%99%82%E9%98%BF%E6%BB%8B%E6%B5%B7%E9%BB%98%E7%97%87/. [in Chinese]
林致明和李奇樺。〈豬腦特定胜肽序列可以治療阿茲海默症〉。《臺灣傳統暨替代醫學協會》，2014年6月13日。2015年7月9日存取。Accessed 9 July 2015. http://www.tatcm.org.tw/%E8%B1%AC%E8%85%A6%E7%89%B9%E5%AE%9A%E8%83%9C%E8%82%BD%E5%BA%8F%E5%88%97-%E5%8F%AF%E6%B2%BB%E7%99%82%E9%98%BF%E6%BB%8B%E6%B5%B7%E9%BB%98%E7%97%87/.

Lloyd, J. B. "The Banquet Theme in Ugaritic Narrative." *Ugarit-Forschungen* 22 (1990): 169–93.

Low, Chai-Hok, and Bruce Nicholls. *The Book of Deuteronomy*. Asia Bible Commentary Series. Manila: Asia Theological Association, 2013.

Luciani, Didier. *Sainteté et pardon*. 2 vols. Bibliotheca Ephemeridum Theologicarum Lovaniensium 185A–185B. Leuven: Leuven University Press, 2005.

Lund, Nils W. *Chiasmus in the New Testament: A Study in the Form and Function of Chiastic Structures*. Peabody: Hendrickson, 1992.

Lundbom, Jack R. *Deuteronomy: A Commentary*. Grand Rapids: Eerdmans, 2013.

———. "The Inclusio and Other Framing Devices in Deuteronomy I–XXVIII." *Vetus Testamentum* 46, no. 3 (1996): 296–315.

Lyu, Weizhen. "The Cause of Alzheimer's Disease Is Found in the Research and 'Eating Brain Benefits Brain' Is Not a Superstition." *Everyday Health*. 11 November 2014. Accessed 9 July 2015. http://news.everydayhealth.com.tw/2014/11/11/13343-%E5%AD%B8%E7%95%8C%E6%89%BE%E5%88%B0%E9%98%BF%E8%8C%B2%E6%B5%B7%E9%BB%98%E7%97%87%E5%85%83%E5%87%B6-%E3%80%8C%E5%90%83%E8%85%A6%E8%A3%9C%E8%85%A6%E3%80%8D%E4%B9%9F%E4%B8%8D%E7%AE%97%E5%AE%8C%E5%85%A8. [in Chinese]

呂維振。〈學界找到阿茲海默症元兇「吃腦補腦」也不算完全迷信〉。《早安健康News》，2014年11月11日。2015年7月9日存取。Accessed 9 July 2015. http://news.everydayhealth.com.tw/2014/11/11/13343-%E5%AD%B8%E7%95%8C%E6%89%BE%E5%88%B0%E9%98%BF%E8%8C%B2%E6%B5%B7%E9%BB%98%E7%97%87%E5%85%83%E5%87%B6-%E3%80%8C%E5%90%83%E8%85%A6%E8%A3%9C%E8%85%A6%E3%80%8D%E4%B9%9F%E4%B8%8D%E7%AE%97%E5%AE%8C%E5%85%A8.

Malina, Bruce J. "Mediterranean Sacrifice: Dimensions of Domestic and Political Religion." *Biblical Theology Bulletin* 26, no. 1 (1996): 26–44.

Malul, Meir. *Studies in Mesopotamian Legal Symbolism*. Kevelaer: Butzon u. Bercker, 1988.

Mann, Thomas W. *The Book of the Torah: The Narrative Integrity of the Pentateuch*. Atlanta: John Knox, 1988.

McCarthy, Dennis J. "Further Notes on the Symbolism of Blood and Sacrifice." *Journal of Biblical Literature* 92, no. 2 (1973): 205–10.

McConville, J. G. *Deuteronomy*. Apollos Old Testament Commentary 5. Downers Grove: InterVarsity, 2002.

———. *Law and Theology in Deuteronomy*. Journal for the Study of the Old Testament Supplement Series 33. Sheffield: JSOT Press, 1984.

McDermott, John J. *Reading the Pentateuch: A Historical Introduction*. New York: Paulist Press, 2002.

McEntire, Mark. *Struggling with God: An Introduction to the Pentateuch*. Macon: Mercer University Press, 2008.

Meier, Samuel A. *Speaking of Speaking: Marking Direct Discourse in the Hebrew Bible*. New York: Brill, 1992.

Merlo, Paolo, and Paolo Xella. "The Ugaritic Cultic Texts–The Rituals." In *Handbook of Ugaritic Studies*, edited by Wilfred G.E. Watson and Nicolas Wyatt, 287–304. Boston: Brill, 1999.

Merrill, Eugene H. *Everlasting Dominion: A Theology of the Old Testament*. Nashville: Broadman & Holman, 2006.

Míguez Bonino, José. "A Covenant of Life: A Meditation on Genesis 9:1–17." *Ecumenical Review* 33, no. 4 (1981): 341–45.

Milgrom, Jacob. "The Case for the Pre-exilic and Exilic Provenance of the Books of Exodus, Leviticus and Numbers." In *Reading Law: Studies in Honour of Gordon J. Wenham*, edited by J. G. McConville and Karl Möller, 48–56. New York: T&T Clark, 2007.

———. *Leviticus 1–16*. Anchor Bible. New York: Doubleday, 1991.

———. *Leviticus 17–22*. Anchor Bible. New York: Doubleday, 2000.

———. *Leviticus 23–27*. Anchor Bible. New York: Doubleday, 2001.

———. "Profane Slaughter and a Formulaic Key to the Composition of Deuteronomy." *Hebrew Union College Annual* 47 (1976): 1–17.

———. "A Prolegomenon to Leviticus 17:11." *Journal of Biblical Literature* 90 (1971): 149–56.

Miller, Barbara Stoler. "Review of 'Sanskrit and Indian Studies: Essays in Honour of Daniel H. H. Ingalls.'" *Journal of Asian Studies* 41, no. 2 (1982): 392–93.

Miller, Cynthia L. *The Representation of Speech in Biblical Hebrew Narrative: A Linguistic Analysis*. Harvard Semitic Monographs. Atlanta: Scholars, 1996.

Miller, J. L. *Studies in the Origins, Development, and Interpretation of the Kizzuwatna Rituals*. Studien zu den Bogazköy-Texten 46. Wiesbaden: Harrassowitz, 2004.

Miller, Patrick D. *The Religion of Ancient Israel*. Library of Ancient Israel. Louisville: Westminster John Knox, 2000.

Modéus, Martin. *Sacrifice and Symbol: Biblical Shelamim in a Ritual Perspective*. Coniectanea Biblica: Old Testament Series. Stockholm: Almqvist & Wiksell International, 2005.

Moraldi, Luigi. *Espiazione sacrificale e riti espiatori: Nell'ambiente biblico e nell'antico testamento*. Rome: Pontificio Instituto Biblico, 1956.

Muthaiyah, Balu, Musthafa M. Essa, Moon Lee, Ved Chauhan, Kulbir Kaur, and Abha Chauhan. "Dietary Supplementation of Walnuts Improves Memory Deficits and Learning Skills in Transgenic Mouse Model of Alzheimer's Disease." *Journal of Alzheimer's Disease* 42, no. 4 (2014): 1197–405. Accessed 9 July 2015. http://content.iospress.com/articles/journal-of-alzheimers-disease/jad140675.

Nelson, Richard D. *Deuteronomy*. Louisville: Westminster John Knox Press, 2002.

———. *Raising Up a Faithful Priest: Community and Priesthood in Biblical Theology*. Louisville: Westminster John Knox, 1993.

Nicholson, Ernest W. "The Origin of the Tradition in Exodus XXIV 9–11." *Vetus Testamentum* 26 (1976): 148–60.

———. *The Pentateuch in the Twentieth Century: The Legacy of Julius Wellhausen*. New York: Oxford University Press, 2002.

Niehaus, Jeffrey J. "The Central Sanctuary: Where and When." *Tyndale Bulletin* 43, no. 1 (1992): 3–30.

———. "Covenant and Narrative, God and Time." *Journal of the Evangelical Theological Society* 53, no. 3 (2010): 535–59.

Nihan, Christophe. *From Priestly Torah to Pentateuch: A Study in the Composition of the Book of Leviticus*. Tübingen: Mohr Siebeck, 2007.

———. "The Holiness Code between D and P: Some Comments on the Function and Significance of Leviticus 17–26 in the Composition of the Torah." In *Das Deuteronomium zwischen Pentateuch und Deuteronomistischem Geschichtswerk*, edited by Eckart Otto and Reinhard Achenbac, 81–122. Göttingen: Vandenhoeck & Ruprecht, 2004.

———. "The Torah between Samaria and Judah." In *The Pentateuch as Torah: New Models for Understanding Its Promulgation and Acceptance*, edited by Gary N. Knoppers and Bernard M. Levinson, 187–223. Winona Lake: Eisenbrauns, 2007.

Noth, Martin. *Exodus*. Translated by J. S. Bowden. The Old Testament Library. Philadelphia: Westminster, 1962.

———. *The Laws in the Pentateuch and Other Studies*. Translated by D. R. ap-Thomas. Philadelphia: Fortress, 1966.

———. *Leviticus: A Commentary*. Translated by J. E. Anderson. The Old Testament Library. London: SCM, 1965.

Olmo Lete, Gregorio del. *Canaanite Religion according to the Liturgical Texts of Ugarit*. Translated by Wilfred G. E. Watson. 2nd English ed. Münster: Ugarit-Verlag, 2014.

———. "Rituales sacrificiales de plenilunio y novilunio (KTU 1.109/1.46)." *Aula orientalis* 7 (July 1989): 181–88.

———. "The Sacrificial Vocabulary at Ugarit." *Studi epigrafici e linguistici sul Vicino Oriente antico* 12 (1995): 37–49.

Olmo Lete, Gregorio del, and Joaquín Sanmartín. *A Dictionary of the Ugaritic Language in the Alphabetic Tradition.* 2 vols. Translated by Wilfred G. E. Watson. Leiden: Brill, 2004.

Otto, Eckart. "Innerbiblische Exegese im Heiligkeitsgesetz Levitikus 17–26." In *Levitikus als buch*, edited by Heinz-Josef Fabry and Hans-Winfried Jüngling, 125–96. Berlin: Philo, 1999.

———. "Scribal Scholarship in the Formation of Torah and Prophets." In *The Pentateuch as Torah: New Models for Understanding Its Promulgation and Acceptance*, edited by Gary N. Knoppers and Bernard M. Levinson, 171–84. Winona Lake: Eisenbrauns, 2007.

Pardee, Dennis. *Les textes rituels*. 2 vols. Ras Shamra-Ougarit 12. Paris: Éditions Recherche sur les Civilisations, 2000.

———. *Ritual and Cult at Ugarit*. Writings from the Ancient World. Atlanta: Society of Biblical Literature, 2002.

Parker, Simon B. "Ugaritic Literature and the Bible." *Near Eastern Archaeology* 63, no. 4 (2000): 228–31.

Parker, Simon B., ed. *Ugaritic Narrative Poetry*. Atlanta: Society of Biblical Literature, 1997.

Patrick, Dale. *Old Testament Law*. Atlanta: John Knox, 1985.

Petersen, Allan Rosengren. *The Royal God: Enthronement Festivals in Ancient Israel and Ugarit?* Journal for the Study of the Old Testament Supplement Series. Sheffield: Sheffield Academic, 1998.

Pitkänen, Pekka. *Central Sanctuary and Centralization of Worship in Ancient Israel: From the Settlement to the Building of Solomon's Temple*. Piscataway: Gorgias, 2004.

Powys, John Cowper. *Enjoyment of Literature*. New York: Simon & Schuster, 1938.

Preuss, Horst Dietrich. "Deuteronomium." *Erträge der Forschung* 164 (1982): 187.

———. *Old Testament Theology*. Vol. 1. Louisville: Westminster John Knox, 1995.

Propp, William H. C. *Exodus 19–40*. Anchor Bible. New York: Doubleday, 2006.

Radday, Yehuda T. "Chiasmus in Hebrew Biblical Narrative." In *Chiasmus in Antiquity: Structures, Analyses, Exegesis*, edited by John W. Welch, 50–117. Provo: Research Press, 1981.

Rainey, Anson F. "The Order of Sacrifices in Old Testament Ritual Texts." *Biblica* 51 (1970): 485–98.

Rappaport, Roy A. *Ritual and Religion in the Making of Humanity*. Cambridge: Cambridge University Press, 1999.

Rendtorff, Rolf. "Is It Possible to Read Leviticus as a Separate Book?" In *Reading Leviticus: A Conversation with Mary Douglas*, edited by John F. A. Sawyer, 22–39. Sheffield: Sheffield Academic, 1996.

———. *The Old Testament: An Introduction*. Philadelphia: Fortress, 1991.

Reyburn, William D., and Euan McG. Fry. *A Handbook on Genesis*. UBS Handbook Series. New York: United Bible Societies, 1997.

Rodd, Cyril S. *Glimpses of a Strange Land: Studies in Old Testament Ethics*. Old Testament Studies. Edinburgh: T&T Clark, 2001.

Rogerson, John W. "The Bible and Theology." In *The Blackwell Companion to Nineteenth-Century Theology*, edited by David Fergusson, 455–67. Hoboken: Wiley-Blackwell, 2010.

Rooker, Mark F. *Leviticus*. New American Commentary 3A. Nashville: Broadman & Holman, 2000.

Ross, Allen P. *Holiness to the LORD: A Guide to the Exposition of the Book of Leviticus*. Grand Rapids: Baker Academic, 2002.

Ruwe, Andreas. "The Structure of the Book of Leviticus in the Narrative Outline of the Priestly Sinai Story (Exod 19:1–Num 10:10)." In *The Book of Leviticus: Composition and Reception*, edited by Rolf Rendtorff and Robert A. Kugler, 55–78. Leiden: Brill, 2003.

Sailhamer, John H. *The Meaning of the Pentateuch: Revelation, Composition and Interpretation*. Downers Grove: IVP Academic, 2009.

———. *The Pentateuch as Narrative*. Grand Rapids: Zondervan, 1992.

Sarna, Nahum M. *Genesis*. JPS Torah Commentary. Jerusalem: Jewish Publication Society, 1989.

Scharfe, Hartmut. "The Great Rituals - Were They Really Meaningless?" In *Sanskrit and Related Studies: Contemporary Researches and Reflections*, edited by Bimal Krishna Matilal and Purusottama Bilimori, 89–97. Delhi: Sri Satguru, 1990.

Schwartz, Baruch J. "The Prohibition Concerning the 'Eating' of Blood in Leviticus." In *Priesthood and Cult in Ancient Israel*, edited by Gary A. Anderson and Saul M. Olyan, 34–66. Sheffield: Sheffield Academic Press, 1991.

Scolnic, Benjamin Edidin. *Theme and Context in Biblical Lists*. Edited by Jacob Neusner, William Scott Green, James Strange, Darrell J. Fasching, and Sara Mandell. South Florida Studies in the History of Judaism 119. Atlanta: Scholars, 1995.

Scroggie, W. Graham. *Know Your Bible: A Brief Introduction to the Scriptures*. London: Fleming H. Revell Company, 1953.

Selman, Martin J. "Sacrifice in the Ancient Near East." In *Sacrifice in the Bible*, edited by Roger T. Beckwith and Martin J. Selman, 88–104. Grand Rapids: Baker, 1995.

Shea, William H. "Literary Form and Theological Function in Leviticus." In *The Seventy Weeks, Leviticus, and the Nature of Prophecy*, edited by Frank B. Holbrook, 131–68. Daniel and Revelation Committee Series 3. Washington D. C.: Biblical Research Institute, 1986.

Sheik, Adam, ed. "Like Nourishes Like." *CantoDict Project*. 22 March 2013. Accessed 9 July 2015. http://www.cantonese.sheik.co.uk/dictionary/words/38236/. [in Chinese]

〈以形補形〉。2015年7月9日存取。Accessed 9 July 2015. http://www.cantonese.sheik.
co.uk/dictionary/words/38236/.

Shen-Nong Limited. "Like Nourishes Like." *Shen-Nong.com*. Accessed 9 July 2015. http://www.shen-nong.com/eng/forum/topic.asp?v_id=301. [in Chinese]

〈以形補形〉。《神農氏》。2015年7月9日存取。Accessed 9 July 2015. http://www.shen-nong.com/eng/forum/topic.asp?v_id=301.

Sherwood, Stephen K., *Leviticus, Numbers, Deuteronomy*. Berit Olam: Studies in Hebrew Narrative & Poetry. Collegeville: Liturgical Press, 2002.

Shorter, Aylward. "Symbolism, Ritual and History: An Examination of the Work of Victor Turner." In *The Historical Study of African Religion*, edited by T. O. Ranger and I. N. Kimambo, 139–49. Berkeley: University of California Press, 1972.

Sivan, Daniel. *A Grammar of the Ugaritic Language*. Handbuch der Orientalistik. Boston: Brill, 2001.

Ska, Jean Louis. *Introduction to Reading the Pentateuch*. Translated by Pascale Dominique. Winona Lake: Eisenbrauns, 2006.

Ska, Jean Louis. "La structure du Pentateuque dans sa forme canonique." *Zeitschrift für die alttestamentliche Wissenschaft* 113, no. 3 (2001): 331–52.

Sklar, Jay. *Sin, Impurity, Sacrifice, Atonement: The Priestly Conceptions*. Hebrew Bible Monographs 2. Sheffield: Sheffield Phoenix, 2005.

Smith, Christopher R. "The Literary Structure of Leviticus." *Journal for the Study of the Old Testament* 70 (1996): 17–32.

Smith, Mark S. *The Priestly Vision of Genesis 1*. Minneapolis: Fortress, 2010.

Smith, William Robertson. *Lectures on the Religion of the Semites*. Rev. ed. London: Adam and Charles Black, 1894.

———. *The Religion of the Semites*. 1894. Reprint. New York: Schoken Paperback, 1972.

Snaith, N. H. "Sacrifices in the Old Testament." *Vetus Testamentum* 7 (1957): 308–17.

Snoek, Joannes Augustinus Maria. *Initiation: A Methodological Approach to the Application of Classification and Definition Theory in the Study of Rituals*. Pijnacker: Dutch Efficiency Bureau, 1987.

Sonsino, Rifat. *Motive Clauses in Hebrew Law*. Society of Biblical Literature Dissertation Series. Chico: Scholars Press, 1980.

Sprinkle, Joe M. *Biblical Law and Its Relevance: A Christian Understanding and Ethical Application for Today of the Mosaic Regulations*. Lanham: University Press of America, 2006.

Staal, F. Rules. *Without Meaning: Ritual, Mantras and the Human Sciences*. New York: Peter Lang, 1989.

Staal, Frits. "The Meaninglessness of Ritual." *Numen: International Review for the History of Religions* 36, no. 1 (1979): 2–22.

Stahl, Nanette. *Law and Liminality in the Bible*. Sheffield: Sheffield Academic, 1995.

Steinberg, Naomi. "The Deuteronomic Law Code and the Politics of State Centralization." In *The Bible and Liberation: Political and Social Hermeneutics*, edited by Norman K. Gottwald and Richard A. Horsley, 365–75. Maryknoll: Orbis, 1993.

Sun, Henry T. C. "An Investigation into the Compositional Integrity of the So-Called Holiness Code (Leviticus 17–26)." PhD diss., Claremont Graduate School, 1990.

Sun, Simiao. *Collection of the King of Medicine*. Edited by Jizuo Zhang and Ruixian Zhang. Reprint. Beijing: Huaxia, 1995. [in Chinese]

孫思邈（唐）。《藥王全書》。張作記和張瑞賢編。北京：華夏，1995。

———. *Invaluable Prescriptions for Ready Reference*. Edited by Tianshi Xiao. 13 vols. Reprint. Taipei: Freedom Press, 2008. [in Chinese]

孫思邈真人（唐)。《千金翼方》。文山遯叟蕭天石編。共13卷。台北：自由出版社，2008。

Talmon, Shemaryahu. "The 'Comparative Method' in Biblical Interpretation: Principles and Problems." In *Congress Volume, Göttingen, 1977*, edited by the Board of Supplements to Vetus Testamentum, 320–56. Leiden: Brill, 1978.

Talstra, Eep. "Deuteronomy 9 and 10: Synchronic and Diachronic Observations." In *Synchronic or Diachronic? A Debate on Method in Old Testament Exegesis*, edited by Johannes C. De Moor, 187–210. New York: Brill, 1995.

"The Analysis of the Difference Between 'Red' and 'Yellow' Words in Chinese and English." 7 June 2008. Accessed 9 July 2015. https://www.getit01.com/p201806112915779/. [in Chinese with English abstract]

〈英漢「紅色」與「黃色」詞彙對比研究〉, 2008年6月7日。2015年7月9日存取。http://www.8u68.com/lunwentiandi/yingyuxiangguanlunwen/xueshuyingyulunwen/show_10679.html.

"The Foundation of Like Nourishing Like." *The Old Sun Digital Press*. 29 February 2012. Accessed 9 July 2015. http://the-sun.on.cc/cnt/lifestyle/20120229/00484_003.html. [in Chinese]

〈以形補形有根據〉。《昔日太陽電子報》, 2012年2月29日。2015年7月9日存取。http://the-sun.on.cc/cnt/lifestyle/20120229/00484_003.html.

Thompson, Deanna A. *Deuteronomy*. Belief: A Theological Commentary on the Bible. Louisville: Westminster John Knox, 2014.

Tidball, Derek. *The Message of Leviticus: Free to be Holy*. The Bible Speaks Today. Downers Grove: InterVarsity, 2005.

Tigay, Jeffrey H. *Deuteronomy*. JPS Torah Commentary. Philadelphia: Jewish Publication Society, 1996.

Tillich, Paul. "The Religious Symbol." In *Symbolism in Religion and Literature*, edited by Rollo May, 75–98. New York: George Braziller, 1960.

Timmer, Daniel C. "Creation, Tabernacle and Sabbath: The Function of the Sabbath Frame in Exodus 31:12–17; 35:1–3." PhD diss., Trinity Evangelical Divinity School, 2006.

———. *Creation, Tabernacle, and Sabbath: The Sabbath Frame of Exodus 31:12–17; 35:1–3 in Exegetical and Theological Perspective*. Forschungen zur religion und literatur des Alten und Neuen Testaments. Göttingen: Vandenhoeck & Ruprecht, 2009.

Tsevat, M. "Studies in the Book of Samuel." *Hebrew Union College Annual* 32 (1961): 191–216.

Turner, Laurence A. *Genesis*. 2nd ed. Sheffield: Sheffield Phoenix, 2009.

Turner, Victor, and Edith Turner. *Image and Pilgrimage in Christian Culture: Anthropological Perspectives*. New York: Columbia University Press, 1978.

Turner, Victor W. *The Ritual Process: Structure and Anti-Structure*. Symbol, Myth and Ritual Series. Edited by Victor Turner. Ithaca: Cornell University Press, 1977.

———. "Symbols in African Ritual." In *Magic, Witchcraft, and Religion: An Anthropological Study of the Supernatural*, edited by Arthur C. Lehmann and James E. Myers, 55–63. Mountain View: Mayfield, 1989.

Tylor, Edward Burnett. *Primitive Culture*. 2 vols. 5th ed. New York: Harper Torchbooks, 1958.

Van der Merwe, Christo H. J., Jackie A. Naudé, and Jan H. Kroeze. *A Biblical Hebrew Reference Grammar*. Biblical Languages: Hebrew. Sheffield: Sheffield Academic, 2002.

VanDrunen, David. "Natural Law in Noahic Accent: A Covenantal Conception of Natural Law Drawn from Genesis 9." *Journal of the Society of Christian Ethics* 30, no. 2 (2010): 131–49.

VanGemeren, Willem A., ed. *New International Dictionary of Old Testament Theology and Exegesis* (*NIDOTTE*). 5 vols. Grand Rapids: Zondervan, 1997.

Vervenne, M. "'The Blood Is the Life and the Life Is the Blood': Blood as Symbol of Life and Death in Biblical Tradition (Gen. 9, 4)." In *Ritual and Sacrifice in the Ancient Near East: Proceedings of the International Conference Organized by the Katholieke Universiteit Leuven from the 17th to the 20th of April 1991*, edited by J. Quaegebeur, 451–70. Leuven: Peeters, 1993.

Vogt, Peter T. "Centralization and Decentralization in Deuteronomy." In *Interpreting Deuteronomy: Issues and Approaches*, edited by David G. Firth and Philip S. Johnston, 118–38. Downers Grove: IVP Academic, 2012.

———. *Deuteronomic Theology and the Significance of Torah: A Reappraisal*. Winona Lake: Eisenbrauns, 2006.

Von Rad, Gerhard. *Deuteronomy*. Philadelphia: Westminster John Knox, 1966.

———. *Studies in Deuteronomy*. Translated by David Stalker. Chicago: H. Regnery, 1953.

Walker, Graham B., Jr. "Noah and the Season of Violence: Theological Reflections on Genesis 6:5–9:17 and the Work of René Girard." *Review and Expositor* 103, no. 2 (Spring 2006): 385–86.

"Walnuts Benefit Brain, Tomatoes Benefit Heart: Nine Amazing Foods Which Support Like Nourishes Like." *People.Cn*. 26 April 2015. Accessed 9 July 2015. http://js.people.com.cn/n/2015/0426/c360306-24636112.html. [in Chinese]

〈胡桃補腦西紅柿護心：以形補形的9種神奇食物〉。《人民網》。2015年4月26日。2015年7月9日存取。Accessed 9 July 2015. http://js.people.com.cn/n/2015/0426/c360306-24636112.html.

Walsh, Jerome T. *Old Testament Narrative: A Guide to Interpretation*. Louisville: Westminster John Knox, 2009.

Waltke, Bruce K. *Genesis: A Commentary*. Grand Rapids: Zondervan, 2001.

Waltke, Bruce K., and M. O'Connor. *An Introduction to Biblical Hebrew Syntax*. Winona Lake: Eisenbrauns, 1990.

Walton, John H. "Equilibrium and the Sacred Compass: The Structure of Leviticus." *Bulletin for Biblical Research* 11, no. 2 (2001): 293–304.

———. "Genesis." In *Genesis, Exodus, Leviticus, Numbers, Deuteronomy*, vol. 1 of *Zondervan Illustrated Bible Backgrounds Commentary*, edited by John H. Walton, 2–159. Grand Rapids: Zondervan, 2009.

Walton, John H., and Andrew E. Hill. *Old Testament Today: A Journey from Ancient Context to Contemporary Relevance*. 2nd ed. Grand Rapids: Zondervan, 2014.

Walton, John H., and Victor H. Matthews. *The IVP Bible Background Commentary: Genesis–Deuteronomy*. Downers Grove: InterVarsity, 1997.

Wang, Yuncen. "The Investigation of Suan Sy-Meau's Gian Jin Yao Fang Based on the Ideology of Contemporary Vital-nourishment." Master's thesis, Feng Jia University, 2006. [in Chinese]

王允岑。〈由現代養生思想探討唐孫思邈《千金要方》〉。碩士論文，逢甲大學，2006。

Warning, Wilfried. *Literary Artistry in Leviticus*. Leiden: Brill, 1999.

Watts, James W. *Reading Law: The Rhetorical Shaping of the Pentateuch*. Sheffield: Sheffield Academic, 1999.

———. *Ritual and Rhetoric in Leviticus from Sacrifice to Scripture*. New York: Cambridge University Press, 2007.

Weinfeld, Moshe. *Deuteronomy and the Deuteronomic School*. Winona Lake: Eisenbrauns, 1992.

———. *The Place of the Law in the Religion of Ancient Israel*. Leiden: Brill, 2004.

Wellhausen, Julius. *Die Composition des Hexateuchs und der historischen Bücher des Alten Testaments*. Berlin: W. de Gruyter, 1963.

———. *Prolegomena to the History of Israel*. Translated by J. Sutherland Black and Allan Menzies. 1885. Reprint. Edited by Harry W. Gilmer. Reprints and Translation Series. Atlanta: Scholars Press, 1994.

———. *Reste arabischen heidentums*. Berlin: Druck und Verlag von Georg Reimer, 1897.

Wells, Bruce. "Exodus." In *Genesis, Exodus, Leviticus, Numbers, Deuteronomy*, 160–283. Vol. 1 of *Zondervan Illustrated Bible Backgrounds Commentary*. Grand Rapids: Zondervan, 2009.

Wenham, Gordon J. *The Book of Leviticus*. New International Commentary of the Old Testament. Grand Rapids: Eerdmans, 1979.

———. "Deuteronomy and the Central Sanctuary." In *A Song of Power and the Power of Song: Essays on the Book of Deuteronomy*, edited by Duane L. Christensen, 94–108. Winona Lake: Eisenbrauns, 1993.

———. *Genesis 1–15*. Word Biblical Commentary 1. Waco: Word, 1987.

———. "The Theology of Old Testament Sacrifice." In *Sacrifice in the Bible*, edited by Roger T. Beckwith and Martin J. Selman, 75–87. Grand Rapids: Baker, 1995.

Westermann, Claus. *Genesis 1–11: A Continental Commentary*. Translated by John J. Scullion. Minneapolis: Augsburg, 1984. Reprint. Minneapolis: Fortress, 1994.

Whybray, R. N. *The Making of the Pentateuch: A Methodological Study*. Sheffield: JSOT, 1987.

Willis, Timothy M. *Leviticus*. Abingdon Old Testament Commentaries. Nashville: Abingdon, 2009.

Wolf, Herbert M. *An Introduction to the Old Testament Pentateuch*. Chicago: Moody, 1991.

Woods, Edward J. *Deuteronomy: An Introduction and Commentary*. Tyndale Old Testament Commentaries 5. Downers Grove: IVP Academic, 2011.

Wright, Christopher J. H. *Deuteronomy*. New International Biblical Commentary on the Old Testament 4. Peabody: Hendrickson, 1996.

Wright, David. P. "Observations on the Ethical Foundations of Biblical Dietary Laws: A Response to Jacob Milgrom." In *Religion and Law: Biblical-Judaic and Islamic Perspectives*, edited by E. Firmage, B. G. Weiss, and John W. Welch, 193–98. Winona Lake: Eisenbrauns, 1990.

———. *Ritual in Narrative: The Dynamics of Feasting, Mourning, and Retaliation Rites in the Ugaritic Tale of Aqhat*. Winona Lake: Eisenbrauns, 2001.

Wright, Marcia. "Nyakyusa Cults and Politics in the Later Nineteenth Century." In *The Historical Study of African Religion*, edited by T. O. Ranger and I. N. Kimambo, 153–71. Berkeley: University of California Press, 1972.

Wyatt, Nicolas. *Religious Texts from Ugarit*. 2nd ed. New York: Sheffield Academic, 2002.

Xiaoyan. "In Terms of Like Nourishes Like, What Is Right and What Is Wrong." *Yangcheng Evening News*. 25 March 2014. Accessed 9 July 2015. http://health.sina.com.cn/hc/2014-03-25/0707129382.shtml. [in Chinese]

曉彥。〈以形補形對在哪錯在哪〉。《羊城晚報》。2015年3月25日。2015年7月9日存取。Accessed 9 July 2015. http://health.sina.com.cn/hc/2014-03-25/0707129382.shtml.

Yang, Ping. "The Preliminary Study of the Symbolic Meaning of the Terminology of Red and White Color in Chinese and English." *Literature Times: Theoretical Academic Version*. July 2008. Accessed 9 July 2015. https://www.ixueshu.com/h5/document/0b6267206c44bdf4c620985a3380db48318947a18e7f9386.html. [in Chinese]

楊平。〈淺談漢英語言中紅白顏色詞語的象征意義〉。《時代文學：理論學術版》，2008年7月。2015年7月9日存取。Accessed 9 July 2015. https://www.ixueshu.com/h5/document/0b6267206c44bdf4c620985a3380db48318947a18e7f9386.html.

Zenger, Erich. "Das Buch Levitikus als Teiltext der Tora/des Pentateuch-Eine synchrone Lektüre mit diachroner Perspektive." In *Levitikus als Buch*, edited by Heinz-Josef Fabry and Hans-Winfried Jüngling, 47–83. Berlin: Philo, 1999.

———. *Einleitung in das Alte Testament*. Stuttgart: W. Kohlhammer, 2006.

Zimmerli, W. "Die Eigenart der prophetischen Rede des Ezechiel: Ein Beitrag zum Problem an Hand von Ez 14:1–11." *Zeitschrift für die alttestamentliche Wissenschaft* 66, nos. 1–2 (1954): 1–26.

Langham Literature, with its publishing work, is a ministry of Langham Partnership.

Langham Partnership is a global fellowship working in pursuit of the vision God entrusted to its founder John Stott –

> ***to facilitate the growth of the church in maturity and Christ-likeness through raising the standards of biblical preaching and teaching.***

Our vision is to see churches in the Majority World equipped for mission and growing to maturity in Christ through the ministry of pastors and leaders who believe, teach and live by the word of God.

Our mission is to strengthen the ministry of the word of God through:

- nurturing national movements for biblical preaching
- fostering the creation and distribution of evangelical literature
- enhancing evangelical theological education

especially in countries where churches are under-resourced.

Our ministry

Langham Preaching partners with national leaders to nurture indigenous biblical preaching movements for pastors and lay preachers all around the world. With the support of a team of trainers from many countries, a multi-level programme of seminars provides practical training, and is followed by a programme for training local facilitators. Local preachers' groups and national and regional networks ensure continuity and ongoing development, seeking to build vigorous movements committed to Bible exposition.

Langham Literature provides Majority World preachers, scholars and seminary libraries with evangelical books and electronic resources through publishing and distribution, grants and discounts. The programme also fosters the creation of indigenous evangelical books in many languages, through writer's grants, strengthening local evangelical publishing houses, and investment in major regional literature projects, such as one volume Bible commentaries like the *Africa Bible Commentary* and the *South Asia Bible Commentary*.

Langham Scholars provides financial support for evangelical doctoral students from the Majority World so that, when they return home, they may train pastors and other Christian leaders with sound, biblical and theological teaching. This programme equips those who equip others. Langham Scholars also works in partnership with Majority World seminaries in strengthening evangelical theological education. A growing number of Langham Scholars study in high quality doctoral programmes in the Majority World itself. As well as teaching the next generation of pastors, graduated Langham Scholars exercise significant influence through their writing and leadership.

To learn more about Langham Partnership and the work we do visit **langham.org**

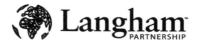

www.ingramcontent.com/pod-product-compliance
Ingram Content Group UK Ltd.
Pitfield, Milton Keynes, MK11 3LW, UK
UKHW031349140325
5003UKWH00023B/115